Mary Baker Eddy

Christian Healer

Mary Baker Eddy

Christian Healer

Yvonne Caché von Fettweis
and
Robert Townsend Warneck

The Christian Science Publishing Society
Boston, Massachusetts, U. S. A.

Authorized literature
of
The First Church of Christ, Scientist

Publisher's Cataloging-in-Publication
(Provided by Quality Books, Inc.)

von Fettweis, Yvonne Caché.
    Mary Baker Eddy: Christian healer / Yvonne Caché von Fettweis
and Robert Townsend Warneck. — 1st ed.
    p. cm.
    Includes index.
    Preassigned LCCN: 97-75056
    ISBN: 0-87510-374-X

    1. Eddy, Mary Baker, 1821–1910. 2. Christian Science—
Biography. I. Warneck, Robert Townsend. II. Title.

BX6995.V66 1997   289.5'092
                                                   QBI97-2248

Mary Baker Eddy

Christian Healer

God has not given us vast learning to solve all the prob-
lems, or unfailing wisdom to direct all the wanderings of
our brothers' lives; but He has given to every one of us the
power to be spiritual, and by our spirituality to lift and
enlarge and enlighten the lives we touch.
—PHILLIPS BROOKS

The secret of my life is in the above.
—MARY BAKER EDDY[1]

INTRODUCTION

Twentieth-Century Biographers Series

*I*N THE CLOSING YEARS of the twentieth century, there is a growing awareness that the hundred years since 1900 will have registered a magnitude and pace of change, in every aspect of human affairs, that probably exceeds any historic precedent. In political, social, and religious institutions and attitudes, in the sciences and industry, in the arts, in how we communicate with each other, humanity has traveled light years in this century.

"Earth's actors," said the Founder of Christian Science, Mary Baker Eddy, "change earth's scenes. . . ." As we look back over the landscape of this century, some towering figures emerge into view: political leaders, scientists and inventors, authors, artists and musicians, social and religious pioneers, industrialists, and many others who helped "change earth's scenes."

Mary Baker Eddy is regarded as a major religious figure of the twentieth century and as a notable example of the emergence of women in significant leadership roles. Although her book *Science and Health with Key to the Scriptures* was published in 1875, in 1992 it was recognized by the Women's National Book Association as one of the 75 major books by women whose words have changed the world. When Mrs. Eddy was inducted into the National Women's Hall of Fame in 1995, it was noted that she had made "an indelible mark on religion, medicine, and journalism."

Mrs. Eddy's works are visible today in virtually every country of the world: in church buildings, in Christian Science Reading Rooms, in the distribution of the newspaper and religious periodicals she established and their derivative broadcast forms, in the wide circulation of her own writings, and most important, in the way hundreds of thousands of people conduct their everyday lives.

Mrs. Eddy wrote only briefly about herself, in a short volume titled *Retrospection and Introspection.* She discouraged personal adulation, clearly hoping that people would find her character and purpose in her own writings rather than in the biographic record. Yet, she came to see the need for an accurate account of her life and gave specific if possibly reluctant acquiescence in the year 1910 to the publishing of the first of the biographies—Sibyl Wilbur's *Mary Baker Eddy.*

As we near the close of a century that directly witnessed some of Mary Baker Eddy's major contributions, The Christian Science Publishing Society, the publishing arm of the church she established, has reexamined the church's obligations to future generations and centuries, in providing an appreciation and understanding of her remarkable career. The Publishing Society now welcomes the opportunity of publishing, and keeping in print, a major shelf of works on Mary Baker Eddy under the general series title: "Twentieth-Century Biographers Series."

Mrs. Eddy's career and works have stirred humanity in the twentieth century and will continue to do so. Perhaps an appropriate introduction for this series is captured in her statement, in the Preface to *Science and Health with Key to the Scriptures:* "The time for thinkers has come." In that spirit, this series of biographies by many different twentieth-century writers is offered to all those who, now and in the future, want to know more about this remarkable woman, her life, and her work.

∼

"A Lifetime of Healing," the first part of *Mary Baker Eddy: Christian Healer,* is expanded from a series that ran in *The Christian Science Journal.* Part Two contains accounts of other healing works by Mrs. Eddy related by people who experienced or saw or were told about them. An appendix also tells something about the experiences of people mentioned in the narrative or who are sources for some of the healing accounts.

CONTENTS

PREFACE

MARY BAKER EDDY was a woman of many talents and she used them very well. She is widely known as the founder of a worldwide religion and the writer of a best-selling book on Christian/spiritual healing. Her life can also be seen as a "rags to riches" American success story. However, most people do not know that before these accomplishments, she was also homeless, friendless, and poor—a single parent who was forced to give up her child for lack of resources. Many women can surely relate to her experiences.

Mrs. Eddy was also socially and politically active for her time. She served as an officer of a temperance society in Lynn, Massachusetts, and on her way to a meeting in February 1866, she fell on an icy street and was seriously injured. Three days later, with friends in the next room waiting for her to die, she turned to the Bible, as she had done since childhood. Reading in the New Testament of Jesus' healing work, she glimpsed God and his relationship to man in an entirely new way—and found herself healed. For the next three years she studied the Scriptures, making copious notes on their spiritual meaning; she actively healed those who were sick; and she began to teach others what had been divinely revealed to her.

What was it like in those early days? As in the days of the early Christians when healing caught the attention of a hungering humanity, Mrs. Eddy's remarkable record of instantaneous healing did the same in her own community—a boy with an infected finger, a lame child on a Lynn beach, followed by many, many more. First, she healed. Then she taught students to heal. And she pored over the Scriptures in an effort to bring out, in writing, the truths of this revelation of what she saw as divine Science. She then wrote *Science and Health*. Mrs. Eddy referred to her book as "the Christian Science textbook," and she said that it ". . . maintains primitive Christianity, shows how to demonstrate it, and throughout is logical in premise and in conclusion."[1]

During the nineteenth century and the first decade of the twentieth century the foundations of the modern world were laid. There were many "firsts." Electricity began to be used for lighting and communication. Automobiles and airplanes were invented. Medical science was discovering germs, bacteria, and viruses. Anesthetics and antiseptics began to be used in surgery. Psychology was invented and became accepted as a therapeutic system. Karl Marx wrote *Das Kapital*. Charles Darwin linked his new concept of evolution to the history of humans. X-rays and the electron were discovered. Albert Einstein formulated the special theory of relativity. The age was demanding logical, "scientific" solutions to problems, and the early Christian Scientists rose to meet those demands through Christian healing.

The assembling of Mary Baker Eddy's record of healing began in her own lifetime, and archivists contributed to this documentation in the following decades. In both her published and unpublished writings, Mrs. Eddy tells of healings accomplished through Christian prayer from childhood and in the years following, before she discovered Christian Science. Her students, in correspondence and reminiscences, tell of her healing work during later years. Mrs. Eddy did reach a point where she publicly announced that she was no longer accepting requests for treatment. This was when she began teaching, and later became fully occupied as Church founder and leader. But the historical record shows clearly that her healing work didn't stop when she gave up her public practice. It continued undiminished.

Beginning in 1992 the authors of this biography began to comb the historical collections of The First Church of Christ, Scientist, in Boston, Massachusetts, searching for every reference to Mrs. Eddy's healing work. The assembled record—her demonstrations of God's healing touch, lifting moral and physical burdens from those oppressed—showed just how foundational her own healing work was to her role as writer and founder.

The authors spent the better part of five years identifying, evaluating, and assembling accounts from Mrs. Eddy's unpublished letters and articles (more than 21,000 of them) and from the reminiscences of others who knew her. They also utilized the findings of former church archivists. Putting accounts of her healing work into two-inch binders, the authors filled eleven binders. Their next step was to read through all of Mrs. Eddy's correspondence and her other unpublished writings in chronological order, to trace the evolution of her thought. The result was documentation of a lifetime of Christian healing spanning almost ninety years. This material was used as the basis of an eighteen-part series of articles titled, "Mary Baker Eddy: A Lifetime of Healing," which appeared in *The Christian Science Journal.*

That series of articles, somewhat amplified, forms the first part of this book. The second part consists of additional healing accounts quoted directly from the original sources. There is also a biographical glossary that provides additional information about people mentioned or quoted in the book.

Following the example of Christ Jesus and his apostles, Mary Baker Eddy saw spiritual, Christian healing as vital to humanity's salvation. From the Bible she saw that this type of healing existed before the days of Jesus of Nazareth, for the Christ, as the saving power of God, had always been present—"Before Abraham was, I am."[2] The ability to heal as Jesus did, quickly and completely, through prayer alone, is found in a life grounded in Christ: a pure and loving thought that correctly understands and completely trusts God as the divine Father-Mother who fully cares for all his offspring throughout His creation. Mrs. Eddy has written, "Now, as then, signs and wonders are wrought in the metaphysical healing of physical disease; but these signs are only to demonstrate its divine origin,—to attest the reality of the higher mission of the Christ-power to take away the sins of the world."[3] She searched the entire Scriptures, seeking answers. Her first teaching documents were exegeses of chapters from both the Old and New Testaments, written in 1866 through 1869.

The idea behind the *Journal* series was both to make her healing work more known, and more importantly, to share the standard for contemporary Christian healing set by her work.

In February 1900, Mrs. Eddy wrote:

> I can look back and see that at the time of the accident although I had no faith in medicine and did not take it, I had faith that God could raise me up. Hence the effect of the Scripture that I read which strengthened my faith and its results in my recovery. And afterwards was seen in the illumination of the spiritual meaning of the Scriptures as given in my books and teachings. All of which is in accord with our Master's precious promise, "If ye have faith as a grain of mustard seed, ye shall say unto this mountain, Remove hence to yonder place; and it shall remove; and nothing shall be impossible unto you." (Matt. 17:20) My experience of the effects of faith was no miracle and nothing impossible to all who have that faith which is followed by spiritual understanding and is equal to avail itself of Christ's promise, not to a select number, but to all who exercise it.[4]

PART ONE

*A Lifetime
of
Healing*

CHAPTER 1

The gifts of childhood
(1821–1843)

As a child, Mary Baker yearned for the tender, loving God who *is* Love.[1] Her reflection of, affection for, and trust in divine Love brought into her experience occurrences which affirmed that God's love does indeed heal. In the beginning her leaning on His care was a matter of simple, strong faith. She witnessed God's grace and care for herself and others when she prayed.

Mary came from a family whose life was centered on the Bible, as was typical of New England families in the early 1800s. Here was a world where formal prayers began and ended the day's labors, prefaced each meal, and embraced all of the Sabbath.

The Baker household was large by today's standards, but about average for that period in the United States. At the time of her birth on July 16, 1821, the family consisted of Mary's parents, Mark and Abigail, her grandmother Maryann Baker, and three brothers and two sisters. Samuel was the oldest at thirteen, followed by Albert (eleven),

George (eight), Abigail (five), and Martha (two). Much of the boys' time was spent in helping with chores on the farm. It was a lively home, often welcoming visitors and thoughtful discussions on both sacred and secular matters, but it was also one that was run on strict Christian principles. Mark was an orthodox Calvinist and Abigail was just as religious, though a good deal more expressive in her understanding of God as Love. However, Mary Baker Eddy's story really begins before she was born.

～

In 1821 the small New Hampshire town of Bow would likely still have been in the cold embrace of a New England winter. Early March winds would have blown across the hills, dipping into the valley, gaining momentum as they crossed the icy river and made their way up the hills on the other side. On the crest of one of these hills, a modest farmhouse sat quiet to the world. Abigail Baker was in the attic gathering wool to spin into yarn. "Suddenly [she] was overwhelmed by the thought that she was filled with the Holy Ghost, and had dominion over the whole earth. At that moment she felt the quickening of the babe, and then she thought 'what a sin I am guilty of—the sin of presumption!' "[2]

The newest member of the family was some months away from making an appearance, and Abigail wondered what would become of this child, whose conception had

The Bow Home
This etching was drawn by Rufus Baker, a cousin of Mrs. Eddy's,
after talks with her about her childhood home.

been unexpected.[3] Abigail's concern arose from the fact that her consciousness had been flooded with thoughts that greatly challenged the theology of her Puritan upbringing—thoughts of the child's special purpose and its spiritual promise. As lovely as these thoughts were to her, they were nothing short of profane in the world of Calvinism into which Mary Baker was soon to be born.

Mrs. Baker would often share her experiences with Sarah Gault, a close friend and neighbor. Mrs. Eddy, recounting this particular incident to members of her household in later years, told them, "[Sarah Gault] was calling on my mother one afternoon and they were praying together." Afterward her mother spoke to Sarah of the thoughts that had been coming to her about this child's spiritual purpose and promise. "My mother said, 'I don't know what I shall do to stop such blasphemy.'" Sarah reminded her that in the Bible it said that God made man in His own image, and made him to have dominion.[4] Abigail found comfort in this.

With thoughts of her mother and her own upbringing, Mrs. Eddy instructed her editor to write an article for *The Christian Science Journal* in 1889. He titled it, "Christian Science and its Revelator." In it we find:

> To-day Truth has come through the person of a New England girl, born of God-fearing parents, in the middle walks of life; . . . gifted with the fullness of spiritual life, and giving from the cradle indications of a divine mission and power, that caused *her* mother to "ponder them in her heart."[5]

And referring to these indications of spiritual discernment and healing ability that marked her from childhood, Mrs. Eddy wrote in a letter in 1899:

> I can discern in the human mind, thoughts, motives and purpose; . . . it is the gift of God. And this phenomenon appeared in my childhood; it is associated with my earliest memories, and has increased with years.[6]

This letter was published in a pamphlet, and in its second edition she added:

> It is a consciousness wherewith good is done and no
> evil can be done . . . and has increased with my
> spiritual increase. It has aided me in healing the
> sick, and subordinating the human to the Divine.

The incidents of healing in Mary's youth were simple but profound. They happened at her home, among her relatives, and in the schoolyard. The healings were linked to her natural outpouring of love for those who needed love most.

Mary loved the animals on her farm. In later years Mrs. Eddy told a member of her household, Irving Tomlinson, that as a girl, she would nurse baby lambs and chicks, and sing hymns to animals in discomfort during the night. It was a healing love, so evident that her father, finding a weakling in the flock, would say "Here is another invalid for Mary." Tomlinson noted, "Then Mary would tenderly take her mild-eyed charge and nurse the fleecy little patient to health and strength."[7] Recalling the time, Mrs. Eddy said, "I would take the little chicks, that seemed sickly or perhaps dying, into the bosom of my dress and hold them until I heard a fluttering sound and found the chicken active and strong and eager to run away, when I would put it down and away it would run."[8]

As Mark Baker knew of his youngest child's abilities, it is not surprising to learn that when Mary's brother George severely injured his leg with an ax and was bleeding badly, her frightened father called on his five-year-old daughter to help. He put her hand on the wound and George stopped crying. Not long after, the doctor arrived and found the bleeding had completely stopped and the wound had already begun to heal. He remarked that he had never seen such an injury heal so rapidly. When asked in later years what her father thought of it, Mrs. Eddy said it disturbed him and he would pray for her.[9]

Mrs. Eddy one time recounted to her household at the supper table a visit she had made to Bow in the 1870s with one of her early students, Miranda Rice. There they had met Mrs. Eddy's cousin, Nancy Baker, who joined them as they walked about the old farm. There was almost a generation between the cousins, and, as in many families, the older woman, Mrs. Baker, was addressed as "Aunt." Mrs. Eddy remembered the experience this way:

> Mrs. Rice thinking to interest my aunt in
> C[hristian] S[cience] told her of many remarkable
> cases of healing wrought through me in Lynn,
> Mass. Mrs. Baker did not express surprise, in fact
> she seemed so calm that Mrs. Rice . . . [pressed my
> aunt to explain her bland] remark. [Mrs. Baker
> said,] "These things do not surprise me concerning

Mary. They are no more wonderful than I had seen
her accomplish before she went away from this
farm a girl of thirteen."[10]

One of those healings was that of George Baker's injured leg. Another healing Nancy Baker herself experienced. As Mrs. Eddy told it, her aunt had come to visit her and was suffering from a severe headache. She asked Mary to pray for her, was healed, and "went home perfectly well."[11]

Evidences of Christian regeneration and healing in Mary's early days followed her to school. Irving Tomlinson recounts in his *Twelve Years with Mary Baker Eddy* that Mary once stood up to a girl who was terrorizing the other children, and the girl's nature was transformed:

The teacher confessed to me that I had done what
whipping had failed to do, for I had completely
changed her character.[12]

In Sybil Wilbur's biography of Mrs. Eddy, she tells of the time a teenage Mary calmed an insane man who appeared at school one day. In relating this incident to Mr. Tomlinson, Mrs. Eddy added that this same man forced his way into their home one morning when the family was at prayer. He rushed up to her father, who was reading from the Bible, and took it away from him. Handing it to Mary he said, "Here! You are the one to read from God's word."[13]

"Many peculiar circumstances and events connected with my childhood throng the chambers of memory," Mrs. Eddy wrote in her autobiographical *Retrospection and Introspection* as introduction to her account of hearing her name called, Samuel-like, repeatedly until she answered, " 'Speak, Lord; for Thy servant heareth.' "[14] Mary's religious upbringing had taught her that all men are God's servants, but her own unique experiences taught her that there was more to serving than what John Calvin had seen. She was learning that *divine service* meant daily deeds in service to a loving God.[15] And that these deeds must include healing the sick was a vital part of her discovery of Christian Science.

Mary Baker, however, did not break free of Calvin's iron grasp without a fearful struggle. Later on in life she recalled asking her mother if Calvin's teaching regarding eternal punishment was true. Mrs. Eddy said, "She paused, then with a deep sigh answered, 'Mary, I suppose *it is.*' What, said I, if we repent and tell God 'we are sorry and will not do so again.' Will God punish us then? Then he is not as good as my mother and he will find me a hard case."[16]

Mrs. Eddy as a child was so troubled by the doctrine of predestination that at one point it caused her to become feverishly ill. God had been gently showing Mary, through experience, that He is ever-present Love, but the theology of her parents' church was trying to teach her something quite different:

My father's relentless theology emphasized belief
in a final judgment-day, in the danger of endless
punishment, and in a Jehovah merciless towards
unbelievers; and of these things he now spoke,
hoping to win me from dreaded heresy.

My mother, as she bathed my burning temples,
bade me lean on God's love, which would give me
rest, if I went to Him in prayer, as I was wont to
do, seeking His guidance. I prayed; and a soft glow
of ineffable joy came over me. The fever was gone,
and I rose and dressed myself, in a normal condition of health. Mother saw this, and was glad.
The physician marvelled; and the "horrible decree"
of predestination—as John Calvin rightly called his
own tenet—forever lost its power over me.[17]

Mary Baker was able to join the Congregational Church a
few years later without compromising her conscience. At her
examination for membership she said she was willing to trust
her spiritual safety to God, as she understood Him, outside the
church, rather than assent to the doctrine of predestination.

The minister then wished me to tell him when
I had experienced a change of heart; but tearfully
I had to respond that I could not designate any
precise time. Nevertheless, he persisted in the
assertion that I *had* been truly regenerated, and

> asked me to say how I felt when the new light
> dawned within me. I replied that I could only
> answer him in the words of the Psalmist: "Search
> me, O God, and know my heart: try me, and know
> my thoughts: and see if there be any wicked way in
> me, and lead me in the way everlasting."[18]

The minister was so touched by her reply, he accepted her into the church.

Mary's willingness to lay herself open to God at all times, following wherever He would guide her, prescribed the fundamental and quintessential standard for a lifetime to come.

CHAPTER 2

God's gracious preparation
(1843–1860)

IN JANUARY 1843 MARY BAKER attended a series of
"revival" meetings that were held alternately at the
Methodist and Congregational churches in Sanbornton
Bridge, New Hampshire, over a period of five weeks. In a
letter to her friend Augusta Swasey, she wrote, "the
meetings were so very interesting . . . almost all of your
acquaintances are now rejoicing in the hope set before
them of higher aims and nobler joys." She went on to
report a large number "who have experienced a change,"
including her married sister, Abigail Tilton:

> Would that you were here to witness with me this
> changed scene! tho I *fear* for *some*, I rejoice with
> *many*, whom I doubt not possess the "pearl" which
> is priceless. And do you not also rejoice with me if
> it were but for *one* sinner that hath repented?
> Doubtless as you feared, there are some who have
> deceived *themselves* by "zeal without knowledge"—
> But methinks we have less to fear from fanaticism,
> than from stoicism; when a question is to be

decided that involves our weal, or woe for *time*
and *eternity.*[1]

It is quite possible that Charles Finney's ideas of
"Christian Perfection" were preached at these meetings. A
Presbyterian minister who had forsaken traditional
Calvinist doctrine, Rev. Finney is considered by some to be
the Father of American Revivalism. He was preaching in
New England at this time, though there is nothing to
confirm his presence at the Sanbornton Bridge revival
meetings. He defined Christian Perfectionism as

> perfect obedience to the law of God. . . .
> Christianity requires that we should do neither more
> nor less than the law of God prescribes. Nothing
> short of this is Christian perfection. This is being
> moral, just as perfect as God. . . . And he has
> created us moral beings in his own image, capable of
> conforming to the same rule with himself. This rule
> requires us to have the same character with him, to
> love as impartially, with as perfect love—to seek the
> good of others with as single an eye as he does. This,
> and nothing less than this, is Christian Perfection.[2]

Ten months after attending these revival meetings, on
December 10, 1843, Mary Baker became Mrs. George
Washington Glover. She had been betrothed to Major
Glover for two years.[3] On December 25 they sailed from
New England to South Carolina to begin their married life

together. The arduous experiences this young New Hampshire woman was soon to encounter would, in later years, be seen by her as "earth's shadows." She would write of them, "The heavenly intent of earth's shadows is to chasten the affections, to rebuke human consciousness and turn it gladly from a material, false sense of life and happiness, to spiritual joy and true estimate of being."[4] And so it was in this way that God prepared her to receive His revelation of Christian Science.

The ship the Glovers were sailing on was in the hands of divine Providence as it tossed perilously on the waves, with the winds shrieking through its masts. A violent storm had descended on the vessel just as it was to pass several sandbars and enter the harbor at Charleston, South Carolina. Below in their stateroom, the young couple knelt in fervent prayer. The captain had just left them. He had never seen such a storm and had no hope that the ship could be saved.

The frightened bride and bridegroom had been full of hope and expectation when they departed New England on Christmas Day. The bride's mother had given them a letter to read during their voyage, and to comfort his new wife George Glover read it to her during the storm. It included a poem, entitled "The Mother's Injunction" by Lydia Sigorney, part of which reads:

> When judgment wakes in terror wild,
> By all thy treasured hopes of Heaven,
> Deal gently with my darling child.

As Mary Baker Eddy told Irving Tomlinson many years later, "When the reading was finished [George] kissed me and took me in his arms for it seemed that the staunch ship would soon sink beneath the waves. Within fifteen minutes thereafter a most remarkable phenomenon occurred. The storm subsided and the waves grew calm and the ship passed [the sand] bars in perfect safety. The captain said that in all his long experience he had never seen anything so wonderful. Thus many a time has God miraculously preserved me."[5]

Seven months later the young bride returned sadly to her family in New England a widow and mother-to-be; George Glover had been stricken with yellow fever and passed away. Mary characteristically turned in prayer to God to sustain her through this trial. Some thirty years later she would write in the First edition of *Science and Health,* in the chapter "Marriage," "but sundering ties of flesh, unites us to God, where Love supports the struggling heart."[6] Human life would continue to be a struggle for Mrs. Glover for many years to come, but with each ordeal she would lean on that divine support through her prayers.

In order to gain some semblance of financial independence from her family, Mary taught in the local academies when her health permitted. On one occasion she had to keep a persistently misbehaving boy after school. Mrs. Eddy, writing of this incident in later years, tells of taking his hand and saying, "I love you, but I must make you suffer for bad conduct and its influence on my pupils." He asked to be punished quickly so he could go. She told him to kneel beside her and she would pray for him. He said it would do no good. Mrs. Eddy then recounts:

> I persisted and he at last dropped on his knees
> beside me, then I prayed. Soon he was sobbing
> and jumped up, implor[ing] me to whip him and
> forgive him. I answered, "the whipping would do
> you no good . . . but my prayer will help you."
> Then I opened the door and he quickly disappeared.

Two days later the boy's mother came to see her; as Mrs. Eddy went on to recount:

> . . . mid smiles and tears she sobbed, "what have
> [you] done to my Willie . . . he's another child. He
> prayed last night and read the Bible, something I
> never could get him to do." That year the dear boy
> joined the Congregational Church of which his
> mother and myself were members.[7]

Children were always dear to Mrs. Eddy's heart throughout her life, and her own son, George, of course, was especially so. As he grew from an infant into childhood, Mary's family became concerned that he was too much for her to cope with alone, considering her delicate health. She would later write of this in *Retrospection and Introspection:* ". . . my little son, about four years of age, was sent away from me, and put under the care of our family nurse. . . . The night before my child was taken from me, I knelt by his side throughout the dark hours, hoping for a vision of relief from this trial."[8] Two years after this separation, she accepted a proposal of marriage from Daniel Patterson. He promised that her son would be restored to her, and they were married on the twenty-first of June 1853. After moving into their new home, he became unwilling to take George in.

In *Retrospection and Introspection* Mrs. Eddy says, "A plot was consummated" to keep her and George apart, and the family caring for him soon moved to Minnesota.[9] The loss of her child caused Mary's fragile health to give way. She became bedridden for months at a time. At this point in her human experience she was literally alone in the wilderness—in her home in the secluded woodlands of North Groton, New Hampshire—far from family and friends. Her only steady companion was a blind teenage girl who served as housekeeper, since Daniel Patterson was often absent for long periods because of his work as a traveling dentist. While he clearly had his weaknesses, they did love each other, and she missed him when he was gone. Even his refusal to let her son join them was in part well intended: he was afraid of the effect on her health of having to care for George. Daniel was kind to Mary and tried to be solicitous of her needs, though he never truly understood them. He would prescribe homeopathic remedies, which would help for a time, but her suffering would always return.

The remedies were familiar ones to Mary. Homeopathic treatment had come "like blessed relief" to her about 1848,

Mrs. Eddy around 1853

when she was in her late twenties. She was introduced to this form of treatment by Dr. Alpheus Morrill, a cousin by marriage.[10] A system for treating disease with minute doses of drugs that in larger amounts would produce symptoms similar to those manifested by the disease, homeopathy was a popular method of that day. Since girlhood Mary had been adhering to one or another of the then current dietetic theories. From her late twenties, she studied textbooks on homeopathy, and after her return from the South she was not only prescribing remedies for herself but also began to do this for others.[11] One very special case took place during the period between widowhood and the first years of her marriage to Dr. Patterson. Mrs. Eddy would later write of it in detail in *Science and Health with Key to the Scriptures.* It was that of a woman with dropsy.[12] The previous physician had given the patient up. Both allopathic and homeopathic methods had been tried, and had failed to bring any relief. Mary took the case and prescribed according to her understanding of homeopathy. There was soon noticeable improvement. At this point she learned that the former doctor had prescribed exactly the same remedy, and she became concerned about overdosing. The patient, however, would not give up the medicine that brought her relief. Without telling the woman, Mrs. Glover administered unmedicated pills instead. Even so, the improvement continued and the case was cured.

Six decades later Mrs. Eddy would speak of that cure as

> . . . a falling apple to me—it made plain to me that
> mind governed the whole question of her recovery.
> I was always praying to be kept from sin, and I
> waited and prayed for God to direct me.[13]

Mrs. Eddy also told Irving Tomlinson that this had been "the falling apple," explaining it as "the enlightenment of the human understanding." She contrasted this with her discovery of Christian Science in 1866, which she described as "the revelation from the divine Mind."[14]

Two facts had become clear as a result of this cure of dropsy: first, the same remedy that had been impotent when administered by a medical physician became effective when *she* prescribed and administered it; second, the unmedicated pills were as effective as the medicated ones. She saw that both the thought of the physician and the thought of the patient were the determining factors in the case, to the exclusion of matter. After receiving the full revelation of Christian Science, Mrs. Eddy would write: "The physician must know himself and understand the mental state of his patient. . . . 'Cast the beam out of thine own eye.' Learn what in thine own mentality is unlike 'the anointed,' and cast it out; then thou wilt discern the error in thy patient's mind that makes his body sick, and remove it, and rest like the dove from the deluge."[15] And so the revelation of Christian Science would move her far beyond material methods as having anything to do with the healing process. The laws of healing rested in divine Mind as the sole physician in every case. During her years of invalidism in North Groton, Mary made a promise to God "that if He restored her to health she would devote her remaining years to helping sick and suffering humanity."[16] Looking back on this promise, decades later, Mrs. Eddy felt that it marked the beginning of a new period in her life. Soon she was given the opportunity to begin her fulfillment of that sacred vow. Shortly after Mrs. Patterson

Photo: Gordon Converse

The North Groton house where Mrs. Eddy lived from 1855–1860

moved to Rumney, New Hampshire, in March 1860, a mother brought her sick baby to Mary, who in later years recounted:

> Mrs. Smith, of Rumney, N.H., came to me with her infant, whose eyes were diseased, a mass of inflammation, neither pupil nor iris discernable. I gave the infant no drugs,—held her in my arms a few moments while lifting my thoughts to God, then returned the babe to her mother healed. In grateful memory thereof Mrs. Smith named her babe "Mary", and embroidered a petticoat for me.[17]

Lifting her thought to God was more natural to Mary than
walking. From a child she had been taught the centrality of
God to everyday life. She knew Him through her daily
prayers and she "love[d] him, because he first loved" her.[18]
She also knew Him through the Bible, which was her
constant companion and daily guide. In 1846, the year she
identified as marking the beginning of her search "to trace
all physical effects to a mental cause,"[19] she had written a
poem about the Holy Scriptures, expressing her awe of
God's communion with man through its sacred pages:

THE BIBLE

Word of God! What condescension,
Infinite with finite mind,
To commune, sublime conception
Canst thou fathom love divine?
Oracle of God-like wonder,
Frame-work of His mighty plan,
Chart and compass for the wanderer,
Safe obeying thy command.
By Omniscience veiled in glory,
'Neath the Omnipresent eye—
Kingdoms, empires, bow before thee,
Sceptic, truth immortal see!
Spare O then the querist's cavil,
Search in faith—obey, adore!
Ponder, pause, believe and "marvel
Not, I say," forevermore.[20]

For this "wanderer" in the wilderness, the Bible was indeed her "chart and compass." She spent much of her time reading it during those lonely years (1856–1862), when she was mostly confined to her bed. Once when Daniel was asked why she had not come to church, he replied, "O, she is at home reading her Bible."[21] Mrs. Patterson was not just reading, she was pondering deeply the Word of God and imbibing its healing message:

> As early as 1862 she began to write down and give
> to friends the results of her Scriptural study, for the
> Bible was her sole teacher. . . .[22]

She described herself then as "a child in the newly discovered world of Spirit"[23]—a world she would spend the rest of her life exploring and leading others into.

CHAPTER 3

Waiting and watching . . . the daystar appears
(1861–1866)

*I*N THE LATE 1850S, the thunderclouds of war were gathering. The United States was wrestling with itself over an issue of morality. The North thought it was a matter of the indissolubility of the Union. The South felt it was the undeniability of states' rights. At the bottom of it all, however, was the immorality of slavery.

Mary Patterson knew all too well about slavery. For her, slavery also meant a material body bound in the chains of chronic illness, under the lash of pain. But unlike the weapons soon to be unleashed on the battlefields of the American Civil War, "the weapons of [her] warfare [were] not carnal, but mighty through God to the pulling down of strong holds."[1] When the war between the North and the South began in 1861, Mary was living in Rumney, New Hampshire, fighting against invalidism. The Bible and prayer were her only weapons. Her neighbors had grown to

2 Cor 10: 4-6

know her as a devout Christian and would seek her counsel in time of trouble. Remembering one such incident, Mary Baker Eddy wrote in later years:

> . . . a mother whose only son was drafted to enter
> the army, came to [me] in tears, told of her trouble
> and her deep concern for her son's moral welfare.
> At that time [my] husband was confined in Libby
> Military prison and [my] only son was in a military
> hospital. . . . But [I] took almost [my] last dollar
> and bought a Bible for the woman's son, wrote a
> scriptural text on the fly leaf and gave it to him.
> He was shot in battle, but the bullet struck the
> Bible and his life was saved. After his return home
> he united with the Methodist Church. He always
> said that Bible and the text written on the fly leaf
> were the cause of his conversion.[2]

Mrs. Eddy told Irving Tomlinson that this soldier came to see her after the war to show her the Bible she had given him:

> Embedded between its covers was a leaden bullet.
> Said the soldier, "That rifle ball was meant for my
> heart, and I have come many miles to show you
> that your goodness saved my life."[3]

Mary's only son, George, was a soldier in the Union Army. At one point during the war, in the latter half of

1862, Mary was struck with the very strong feeling that something terrible had happened to her son. True to her nature, she prayed at once specifically for his safety and well-being. Soon thereafter she received a message that George had been shot in the neck. At first the doctors thought the wound was fatal, but quite suddenly the danger passed, and his recovery began.[4]

When Mary learned that her husband, Daniel, had been taken prisoner of war, she went to see his family in Maine. Frances Thompson Hill relates in her reminiscence, "During the time that her husband was in Libby prison Mrs. [Patterson] visited the [Patterson] home, spending several weeks there. [Daniel's niece] said that she had been told by her father that Mrs. [Patterson] wrote a great deal and kept quietly to her room, but that her loving thought had healed one of their livestock."[5] Her concern for her husband is quite evident in a poem she wrote during this period. The last two verses of "To a Bird Flying Southward" read:

> Oh! to the *captive's* cell I'd sing
> A song of hope—and *freedom* bring—
> An olive leaf I'd quick let fall,
> And lift our country's blackened pall;
> Then homeward seek my frigid zone,
> More chilling to the heart *alone*.

> Lone as a solitary star,
> Lone as a vacant sepulchre,

Yet not alone! my Father's call—
Who marks the sparrow in her fall—
Attunes my ear to joys elate,
The joys I'll sing at Heaven's gate.[6]

Several months before Daniel Patterson had left for the South, he had received a circular from a doctor in Portland, Maine, who gave no medicine but effected cures by talking to the patient. Daniel wrote to this doctor, Phineas P. Quimby, in the hope that he would come to treat Mary. Dr. Quimby could not come, so Mary went to him in October 1862, full of hope and expectation. His treatment consisted of explaining the psychological origin of her illness and then, after first dipping his hands in water, rubbing her head vigorously. "At first my case improved wonderfully under his treatment,"[7] Mrs. Eddy would later write. So great was the improvement that she felt it must be of God. Her Puritan upbringing and natural inclination toward the Divine were so strong that she could not conceive of any other source for something that had such a remarkable effect on her. But being made well, as marvelous as that was, was not enough for Mary; she must know *how* the healing was done. Dr. Quimby, however, could not tell her. He did not know himself.

Over the next three years, Mrs. Patterson made a number of visits to Portland. To her disappointment, she had found that Dr. Quimby's cure was not permanent, and further treatment was necessary. But her motivation for these trips actually lay more in the hope of gaining an understanding of the cause behind the powerful effect. She would have long conversations with Dr. Quimby and afterward write of the insights that came to her from their discussions. Her writings, naturally, were permeated with references to God and lessons from her Bible study. Mary did not realize at this time that Dr. Quimby was a mesmerist and not at all inclined toward religion. In talking with patients he simply found it most effective to speak in terms of whatever subjects interested them most, not caring whether it was religion, spiritualism, or even witchcraft, as long as he could hold their attention.[8]

During her visits to Portland, Mary's own healing work grew stronger. In later years she told her personal secretary, Calvin Frye, of healing a man, in Dr. Quimby's absence, who was in leg braces and suffering greatly.

> . . . a man was brought to the International Hotel
> who had met with an accident which had injured
> . . . his spine and had broken both his legs above
> the knees. Dr. Q[uimby] had treated the case twice
> but one day the patient was suffering intensely and
> Dr. Q[uimby] was away. The landlord came to Mrs.
> E[ddy] (then Mrs. P[atterson]) and asked her if she
> would not go and see the patient. She was surprised
> at his request & asked his reason for the strange
> request of her. He said that Dr. Q[uimby] had told
> him many wonderful things about her and he was
> curious to have her go and see what she could do
> for the case. She went and stood inside the door of

the sick room & said to the patient, "Why don't
you get up?" He turned his head and looked at
her surprised then turned his head and looked up.
She said again, "Get up." He got up and walked
about the room, the wooden splints on his limbs
clattering at every step and he came to the door and
bowed her out.[9]

When [Dr. Quimby] returned and found this
case so changed he was quite aroused over it and
told Mrs. Eddy never to do anything for another of
his patients unless he asked her to.[10]

In describing this healing to her household in 1902,
Mrs. Eddy told them that when she was first asked to help
she didn't think she could, but then the thought came to
her, "God can do it. I went to his bed side and lifted my
thought silently to God.". One of the household asked,
"This was not your only case of healing while with Dr.
Quimby, was it?" She answered:

No indeed, there was a young woman whom he
had given up to die with consumption. . . . I visited
her, called upon God to help her, and when
[Quimby] visited her two days later, he declared
that she no more had consumption than he did.

One of her listeners asked, "How was the healing wrought,
not in the way that Dr. Quimby practiced?" Mrs. Eddy
replied, "No, not at all. I used no material means whatever.

I could not tell how the healing was done. I only know that God did it."[11]

Another case brought to Dr. Quimby was that of a man who had been run over by a train. Mrs. Eddy recounted, "Both limbs were shattered and his condition was so pitiable that Quimby would not stay in the room with him, but he said to me, 'Mrs. [Patterson] you go and see if you can't help him.' I went to the door, lifted my eyes to heaven, breathed a prayer, and the man rose up healed."[12]

Early in 1864, during one of her visits to Portland, Mary met Sarah Crosby and Mary Ann Jarvis, patients of Dr. Quimby. In the spring of that year, she stayed two months with Miss Jarvis in her home in Warren, Maine. During this visit, Mary healed Miss Jarvis of consumption and the suffering brought on by "east winds." She later described this healing in her book *Science and Health:*

> A woman, whom I cured of consumption, always
> breathed with great difficulty when the wind was
> from the east. I sat silently by her side a few mo-
> ments. Her breath came gently. The inspirations were
> deep and natural. I then requested her to look at the
> weather-vane. She looked and saw that it pointed due
> east. The wind had not changed, but her thought of
> it had and so her difficulty in breathing had gone.
> The wind had not produced the difficulty. My
> metaphysical treatment changed the action of her
> belief on the lungs, and she never suffered again
> from east winds, but was restored to health.[13]

In late summer and early autumn, Mrs. Patterson spent about three months with Mrs. Crosby in her home in Albion, Maine. During that visit Sarah was taking down a bottle of vitriolic acid from a high shelf when the bottle broke and the acid spilled on her face. A doctor was called, but he could do nothing for her. In fact, he thought she might die. Sarah then put herself in the hands of her guest, who told her to go lie down. She went to sleep while Mary prayed. Two hours later she woke to find the pain gone and her face showing no signs of the accident.[14] Sometime after Mary went home, Sarah wrote her about a problem she was having with one of her eyes. Another letter soon followed:

Photo: Preble at Waterville, Maine

Mrs. Eddy in 1864

Since the accident to my eye, it has been so
exceedingly sensitive to the light, I have shaded it,
unable to do any writing or sewing of any note.
The Sunday I mailed you a letter I suffered a great
deal with it; Monday it was painful until towards
night, when it felt better; Tuesday it was *well,* and I
have not worn my shade over it since a week ago
Monday, and I have read, sewed, and written, and
still all is well. . . . I told a friend the other day you
had cured my eye, or perhaps my fear of my eye,
and it is so; . . .[15]

By this time, Mary was living in Lynn, Massachusetts. Her husband had escaped from the military prison and on his return based his dental practice in that town. In the autumn of 1865 they moved to the neighboring town of Swampscott and together joined the Good Templars in Lynn. Mary soon became the presiding officer of the women's branch of that temperance association.

On a bitterly cold night, the first day of February 1866, Mary walked with friends to a temperance meeting in Lynn. She slipped on the ice-covered street and fell with such force as to injure herself severely. Rendered insensible by the fall, Mary was carried to a nearby house and a doctor was called. His examination showed her to be suffering from a concussion and internal injuries, including possible spinal dislocation. The next day, at her request, she was moved to her home in Swampscott, in what the newspapers described as a very critical condition. The doctor left her some homeopathic medicine, which she did not take, having learned years before that material remedies had no real curative power. Instead, her healing rested in "that consciousness which God bestows."[16]

On the third morning after the accident, a Sunday, Mary's pastor visited her. She asked him to return in the afternoon. He said he would, even though he didn't expect her to live that long. When he had gone, she asked those attending to leave her for a while. Mary felt totally alone, bereft of all human aid. Her husband was absent, away on a trip to New Hampshire. There was no *person* left to whom she could turn for help. But Mary knew God to be "a very present help in trouble"[17] and she turned to her Bible. In early editions of *Science and Health,* Mrs. Eddy stated that she read from the third chapter of Mark:

> . . . where our Master healed the withered hand on
> the Sabbath day. As we read, the change passed over
> us; the limbs that were immovable, cold, and
> without feeling, warmed; the internal agony ceased,
> our strength came instantaneously, and we rose
> from our bed and stood upon our feet, well.[18]

She dressed, and walked into the next room to the utter astonishment of those waiting for her to die. When she greeted her pastor at the door that afternoon, he thought he was seeing an apparition. The doctor was sent for, but he could only express his incredulity at her improvement. When she told him she had not taken any of the medicine

23 Paradise Road, Swampscott, Massachusetts,
where Mrs. Eddy lived when she was healed in 1866

he had left, his disbelief seemed to strike at her and she felt
suddenly weakened and could no longer stand.

After the doctor left, Mary again turned to her Bible.
Reading from the ninth chapter of Matthew—the healing
of the palsied man confined to his bed—Jesus' words
"Arise, and walk" spoke to her across the centuries. Again
she arose in strength, and the claim of relapse dissolved.
This recovery was so significant because of what it revealed
to her about the spiritual nature of life. She glimpsed ". . .
Life in and of Spirit; this Life being the sole reality of
existence."[19] She later described her recovery as "the
revelation from the divine Mind."[20] This revelation was

both the discovery of divine Truth and the fulfillment of Biblical prophecy of the Comforter promised by Jesus.[21]

Christian Science came to mankind from God through the window of Christ-healing. Mary Baker Eddy was the "transparency for Truth" through which the light of divine Love shone.[22] From birth, God had been preparing her for this mission, nurturing her growth "into such a fitness for it."[23] As her understanding of the divine revelation increased, Mrs. Eddy saw that the discovery of the divine Truth that had been revealed to her through Christ-healing could only be sustained in this world *by* such healing. God's assignment for her was to share with mankind the "science" behind her healing. In the divine light of her revelation, the Bible she knew so well became a new book to her, a textbook that needed to be studied and then put into practice through spiritual healing, as Christ Jesus had practiced two thousand years earlier.

CHAPTER 4

The pioneer alone: a mission revealed
(1866–1868)

ONE MORNING, JUST A FEW MONTHS after her revelatory healing, Mary's husband told her, "You need not expect me home to dinner. I have some business and I may be gone for several days." That day Daniel Patterson eloped with another woman, one of his dental patients. The woman's husband pursued them and brought his wife home. Some days after, this woman turned up at Mary's door looking pale and very haggard. Mrs. Eddy, in recounting this episode to Irving Tomlinson years later, said she asked the woman:

> For what . . . have you come to me? You, who
> have robbed me of my good husband and desolated
> my happy home. You, who have disgraced yourself
> and your family. Why *have* you come to me? She
> replied, "I come to you because of what your
> husband has told me of you. I knew you must be
> a good woman and I felt you would help me."
> I asked her what I could do for her. She said,

"My husband has locked me in a room and only gives me each day a crust [of bread] and cold water, and I know he means to kill me. Today with the help of the servants I escaped through a window to come to you and ask you to go to my husband and ask him to forgive me." I told her that I would do all that I could for her.

The following day I went to her husband's factory, for he was a wealthy man and the family was one of the leading families in the social circles of Lynn. I did not find him in and was told that he had gone on business to Boston. On returning home I wrote him a letter. That night he called at my house. I met him at the door. He said, "I received your letter and I desire to ask if you have really forgiven your husband and can you forgive my wife her cruelty to you." I answered, "I forgive them both and I ask you to forgive them." Then he left me and my heart went with him. I do not know but that I went to God in prayer for that husband and his home. Soon after, I heard that his wife was at the table, for the cruelly wronged husband had forgiven her and their home was again a happy one.[1]

Unfortunately, the same could not be said of Mary's home. Though she accepted Daniel back, he deserted her again a few months later. When he tried to return once more, she told him he could not.

For a period of time he sent her money to pay part of her living expenses, but eventually it stopped. Though having no choice at the time, living off the benevolence of friends was very difficult for Mary Patterson. She had been raised to believe that "the noblest charity is to prevent a man from accepting charity."[2] In 1866 alone, she would change her residence ten times. This period of her life was certainly illustrative of Jesus' words, as recorded in Luke 9, to the man who promised to follow him wherever he went: "Foxes have holes, and birds of the air have nests; but the Son of man hath not where to lay his head."[3]

To follow faithfully the daystar of Christian healing places extraordinary demands on those who would walk in the way Christ points out, who would gain a practical understanding of divine healing. Mary, however, had learned from the gospel that "no man, having put his hand to the plough, and looking back, is fit for the kingdom of God."[4] And as her Way-shower, Christ Jesus, was tempted in the wilderness, so did temptation come her way. Abigail, her elder sister, wrote with an offer to provide a home and income, but added, "There is only one thing I ask of you, Mary, that you give up these ideas which have lately occupied you, that you attend our church and give over your theory of divine healing." Once before Mary had been told she had to give up what she cherished most—her own son. That time she had had neither the strength nor understanding to resist. This time, with the divine revelation firmly in thought, the babe of Christian healing in her grasp, she replied, "I must do the work God has called me to."[5] With the light of this revelation had also come a recognition of the divinely appointed mission. Not only did she feel God-impelled to gain a demonstrable understanding of what had been revealed; it was also imperative that she impart this understanding to others.

For most of her adult life, Mary had been searching for an understanding of how to heal physical ailments—not just improvement, but complete cure. From her study of homeopathy and of Phineas Quimby's human mind methods, she had become convinced that all ailments have a mental nature and that their treatment rests solely in the mind. Now with the divine revelation she had received at the time of her own spiritual healing, it had been shown her that the Mind one needed in treating disease must be the divine Mind, God, and no other. And what made divine healing superior to all other methods was that it not only cured the illness, but it inevitably made the patient better morally, as well.

Friends and acquaintances found it difficult to have Mrs. Patterson live with them for any length of time. While they loved the sweetness of her healing work, digesting the revolutionary ideas she eagerly shared with them was difficult for the less spiritually minded. She herself was

wrestling with the question "how can sinful mortals prove
that a divine Principle heals the sick, as well as governs the
universe, time, space, immortality, man?"[6] To answer this
question, she spent most of her time from the summer of
1866 through the winter of 1869–1870 in hour after hour
of Bible study, and writing down, from the perspective of
the revelation, what she was learning.[7]

At first, Mary was almost overwhelmed by the
immensity of the task before her. She would later say of her
thought at this time,

> . . . it looked as if centuries of spiritual growth were
> requisite to enable me to elucidate or to demon-
> strate what I had discovered: but an unlooked-for,
> imperative call for help impelled me to begin this
> stupendous work at once, and teach the first
> student in Christian Science.[8]

The "call for help" came to her in the form of a child with
an inflamed infected finger:

> [Dorr Phillips] had a bone felon which kept him
> awake at night and out of school during the day.
> Mrs. Patterson had not been to the Phillips house
> for several days, and when she did go and found the
> boy in agony walking the floor, she gently and
> sympathetically questioned him.

"Dorr, will you let me heal that felon?"

"Yes, indeed, Mrs. Patterson, if you can do it," replied the lad.

"Will you promise not to do anything for it or let any one else, if I undertake to cure it?"

"Yes, I promise, and I will keep my word," said Dorr Phillips. He had heard his father and their friend discuss divine healing many times, and had a boy's healthy curiosity to see what would happen if all this talk was actually tried on a wicked, tormenting, festering felon that was making him fairly roar with rage one minute and cry like a girl the next.

That night the boy stopped at his sister Susie's house. "How is your finger?" she asked solicitously.

"Nothing the matter with my finger; it hasn't hurt all day. Mrs. Patterson is treating it."

"What is she doing to it? Let me look at it."

"No, you'll spoil the cure. I promised not to look at it or think about it, nor let any one else touch it or talk about it. And I won't."

The brother and sister looked at each other with half smiles. They were struggling with skepticism.

"Honest, Dorr, doesn't it hurt?"

"No."

"Tell me what she did."

"I don't know what she did, don't know anything about this business, but I'm going to play
fair and keep my word."

The boy actually forgot the felon and when his
attention was called to the finger it was found to be
well. This strange result made an impression on the
family. No one quite knew what to say, and they
were scarcely ready to accept the healing of a sore
finger as a miracle.

"But it is not a miracle," said Mary Baker. "Nor
would it be if it had been a broken wrist or a
withered arm. It is natural, divinely natural. All life
rightly understood is so."[9]

Radical, uncompromised reliance on God's healing grace
had become her standard. It was to base what she would
teach to others as the only standard for Christian healing.

In later years, Mrs. Eddy told her students, "for the first
four years [after the discovery of Christian Science] my
healing work was not acknowledged although I healed
constantly."[10] Another of her first healings also involved a
child. Margaret E. Harding recounted what the child's
mother told her:

Sometime during . . . 1866 Mrs. Norton drove
her young son, George, to Lynn Beach for a day's

outing. At the time George was about seven years of age and had been carried on a pillow since birth, having been born with a deformity commonly know as club-feet, both feet being turned backward, and consequently he had never walked.

Mrs. Norton laid the child upon the pillow on the sand and left him alone while she hitched the horse and went for water. On her return shortly the child had disappeared and the mother searched bewilderedly about, only to find him down by the water and walking with a woman holding his hands, which she released a moment later and George stood alone. Later he took a few steps and from that time was able to walk. The strange woman and the mother both looked into each other's eyes, a little and thanked God for this seemingly miraculous healing. . . .

At the time of the incident, the boy told his mother that the strange lady was walking by, and seeing him stretched upon the pillow with his feet covered, asked why he was not playing with the other children there. He told her he had never walked, and she lifted the shawl and saw why. She put her hands under his arms, and while he protested his inability to do so, told him to stand, and when he was lifted to an upright position, she

guided his feet with her own, supporting him the
while he took his first feeble steps into freedom.

I need not add that the strange lady was Mrs.
Mary B. Glover, who afterwards became Mrs. Eddy,
and the founder of Christian Science.[11]

There is a record of three other healings that were
accomplished by Mrs. Eddy during the last half of 1866:
Dorr Phillips's mother, Hannah, who had dislocated her
hip;[12] a young man delirious with fever;[13] and James
Wheeler who, like Dorr, suffered from a finger felon. Mrs.
Eddy wrote about Mr. Wheeler's healing in later years, "the
day that his physician, an M.D., had proposed to amputate
his finger I asked to be allowed to treat him. My request
was granted. With one mental treatment the finger was
healed. . . ."[14] She shared details of this healing with Irving
Tomlinson:

> [Mr. Wheeler] was antagonistic to Science, but his
> wife was friendly. . . . His wife had already told me
> of his agony and had asked me to help him. He had
> his hat on waiting to take the carriage to visit the
> surgeon. I said to him, "Will you allow me to stand
> here a few minutes before you go and think about
> your finger?" He replied, "If you will be quick, I
> will." I stood in thought for perhaps five minutes

when he said, "There is not a bit of pain or soreness
in my finger." I said, "Take the cloth off and leave
it unbandaged." He did so and in a half hour, after
rubbing his finger and saying, "It doesn't hurt a
particle," he went out, got in his carriage and went
about his business never feeling any inconvenience
from the finger thereafter.[15]

In the fall of that year, Mrs. Patterson met Hiram
Crafts and his wife at a boarding house where she was
staying in Lynn. In Hiram, she found her first student.
She moved to his home in East Stoughton in order to
teach him. While she still had her notes made years earlier
from her discussions with Dr. Quimby, they were not
what she used to teach from. She turned to the Bible. To
teach Hiram she wrote out an explication of chapters 14
through 17 of Matthew's Gospel. For example, of
Matthew 15:2, where the Pharisees ask Jesus why his
disciples break tradition by eating without first washing
their hands, she commented:

> An enquiry of Error why Truth hath left the
> traditions of elders, in that it takes no matter form
> in healing the sick.

For Matthew 15:24, where Jesus tells his disciples that he is
sent to Israel's lost sheep, her notes read:

Then the truth answered, "I am sent by wisdom to save those ideas so misguided as to be lost in error, for such science has come to save."[16]

Mrs. Eddy around 1867

Tintype: Morris Allard Davis

As early as 1867, Mary Baker Eddy began work on a class-book that would become the centerpiece for teaching Christian Science for all time. Over the next few years it would evolve into "The Science of Man, by which the sick are healed. Embracing Questions and Answers in Moral Science." This is the pamphlet she refers to on page ix of *Science and Health with Key to the Scriptures.* It would eventually be incorporated into the Third edition of *Science and Health* as the chapter "Recapitulation."

While in East Stoughton, Mrs. Patterson healed James Ingham of consumption. His testimony appeared in the First edition of *Science and Health* (p. 338):

> I was suffering from pulmonary difficulties, pains in the chest, a hard and unremitting cough, hectic fever, and all those fearful symptoms that made my case alarming. When I first saw Mrs. Glover, I was reduced to such a state of debility as to be unable to walk any distance, or to sit up but a portion of the day; to walk upstairs gave me great suffering from breath. I had no appetite, and seemed surely going down the victim of consumption. I had not received her attention but a short time, when my bad symptoms disappeared, and I regained health. During this time, I rode out in storms to visit her, and found the damp weather had no effect on me. From my personal experience I am led to believe the science by which she not only heals the sick

but explains the way to keep well, is deserving the
earnest attention of [the] community; her cures
are not the result of medicine, mediumship, or
mesmerism, but the application of a Principle that
she understands.

In the spring of 1867, the Crafts and Mrs. Patterson
moved to Taunton. There, Hiram advertised his services as
a healer in the local newspapers. In later years, he wrote of
Mrs. Eddy's teaching:

About rubbing the head &c. Mrs. Eddy never
instructed me to rub the head, or body, or
manipulate in any forme. But when I was a
Spiritualist, I used to use water and rub the head,
limbs and body. So, sometimes when I was studying
with her I would try it, but I did not say anything
to her about it. . . .
We used nothing outside of the New
Testament, she had no manuscripts of any kind
until after I had been studying six months.[17]

While Hiram eventually gave up his belief in
spiritualism, his wife could not. Mrs. Crafts came to resent
her husband's teacher, and Mary saw the wisdom of
moving on. But before finally leaving, Mary made a trip to
Sanbornton Bridge, New Hampshire. While there she
healed her niece, Ellen Pilsbury, who was dying of enteritis,

95 J.H.   CRAFTS. HIRAM S

Hebron N H Feb 23 1902

Mr C. A. Frye

Dear Sir

I have had all of the manuscript
recopied. I think it is all right.
I sincerely hope it will stand
inspection. will mail it monday.
I sent the Negatives by Exp⁷.
I began study with Mrs Eddy
in aug 1866. and finished my
studies aug 1867.

            Mrs Patterson never
called on Mrs Eddy while she
was with me. she had some
corespondence with him. of
what nature I did not know,
I should say that she was pretty
well deserted in 1866,

CRAFTS, HIRAM S. 1/2/72

about rubing the head &c.
Mrs Eddy never instructed
me to rub the head. or body.
or manipulate in any forme.
But when I was a Spiritualist.
I used to use water and rub the
head. limbs and body.
So. sometimes when I was
studying with her I would
try it. but I did not say
anything to her about it.
Be wise as a Serpent. and harmless
as a Dove.
        We used nothing outside
of the New testament. she
had no manuscripts of any kind
until after I had been studying
six months.
                Fraternally your
    Hiram S Crafts

and had been given up by the family's medical physician (see pages 223–224). Neither Mary's visit, nor this healing, however, did anything to quiet her family's opposition to her "science."

Sibyl Wilbur's account of this opposition, bred of familiarity, compared it to the opposition Jesus faced "when in Nazareth. 'Is not this the carpenter's son?' they asked, and, 'Are not his brothers and sisters here with us?'" Mrs. Eddy was touched by this reference in Wilbur's biography, telling Irving Tomlinson, "Yes, it was even so."[18] This visit effectively ended Mary's relations with her sisters. A brother, too, would refuse to accept her aid and soon pass on. She returned to Taunton for a short time, and then found a home with Mary Webster in Amesbury. Here, she met her second student, nineteen-year-old Richard Kennedy.

While living at Mary Webster's, Mrs. Patterson continued working on a verse-by-verse explication of the book of Genesis. In her introductory remarks to this work, she speaks of the "science" she has discovered: "we . . . find the blessed statement of this science contained in the Bible, and its full demonstration in casting out error, and healing the sick."[19] When she wrote this she first placed "healing the sick" before "casting out error" and then switched their order. The third verse in the one hundred and third Psalm would have confirmed this choice. She had been healed of an illness during her childhood when her brother Albert had

25 Of old hast thou laid the foundation of the earth: and the heavens *are* the work of thy hands.

26 They shall perish, but thou shalt endure: yea, all of them shall wax old like a garment; as a vesture shalt thou change them, and they shall be changed:

27 But thou *art* the same, and thy years shall have no end.

28 The children of thy servants shall continue, and their seed shall be established before thee.

PSALM CIII.

1 *An exhortation to bless God for his mercy,* 15 *and for the constancy thereof.*

A Psalm of David.

BLESS the LORD, O my soul: and all that is within me, *bless* his holy name.

2 Bless the LORD, O my soul, and forget not all his benefits:

3 Who forgiveth all thine iniquities; who healeth all thy diseases;

4 Who redeemeth thy life from destruction; who crowneth thee with lovingkindness and tender mercies;

5 Who satisfieth thy mouth with good *things;* so *that* thy youth is renewed like the eagle's.

6 The LORD executeth righteousness and judgment for all that are oppressed.

7 He made known his ways unto Moses, his acts unto the children of Israel.

8 The LORD *is* merciful and gracious, slow to anger, and plenteous in mercy.

K   145

read the psalm aloud to her: "[the Lord] forgiveth all thine iniquities; . . . [He] healeth all thy diseases."[20] Mary knew that the sick could be healed with her "science" only as the Truth of being first cast out error or sin in the thought of both the physician and the patient. And she knew that turning to God in prayer was the only way to do this.

CHAPTER 5

Moral Science
(1868–1870)

*I*N 1868 MRS. GLOVER, as she was then calling herself, was seeking a thorough understanding of the Principle and rules of the divine Science that had healed her. The Bible had become her only textbook and she was healing others in accord with the divine laws she was discovering in those Scriptures.

A telegram for "Mrs. Mary B. Glover" arrived at the Websters' on May 30, a Saturday. It was from Manchester, New Hampshire. "Mrs. Gale is very sick, please come Monday morning if possible. Answer yes or no." Her friends had come to think of her as a healer at this time. Mrs. Glover packed her bag immediately and went to see Mary Gale. When she arrived, the doctors informed her there was no hope, Mrs. Gale could not live. She was dying of pneumonia. Mrs. Glover healed her on the spot.[1] This healing is referred to in Mrs. Eddy's book *The First Church of Christ, Scientist, and Miscellany* on page 105. In later years when asked by a student what had prompted her to write *Science and Health with Key to the Scriptures*,

Mrs. Eddy told her about this healing. The student, Clara Shannon, relates in her reminiscence:

> . . . when [Mrs. Glover] entered the room the patient was propped up with many pillows, and could not speak. Our Leader saw that what she needed was an arousal, and [taking away the pillows] told her that she could get up and that she would help her dress. [Mrs. Gale] was instantaneously healed and well. . . .
>
> One of the doctors, an old, experienced physician witnessed this, and he said, "How did you do it, what did you do?" [Mrs. Glover] said, "I can't tell you, it was God," and he said, "Why don't you write it in a book, publish it, and give it to the world?" When she returned home she opened her Bible, and her eyes fell on the words "Thus speaketh the Lord God of Israel, saying, Write thee all the words that I have spoken unto thee in a book." Jeremiah 30:2.[2]

On returning to Amesbury, Mary found that Mrs. Webster's son was bringing his family to stay in the house for summer vacation. All the boarders were forced to move. Mary's next home was with Sarah Bagley, who introduced her to the poet John Greenleaf Whittier. She healed him of consumption when they met.[3]

After two months Mary moved again. This time she found a home south of Boston with the Wentworth family in Stoughton. Mary had met the Wentworths previously when she was living with her first pupil, Hiram Crafts, and his wife. She had healed Mr. Wentworth of sciatica, and his daughter, Celia, of consumption. These healings prompted Mrs. Wentworth to ask Mrs. Glover to teach her how to heal. Mrs. Eddy would later write about her experience with the Wentworths:

> When I was called to go teach Mrs. Sally Wentworth at Stoughton I did so at a great sacrifice. They were *very* poor. Mr. Wentworth was a shoemaker by trade but had been sick for a long time & unable to work. I healed him of socalled incurable hip-disease in one treatment.
>
> They had scarcely enough money with which to provide food and lived in a house black for want of paint with a great boulder directly front of their door. I paid for having the house painted and for making a lawn front of their house. I healed Mr. & Mrs. Wentworth and their 2 girls free of charge, taught Mrs. W. & remained in their family & directed & assisted her in getting up a practice. She told me when I left their home that she was averaging $50 per week from her practice at healing. . . .

> I had an agreement with Mrs. Wentworth that
> she should give me rent and board while with them
> and pay me a percentage on her practice in return
> for teaching her, but . . . I never received any
> money from her.[4]

Mary healed Mrs. Wentworth's chronic throat disease, and her younger daughter, Lucy, of deafness. And in addition to his hip trouble, she healed Alanson Wentworth of smoking and chewing tobacco. Also during her stay in Stoughton, Mrs. Glover healed John Scott, within an hour, of enteritis and bowel stoppage. This healing is related on pages 69 and 70 of *Miscellaneous Writings:*

> I was once called to visit a sick man to whom
> the regular physicians had given three doses of
> Croton oil, and then had left him to die. Upon my
> arrival I found him barely alive, and in terrible
> agony. In one hour he was well, and the next day he
> attended to his business. I removed the stoppage,
> healed him of enteritis, and neutralized the bad
> effects of the poisonous oil. His physicians had
> failed even to move his bowels,—though the won-
> der was, with the means used in their effort to
> accomplish this result, that they had not quite
> killed him. According to their diagnosis, the exciting
> cause of the inflammation and stoppage was—eating

smoked herring. The man is living yet; and I will send his address to any one who may wish to apply to him for information about his case.

Now comes the question: Had that sick man dominion over the fish in his stomach?

His want of control over "the fish of the sea" must have been an illusion, or else the Scriptures misstate man's power. That the Bible is true I believe, not only, but I *demonstrated* its truth when I exercised my power over the fish, cast out the sick man's illusion, and healed him. Thus it was shown that the healing action of Mind upon the body has its only explanation in divine metaphysics.

Especially interesting for what it adds to this account, is the write-up of it in the *Boston Traveller* in 1900:

. . . Remarkable as was the man's physical healing, even more remarkable was the transformation in his thought and life. His wife told Mrs. [Glover] a few days later that she had never before seen him [hug] his children as other fathers did, but on the night of his recovery he called them to him, and taking them in his arms he told them that he loved them; and with tears rolling down his cheeks he said to his wife, "I am going to be a better man." It is not strange that the happy wife said to Mrs. [Glover],

"Oh, how I thank you for restoring my husband to
health, but more than all, I am grateful for what
you have done for him morally and spiritually."[5]

It was this aspect of moral regeneration that set Mrs.
Glover's "science" apart from any other healing method. She
saw it as the most important part, which very likely caused
her originally to call her discovery Moral Science. This
name first appeared in the title of her teaching manuscript:
"The Science of Man, by which the sick are healed.
Embracing Questions and Answers in Moral Science." She
completed this work while at the Wentworths'.

In this manuscript Mrs. Glover had written, "The sick
have only to waken from this dream of life in matter—of
pain, and disease in matter, yea, of sensation in matter that
you call personal sense, to realize themselves well: but to
break up this illusion requires much growth on your part,
much progress from sense to Soul."[6] She followed this
statement a little further on with:

Ques. What is the proper method and the one Jesus
employed to heal the sick?
Ans. To cast out error with truth; and this heals the
sick, and is Science, and no other process is.
Ques. How can I succeed in doing this so that my
demonstration in healing shall be wonderful and
immediate?

Ans. By being like Jesus, by asking yourself am I
honest, am I just, am I merciful, am I pure?

In a sermon she gave in Boston several years later, Mrs.
Eddy shared with the congregation one of her early healing
works:

> I had an interview this last week with a
> gentleman who had escaped from a mad-house in
> 1868. He was a raving maniac, and they were in
> pursuit of him. He stopped at the place where I
> boarded, and the lady ran for me and said, "I am
> well nigh frightened to death; won't you come?
> Here is a maniac threatening our lives. My daughter
> has fled, and I am come for you."
> I went with her. He took a chair, and poised it,
> but I looked upward, and he dropped the chair, and
> asked if I had something to say to him. I said I had,
> all from the spiritual side, "The first thing is you
> have no disease of the brain; you need never have
> been in the insane hospital." Then came the
> comfort and relief, and the poor maniac fell on his
> knees before me; he was cured. I saw him last week,
> married, the father of children, a well man. He
> never was insane after that.
> Now I feel like asking your forgiveness for
> what I am saying, you must think it so perfectly

incomprehensible. He said to me last week, "Do you remember, Mrs. Eddy, when I sat at your feet and you toyed with my curls. I said what are you doing and you said, I am anointing your hair with oil, and," he continued, "my hair was covered with oil; for months I could feel it like dew upon my head."

I remembered it; I remembered that when he fell before me, I reached out my hand in benediction. It touched his head, and he said, "What are you doing?" [I replied,] "Anointing your head with oil." I meant what David said, "He anointed my head with oil, so that my cup runneth over." I meant the anointing of Truth like the dew or the gentle rain, coming upon that poor, agonized brain, and he thought it was hair-oil and that I was toying with his hair!⁷

After a year and a half at the Wentworths', Mary went back to Amesbury to teach Sarah Bagley. While there she met with Richard Kennedy, her second student whom she had taught two years earlier. Mr. Kennedy was twenty-one years old and very eager to start in the full-time practice of healing. He convinced Mrs. Glover to form a teacher/practitioner partnership with him. He would treat patients and she would guide his practice. Before agreeing to this Mary said to him, "Richard, this is a very spiritual life that Mind Science exacts, and the world offers many alluring temptations. You know but little of them as yet. If you follow me you must cross swords with the world. Are you spiritually-minded enough to take up my work and stand by it?"[8] With more enthusiasm than wisdom, he assured her he was.

Because she saw the need to establish her student's practice in a larger town, Mrs. Glover and Mr. Kennedy moved to Lynn in May 1870. Her hope was that Richard's practice would prompt calls for teaching. As can be seen from her letter to Sarah Bagley in July, she was not disappointed:

> I have all calling on me for instruction, and why, if I
> am not better than others I am not fit to teach God
> beyond them and could not. Richard is literally
> overrun with patients, as soon as it was known that I
> had brought a student here the people began to
> throng him. We had had some fine presents from
> the sick who were healed. I had a *magnificent* hat
> given me & a sash that was at least 10 dollars & the
> hat was more, and several other beautiful presents.
> On the 4th we had some excellent cherries sent in.
> We enjoy our *moments* of leisure more than can be
> named. In the evening of the 4th our rooms were
> filled with company to hear the concert given on the
> Common by the brass band.[9]

Mary's guidance of her student's practice was more active than passive. Richard Kennedy did not have the confidence to treat his patients without resorting to physical manipulation, rubbing the head or stomach. Though she never used this method herself, Mrs. Glover allowed it to continue with the hope that he would grow out of it. He never did. A girl who knew her during this period wrote, "Mrs. [Glover] used to do the treating and Dr. Kennedy the rubbing."[10] And Mrs. Eddy wrote in a letter in 1888:

> When my second student went into practice I did the healing for him sitting in a cold gloomy ante-room while he was in the front office as the physician. This I did because my first student stopped his practice the first year, so great was the persecution, and to get one started I had to do the work at first, and not be seen in doing it.
>
> I was pleased with this out-of-sight labor, liked it much better than to be in front. . . .[11]

In 1909, Mrs. Eddy told Irving Tomlinson more about what her life was like during that time:

> . . . At one time in Lynn I had something like one hundred cases, but a student was perceptively the practitioner. I refused to take patients because I was

carrying the Cause and my time was occupied with
many other matters.

I remember one case brought to the rooms well
nigh prostrated and one which had been given up
as hopeless. I happened to be in the ante-room
when the only seat was an upturned tub. Down I
sat upon it, silently treated the patient, and she left
fully healed.[12]

The "many other matters" Mrs. Glover was concerned
with at that time involved teaching, writing, and counseling.
In August 1870 she taught her first class of six students.
Three months later, she taught another class of similar size.
Samuel Putnam Bancroft was a member of that class, and
wrote extensively of his experiences with his teacher during
this period. True warmth and appreciation flow through his
words as he describes what it was like to be taught by Mrs.
Glover, of her great concern for the welfare and progress of
her students. At one point she saved the life of his young
child, who was severely ill.[13] Mr. Bancroft writes:

Mrs. [Glover] did not claim to be a teacher of
religion, however, but of a method of healing the
sick without the use of medicine. That was what
induced us to study with her. The object of some
was to regain health; of others, to commercialize the
knowledge acquired. They considered it a sound

business proposition. Her religious views, while not
concealed, were not capitalized. Later, we learned
that our success or failure in healing depended on
the purity of our lives, as well as on the instruction
she gave us.[14]

Her continuing Bible study furnished a strong
foundation. In order to facilitate her teaching, Mary also
wrote papers for her classes. "The Soul's Inquiries of Man,"
"Spiritualism," and "Personal Sense" were some of the
titles. She used these in conjunction with her teaching
manuscript, *The Science of Man*. Occasionally a question
would be asked in class that the teacher felt was important
enough to answer in writing. One of these was from Mr.
Bancroft, who asked how they should metaphysically view
the process of teaching. As part of her answer, Mrs. Glover
wrote:

When I teach science it is not woman that
addresses man, it is the principle and soul bringing
out its idea. . . . My scholars may learn from me
what they could not learn from the same words if
uttered by another with less wisdom than even my
"grain of mustard seed," hence, it is not the words,
but the amount of soul that comes forth to destroy
error.[15]

For Mary, the ability to heal came from far more than an intellectual understanding of metaphysical concepts. It was a matter of whether spiritual sense or material sense governed the practitioner. Without the spiritual aspect, the healing practice turned into a mesmeric exercise of one human mind controlling another. This is why she kept stressing to her students the need for greater goodness and purity in their thought and lives. As she stated in a further revision of *The Science of Man,* "A student of Moral Science, and this is the Science of man, must be a pure and undefiled Christian, in order to make the most rapid progress in healing. . . ."[16] Mary Gatchell, who lived for a time in the same house as Mrs. Glover, described her as "the purest minded woman I ever knew."[17] This is how Mary could instantaneously heal a badly deformed man sitting on the sidewalk in Lynn by simply telling him that God loved him. Mrs. Eddy described this healing to a member of her household in 1907:

> . . . I was walking along the street . . . and saw this
> cripple, with one knee drawn up to his chin; . . .
> The other limb was drawn the other way, up his
> back. I came up to him and read on a piece of
> paper pinned on his shoulder, "Help this poor
> cripple." I had no money to give him so I
> whispered in his ear, "God loves you." And he
> got up perfectly straight and well. He ran into

[Lucy Allen's] house and asked who that woman is, pointing to [me.] The lady told him, "it is Mrs. Glover." [He replied,] "no it isn't, it's an angel."[18]

In *Science and Health,* Mrs. Eddy writes that one "must prove, through living as well as healing and teaching, that Christ's way is the only one by which mortals are radically saved from sin and sickness."[19] Before she wrote the words, she lived them.

CHAPTER 6

Teacher, counselor, author
(1871–1874)

As MARY BAKER EDDY WENT FORWARD in her life as teacher, author, and founder, sharing Christian Science with mankind, she never stopped healing. In fact, she would not have been able to carry out the duties that each of these divinely motivated roles demanded, without her God-given ability to heal. It permeated everything she did.

In 1871, Mrs. Glover was conducting classes in Moral Science. She taught in the evenings in the same building where she also lived, Susie Magoun's school for young girls. One day Miss Magoun told her about a girl in her school who was mute, but could hear perfectly well. Mrs. Eddy wrote about this in 1898:

> The next time the child passed my door on her way
> to school I met her and spoke a few words to her.
> When the question came around to her in class she
> astonished the whole school by promptly answering
> in a clear strong voice.[1]

This ability to heal quickly and completely was what Mrs. Glover was striving so earnestly to teach to those interested in learning. For the most part they came from the working-class people of Lynn. The price she put on her lessons was $300, about one third of a worker's annual salary. In today's economy the fee would be equivalent to about $9,000. Not only did this show the value she placed on what she was teaching, it also helped to ensure that the student's interest was deep and abiding, and not just a matter of idle curiosity. However, she did take a number of students at a reduced fee, and some needy students were taught gratuitously if she felt they were sincere. For Mary, her discovery of divine Science, which had come as a revelation from God, was a "pearl of great price."[3] And scientific Christian healing was a lifework, not simply another way to earn a living. She knew that a total commitment was essential to success in this healing work.

Mrs. Glover taught only one class in 1871. It was held in April. The rest of her time was taken up in counseling and supporting her students in their healing practices. Caring for one's pupils after formal lessons have been completed remains to this day, at Mrs. Eddy's impetus, a moral imperative on teachers of Christian Science.[3] Mary watched over her students as if they were her own children, and hoped that their practices would decrease the continual call on her personally to do healing work. This, however, was not the case in the beginning. As she wrote in 1901:

> I could not at first make a student see how to
> heal the sick with prayer alone for each student that
> I taught thirty years ago was not enough of a
> Christian to pray with sufficient faith and under-
> standing to heal the sick.

So she told her students "to practice as best they could," working with what they did understand. Some resorted to rubbing the heads of their patients. Mrs. Eddy continued:

> This went on till I had gained a clearer sense of
> the divine Principle of Science through which I
> learned it was impossible to practice it by any
> material method of manipulation. Then I hastened
> to instruct my students not to lay hands on the sick
> but to accept only the spiritual interpretation of that
> Scripture, namely, to apply through prayer the power
> of God to heal the sick & by that time some of them
> had grown to the point of spiritual understanding
> sufficiently to take in my meaning. . . .[4]

As she waited for the spiritual growth of her pupils, Mrs. Glover naturally continued to respond to calls for healing. At one point, she was asked to help a man with a severe fever who had refused to eat anything for a week. His two physicians declared he would die. When she entered his room, the man was delirious. He was saying, "This tastes

Photo: W. T. Bowers

Mrs. Eddy in 1871

good and that tastes good," but there was no food in the room. Mrs. Glover said to the doctors, "With that consciousness he can live without eating anything." When they laughed at her, she replied, "Well, then he *can* eat," and immediately he was in his right mind. He recognized someone in the room and asked for something to eat. After finishing his meal, he dressed, went outside, and was completely well. Many years later, Mrs. Eddy told a member of her household that she had not given any thought to the man's physical condition, only to the fact that "'God is all,' and shut out what the physicians had said and everything else from the [material] sense side."[5]

In healing, Mrs. Eddy could speak with authority because of the depth of her spiritual understanding and her compassion tempered with the need to reach her patient. She recounted to the same individual another healing that occurred during this period:

> A lady in Lynn was so angry at me she would not speak to me after healing her daughter because she said I spoke disrespectfully to her dying daughter. The physicians had said there was only a little piece of her lung left and she was dying. I was called and there were spiritualists around. I tried to reach her thought, but no, could not get at it. So I said, "Get out of that bed." Then I called to those in the other room, "Bring her clothes." The girl got up and was well; never even coughed again. . . . I speak sharply sometimes, but the thought must *move.*[6]

Mrs. Glover herself never practiced physical manipulation in her own healing work. But when she told her students, at the beginning of 1872, that they must drop it completely from their practice, this caused a stir with some of them. Her second student, Richard Kennedy, refused to comply. She tried for a time to make him see the importance of taking this step, but he would not change his ways. So they dissolved their formal partnership that had been agreed on when they first came to Lynn together two years earlier.

Also, at the beginning of 1872, another former pupil, Wallace Wright, used a Lynn newspaper to attack Mrs. Glover's teaching and practice, calling it mesmerism. In her response she made her first public statement about her "science" through the same newspaper. Wright's published reply prompted a second statement, which Mrs. Glover titled, "Moral Science and Mesmerism." She ended this letter "To the Public" this way:

> I am preparing a work on Moral and Physical Science, that I shall submit to the public as soon as it is completed. This work is laborious, and I have not much opportunity to write, hence the delay in publishing. I withhold my MSS. from all eyes but my students', first, because they are mere outlines of my subject, that require me to fill up by explanation, and secondly, because I think the mass of minds are not yet prepared to digest this subject.[7]

The "work" she was preparing would become the textbook for her "science." In March of 1872, she held one more class and then stopped teaching in order to devote her entire effort over the next three years to the writing of *Science and Health*.

When Mary had first considered the problem of what to do for her students, having taken away their crutch of physical manipulation, she did not immediately see the solution. She wrote about this years later on the flyleaf of one of her Bibles:

> Before writing *Science and Health with Key to the Scriptures* I had asked God for weeks to tell me what next I should do and each day I opened the Bible for my answer, but did not receive it. But when I grew to receiving it I opened again and the first verse I looked at was in Isaiah 30:8.[8]

This verse reads, "Now go, write it before them in a table, and note it in a book, that it may be for the time to come for ever and ever."

Mrs. Eddy told Irving C. Tomlinson in 1900 that it was important to include in a biographical piece he was

Jan. 20, 1872

For the Transcript.

Mr. Editor:—I casually noticed in the *Transcript* an attack by W. W. Wright on the Moral and Physical Science that I teach, in which he states it is mesmerism, and that the MSS. he holds prove this. Mr. Wright is under a three thousand dollar bond not to show those MSS. Can he annul this agreement and *practice* or *understand Moral* Science? But the same MSS. are in the hands of other of my students in this city, who will answer this question, and if the reader of his article, or any one desiring to learn this Science, will call on me, at 29 South Common street, they shall have the opportunity to judge for themselves, as I will satisfy them on this point; or, if I am out, one of my former students, Dr. Kennedy, with whom I am in business, will answer this question of Moral Science.

Mr. Wright says his principal reason for writing on this subject was to prevent others from being led into it. Here he is honest. 'Tis but a few weeks since he called on me and threatened that, if I did not refund his tuition fee and pay him two hundred dollars extra, he would prevent my ever having another class in this city. Said he, "My simple purpose now is revenge, and I will have it,"—and this, too, immediately after saying to individuals in this city that the last lesson the class received, of which he was a member, was alone worth all he had paid for tuition. The "whistle" was not so "dear" then. Very soon after this, however, I received a letter from him, requesting

Lynn Transcript

me to pay him over and above all I had received from him, or, in case I should not, he would ruin the Science. I smiled at the threat, and told a lady at my side, " If you see him. tell him first to take a bucket and dip the Atlantic dry, and then try his powers on this next scheme." The student in Knoxville, to whom he referred, wrote me :—" Mr. Wright puts a false construction on the Science, but says ' he does not question its *morality* and *Christianity*.' " Also, in his letter to me he never referred to mesmerism, but said, (here I copy *verbatim*) :—" While I do not question the right of it, it teaches a deprivation of social enjoyment if we would attain the *highest* round in the ladder of Science." Was not this the " side " referred to in his newspaper article, in which he said, " Had I been shown both sides nothing could have induced me to take it up "?

Christianity as he calls it at one time, and mesmerism at another, cannot be the " two sides," for these are separated by barriers that neither a geometrical figure nor a malicious falsehood would ever unite.

My few remaining years will be devoted to the cause I have espoused, viz :—to teach and to demonstrate the Moral and Physical Science that can heal the sick. Well knowing as I do that God hath bidden me, I shall steadfastly adhere to my purpose to benefit my suffering fellow beings, even though it be amid the most malignant misrepresentation and persecution.

MARY M. B. GLOVER.

In response to Wallace Wright's article, Mrs. Eddy wrote this Letter to the Editor to the Lynn Transcript. It was published January 20, 1872.

working on something she considered to be a significant "epoch" in her life. At age seven when her friends asked what she was going to do when she grew up, she replied, "Write a book."[9] And it turned out to be not just *any* book filled with good thoughts and theories, but a hands-on textbook that would explain the "science of Life"[10]—a textbook that makes this "science" something a student can practice in his daily life, enabling him, entirely through prayer, to overcome the problems of material living, whether they be moral, mental, or physical. However, the author made a demand on the student: ". . . those who would learn this science without a high moral standard will fail to understand it until they go up higher."[11] Mr. Wright, who had attacked her in the newspaper, was one who felt that too much was being asked in order to go up higher. In a letter to her he had complained, "While I do not question the right of it, it teaches a deprivation of social enjoyment if we would attain the *highest* round in the ladder of Science."[12]

Mrs. Glover did counsel her students in line with Christ Jesus' teaching that while they may be "in" the world, they must not be "of" the world.[13] Her life was certainly an example of this. Every waking hour of her day was devoted to "Science." Although she planned most of it to be spent in writing, calls for help came to her constantly, and she could not refuse those in need. One can see the blessing this brought to her writing, however, as she included some of these healings in the First edition of her textbook:

The following is a case of heart disease described in a letter from a lady at New York. ". . . The day you received my husband's letter I became conscious, for the first time for forty-eight hours; my servant brought my wrapper and I rose from bed and sat up. The attack of the heart had lasted two days, and no one thinks I could have survived but for the mysterious help I received from you. The enlargement of my left side is all gone and the M.D.'s pronounce me entirely rid of heart disease. I have been afflicted with it from infancy, until it became organic enlargement of the heart and dropsy of the chest. I was only waiting, and almost longing, to die; but you have healed me; and yet how wonderful to think of it, when we have never seen each other! We return to Europe next week. I feel perfectly well."[14]

and

The following is from a lady in Lynn: "My little son, one year and a half old, was a great sufferer from disease of the bowels, until he was reduced to almost a skeleton, and growing worse constantly; could take nothing but gruel, or some very simple nutriment. At that time the physicians had given him up, saying they could do no more for him, but you came in one morning, took him up from the cradle in your arms, kissed him, laid him down again and went out. In less than an hour he called for his playthings, got up and appeared quite well. All his symptoms changed at once. For months previously nothing but blood and mucous had passed his bowels, but that very day the evacuation was natural, and he has not suffered since from his complaint, and it is more than two years since he was cured. Immediately after you saw him, he ate all he wanted, and one thing was a quantity of cabbage just before going to bed, from which he never suffered in the least."[15]

There's more to this last healing than appeared in the First edition of *Science and Health.* When Mrs. Glover came to the home, she also found the woman's husband confined to his bed with rheumatism and a little daughter who was deaf. By the time she left the house, less than half an hour after she had arrived, both of these cases had been healed, too.[16]

Many years later Mrs. Eddy told one of her students about this experience, which prompted the question "When will we be able to do work like that?" Looking off in the distance, Mrs. Eddy replied, "It is Love that heals, only Love!" The student, Miss Nemi Robertson, repeated the question, "But when will *we* be able to do such work?" This time her teacher looked directly at her and said quietly, "When you believe what you say. I believe every statement of Truth that I make."[17] And she recorded those statements of Truth in her textbook, *Science and Health with Key to the Scriptures,* so that all who study them may be purified, and heal as she did.

CHAPTER 7

The *"cause of Truth"*
(1875–1879)

BETWEEN 1872 AND 1875, Mary Glover was writing the textbook to explain the Science she had discovered in 1866 through divine revelation.[1] Since that discovery, she had been intensively studying the Bible, healing the sick through prayer alone, and teaching others how to heal. She suspended teaching in 1872 in order to devote her full time to writing *The Science of Life*. This was the original title for her work, which she changed after learning of a book with that same title already in print. Mrs. Eddy later wrote of this:

> Six weeks I waited on God to suggest a name for the
> book I had been writing. Its title, Science and
> Health, came to me in the silence of night, when the
> steadfast stars watched over the world,—when
> slumber had fled,—and I rose and recorded the
> hallowed suggestion. The following day I showed it
> to my literary friends, who advised me to drop both
> the book and the title. To this, however, I gave no
> heed, feeling sure that God had led me to write that
> book, and had whispered that name to my waiting

hope and prayer. It was to me the "still, small voice"
that came to Elijah after the earthquake and the fire.[2]

At the beginning of 1875, Mrs. Glover was boarding
with Amos Scribner and his wife at 7 Broad Street in Lynn,
Massachusetts. One night, Mr. Scribner was called to stay
with a friend who had been very ill for some time with two
kinds of fever. He was reluctant to go because the friend
was now said to be dying. Years later, Mrs. Eddy wrote
about that evening:

> When I heard of the circumstances I said to
> him, "go & I will heal him for you." I also told him
> the signs that he would see as my work on the case
> progressed. He said, "well supposing when I get
> there he is dead?" I said, "he won't be, & at 9 (this
> was 7) I will cure him if you will ask every one but
> yourself to leave the room."
>
> "But," he said, "supposing he is dying before
> then?"
>
> "Then I will cure him at that time."
>
> He had seen me heal his wife of child bed fever
> & his son of choler infantum & had utter confi-
> dence in my ability & said, "I will go." When he
> arrived there the man was very low & he soon
> requested all to leave the room that he might have
> the man wholly in his care.
>
> Soon the man opened his eyes & said, "hello!
> Amos! Is that you, how glad I am to see you."

A[mos] said, "would you not like to get up?" He
said, "yes, it is rather early to go to bed," & he got
up & dressed himself & then wanted something to
eat. The next day he was out of the house perfectly
well.

This case was so well known that people would
gather on the corner of streets & talk about [it,] the
whole city was shocked by it.[3]

In the Preface of her soon-to-be-published book, Mrs.
Glover would write, ". . . we propose to settle the question
of 'What is Truth?' on the ground of proof. Let that
method of healing the sick and establishing Christianity, be
adopted, that is found to give the most health, and make
the best Christians. . . ."[4] Her "method of healing"—
demonstrating the reality of the divine Science that had
been revealed to her by God—did "give the most health,
and make the best Christians"; it treated the whole man,
transforming human character while it healed the body.
This defines what Christian Science healing can
accomplish.

On October 30, 1875, Mrs. Glover's book, *Science and
Health,* was published in its First edition of one thousand
copies. The months leading up to that luminous day had
been exceedingly full. In the spring and summer, Mary had
been occupied with not only correcting printer's proofs but
also adding her observations on mental malpractice to the
book's last chapter, "Healing the Sick." She described the
writing of this addition as a "painful task,"[5] but one she had

No. 8, now 12, Broad Street,
Lynn, Massachusetts.
The skylight window
is in the attic room where
Mrs. Eddy wrote.

SCIENCE

AND

HEALTH.

BY

MARY BAKER GLOVER.

BOSTON:
CHRISTIAN SCIENTIST PUBLISHING COMPANY.
1875.

The title page of the
First edition of *Science and Health*

PREFACE.

———

LEANING on the sustaining Infinite with loving trust, the trials of to-day are brief, and to-morrow is big with blessings. The wakeful shepherd tending his flocks, beholds from the mountain's top the first faint morning beam ere cometh the risen day. So from Soul's loftier summits shines the pale star to the prophet shepherd, and it traverses night, over to where the young child lies in cradled obscurity that shall waken a world. Over the night of error dawn the morning beams and guiding star of Truth, and " the wise men are led by it to Science, to that which repeats the eternal harmony reproduced in proof of immortality and God. The time for thinkers has come; and the time for revolutions, ecclesiastic and social, must come. Truth, independent of doctrines or time-honored systems, stands at the threshold of history. Contentment with the past, or the cold conventionality of custom, may no longer shut the door on science; though empires fall, " He whose right it is shall reign." Ignorance of God should no longer be the stepping-stone to faith; understanding Him " whom to know aright is Life " is the only guaranty of obedience.

Since the hoary centuries but faintly shadow forth the tireless Intelligence at work for man, this volume

3

The opening page of the
First edition of *Science and Health*

become convinced was necessary to alert readers to the danger of straying from Christian healing into mesmerism. These sixteen pages were written at 8 Broad Street, her new home in Lynn. Mary had purchased the house in March and resumed teaching in April, using the front parlor as her classroom. A month after this, on May 23, she delivered a lecture entitled "Christ Healing the Sick" at Concert Hall on Market Street in Lynn. This was her first public address on Christian Science.

Whether teaching or lecturing, *healing* was at the center of all Mary's efforts. She wrote a prospective student in 1876 about her teaching, ". . . if I do not make [pupils] capable of healing I will refund the money to them."[6] To her, teaching was not about pupils' learning previously unknown facts; its purpose was to produce students who could heal through Christian prayer alone. Though it became necessary to gradually move from a public to a private practice of spiritual healing as the demands of establishing the Christian Science movement grew, Mrs. Glover's own healing work continued as calls for help kept coming. One of these was from the son of a widow in Lynn; he had a degenerative shinbone. The boy's doctor had prescribed an opiate, which he took every two hours, to dull the pain. When Mrs. Glover came to him, the day he was to have his leg amputated,[7] there was a question whether he would live. She wrote about the results:

> The next day after my visit he was out on the street,
> took no more morphine, and that winter attended

the dancing school. About a month after I healed
him, he called on me and I noticed that his foot
turned unnaturally outward. I immediately changed
that and he walked across the floor with the foot in
its natural position.[8]

In 1901, Calvin Frye, Mrs. Eddy's private secretary, wrote in
his diary that she had spoken of this healing to him and said,
"I knew that if he died he would awake to find he had not
that disease and I wanted to wake him to it *before he died.*"[9]

Waking thought to the truth about the allness and
goodness of God, and of man as His perfect reflection, is
central to Christian Science. It produces healing and
motivates all the activities that are undertaken in its
name. Awakening mankind to divine Truth was certainly
behind the writing of *Science and Health,* but its author
was not content simply to produce the book and then
leave the outreach of its message to the whim of public
interest. Mary Baker Glover understood it to be part of
her divinely appointed mission to see that the book's
message reached all that "hunger and thirst after
righteousness"—purity, health, and wholeness—so that
"they shall be filled."[10] And so, a month and a half after
her book appeared, we find her writing to a student about
"our glorious cause."[11] What had started out more than
thirty years earlier as a search for true health, had,
through God's gracious preparation, transformed an
invalid into a healer, teacher, author, and now founder of
the "cause" of Christian Science.

In 1876, one of Mrs. Glover's primary concerns was getting *Science and Health* in the hands of the public. She appointed Daniel Spofford, one of her students, as publisher, to be responsible for the sale of the book.[12] In May she wrote him, ". . . what you most need is Love, *meekness,* and charity, or patience, with everybody. These things would increase your success. . . ."[13] And a year later she wrote him of her need "to get students into the field as practitioners and their healing will sell the book and introduce the science more than aught but *my* lecturing can do."[14]

And, of course, her public speaking healed, too. She makes reference to this in her autobiography, *Retrospection and Introspection,* where she writes, "Our last vestry meeting was made memorable by eloquent addresses from persons who feelingly testified to having been healed through my preaching. Among other diseases cured they specified cancers."[15] Mrs. Eddy was referring to a series of afternoon sermons she had given in the Tabernacle Baptist Church in Boston, beginning November 24, 1878.

Several significant events took place in the three intervening years since her book had been published. In March of 1876, she met Asa Gilbert Eddy, her future husband, who came to her for healing of heart disease. After they married on January 1, 1877, she wrote a pupil:

> I need not vindicate this step to a student who
> knows the interest of the cause of Truth is all the
> earthly interest I possess, and with a view to
> promote this cause and to find in union there is

strength, to bring another into my department of
labor and last though not least to unite my life to
one whom I know will bless it. I have changed its
tenor after so many years of struggles *alone.*

Last Spring Dr. Eddy came to me a hopeless
invalid, I saw him then for the first time, and but
twice. When his health was so improved he next
came to join my class. . . . In four weeks after
he came to study he was in practice doing well,
worked up an excellent reputation for healing and
at length won my affections on the ground alone of
his great goodness and strength of character.[16]

Gilbert Eddy became the first of her students to announce
himself to the public as a "Christian Scientist." The
publication of *Science and Health* had established "Christian
Science" as the permanent name for the divine revelation
Mrs. Eddy taught and for "the cause of Truth" she led.

Also significant in the development of this "cause" was
the organization of students into the Christian Scientist
Association on July 4, 1876. Through her Association,
Mrs. Eddy was able to continue the spiritual education of
her pupils at regularly held meetings. She cared deeply
about her students, who would turn to her for help when
unable to meet a challenge alone. In one instance, a mother
of six months had been driven by the ceaseless crying of her
baby to appeal to her teacher for relief. Mrs. Eddy spoke of
this in a class she taught in 1888. A member of that class
later wrote in her reminiscences:

Mrs. Eddy said she returned to the home with the mother, took the baby on her lap, and asked the mother to leave the room. The child cried and screamed terribly, and Mrs. Eddy silently declared the truth, but did nothing else. She said the struggle went on until it seemed as if the baby might die, but she continued to know that the real child could not die and that error had no life and that it could not continue to manifest itself. After a short time the child stopped its screaming and crying and went to sleep, and this was the end of that error. Mrs. Eddy went on to explain to the class that the mother, before the birth of her child, had been treating a patient who had a violent temper, and that the mother had not taken the precaution of protecting herself or her unborn child.[17]

The need to defend her own "child," the newborn "cause of Truth," was something Mrs. Eddy was keenly alert to. The materialistic, or worldly, thought of others resisted this "cause" to the point of trying to destroy it. Such was the case when Gilbert Eddy was falsely charged on October 29, 1878, with being party to a conspiracy to murder Daniel Spofford. Three months later the malicious lie was exposed and the charge was dismissed as having absolutely no validity. In March 1879, Mrs. Eddy wrote a friend:

The cause is prospering again, rising up slowly from the awful blow of malice and falsehoods dealt it last

Autumn—in which two of my students (one, my
darling husband) were so shockingly belied and I
dragged into the newspaper articles. It was got up
by Spofford to stop the sale of my Book after I took
from him the license to sell it because of some
shocking immorality and his broken agreement. . . .
My husband became publisher of the Second
edition of my work and it had been issued but a
week when the blow fell.[18]

Mrs. Eddy had begun this letter by relating how she was
then currently conducting regular Sunday services in

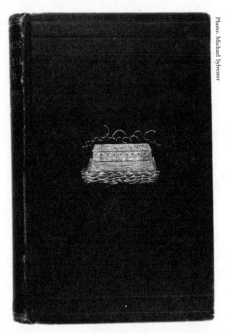

The Second, or Ark, edition of *Science of Health*

Boston at the Parker Memorial Building. In less than a month, she and her students would organize the Church of Christ (Scientist), "designed to perpetuate the teachings of Jesus, to reinstate primitive Christianity, and to restore its lost element of healing."[19] Materialism's attempt to ruin "the cause of Truth" had proved impotent. Mrs. Eddy swerved not, nor slowed, in leading this healing cause forward under divine direction.

CHAPTER 8

Pastor
(1879–1881)

ON APRIL 12, 1879, at Mary Baker Eddy's home in Lynn, Massachusetts, the Christian Scientist Association of her students met:

> On motion of Mrs. M. B. Glover Eddy, it was
> seconded & unanimously voted, that we organize a
> church to be called Church of Christ.[1]

It was subsequently discovered that another congregation in the state had already incorporated under that name, so in August, Mrs. Eddy's students obtained a charter for the Church of Christ (Scientist). During that same month, rules and regulations were drawn up to govern the new Church. One of these rules was:

> The Pastor of this Church must be able to heal the
> sick after the manner of Christian Science, must be
> strictly moral, and an earnest and devoted follower
> of Christ.[2]

Mrs. Eddy had been conducting Sunday services in Boston since the previous November, and the congregation naturally called her to preach for the new Church that August. She certainly met all of the moral and spiritual qualifications as a Christian healer.

During this period a suffering child turned up one day on Mrs. Eddy's doorstep in Lynn. Many years later, Mrs. Helen M. Grenier wrote of this incident:

> I was a little girl at the time, with a child's natural antipathy for medicine, as well as an inherent dread of doctors, and being taken suddenly ill with an agonizing pain in my side, decided to keep my suffering to myself. The eyes of love are keen, however. My mother noticed my unusual pallor and listlessness and questioned me, with the result that a physician was to be called next day unless I was much improved. I grew worse instead of better and set my wits to work to find a way out of the difficulty.
>
> In visiting a relative on Broad Street I had often noted a house on which was a sign decorated with a gold cross and crown. A woman doctor lived there, it was said, and in my desperation I reasoned thus: "If I must have a doctor I will go to the lady on Broad St. The sign shows she is a Christian and a Christian woman—even if she is a doctor—

wouldn't hurt a little girl" Accordingly I ran away and went to see Mrs. Eddy.

I have never forgotten Mrs. Eddy's gracious womanliness as she met me and led me to a seat, saying "dear child, did you wish to see me?" After a few generalities she closed her eyes for a brief period. She asked me no questions as to symptoms, ailment etc., but taking my hand said "if you are not better tomorrow come and see me again." As I rose and asked the fee she simply said, "Nothing, dear."

I could not understand it. It was so unusual. No questions asked—nothing done to my body— no medicine and no money, and yet—the pain was gone! I knew nothing whatever about Christian Science and nothing was said regarding it either by Mrs. Eddy or her husband, who met me at the door. I was filled with wonder at the loving kindness of the people who were so good to a little girl, but I no longer wondered at the beautiful cross and crown over the door and in my heart enshrined them as true Christians.

That treatment has never been paid for except in love and grateful appreciation. I was perfectly healed in that one treatment and walked—or rather—*ran* all the way home.[3]

Mrs. Eddy especially cherished the childlike thought. This can be seen in the friendship she developed with fifteen-year-old Alice Sibley, whom she had met through one of her students. On September 14, 1879, Mrs. Eddy wrote her:

> Darling Alice, keep yourself pure from con-
> tamination. Let not the grosser element of other
> people's thoughts touch the finer fabric of thine
> own to interweave a single thread not golden. Aim
> at all that is exalted, put aside as worthless all that
> degrades or can only dim the luster of the jewel of
> mind. Let the perfect thought be the parent of the
> perfect deed, keep the fountain of mind unsullied
> by a single wrong thought, carelessly cherished, and
> then the bright promise of your sweet girlhood will
> meet the expectancy of riper years and of those who
> so tenderly love thee.[4]

Two months later, Mrs. Eddy's own child, George Glover, came to visit her in Boston. They had not seen each other in twenty-three years. Mr. and Mrs. Eddy had moved to the city in November, primarily to be closer to the Church's services, which were held first in Charlestown, and then in downtown Boston at Hawthorne Hall. Though mother and son held a deep affection for each other, their opposite outlooks on life created a gulf between them that could not be spanned. He was a gold prospector in the Black Hills of the Dakota Territory, while she had already found her gold in the kingdom of God. Before returning home, George mentioned to his mother that his three-year-old daughter, Mary, had crossed eyes. She told him, "You must be mistaken, George, her eyes are all right." Later on the granddaughter wrote: "When he returned to our home in Deadwood, and during a conversation with my mother at my bedside while I was asleep, they awakened me and discovered that my eyes had become straightened. Mother has a picture of me taken before this incident showing my eyes crossed."[5]

In April 1880, Mrs. Eddy delivered a sermon titled "Christian Healing." The following month it appeared as a pamphlet, becoming the first of her works, after *Science and Health,* to be published for the public. In it she cautioned her followers: "See to it, O Christian Scientists, ye who have named the name of Christ with a higher meaning, that you abide by your statements, and abound in Love and Truth, for unless you do this you are not demonstrating the Science of metaphysical healing."[6] This was a problem Mrs. Eddy had seen almost from the beginning of her teaching efforts. So many early students, though grasping somewhat her "Science," found it difficult to "abide by" and "abound in" the righteousness that Christian metaphysics demands. Wrong or failed actions undermined their healing practice, which in turn removed their support of the work she was doing to establish the Cause of Christian Science. It was this lack of support that caused Mrs. Eddy to consider resigning from the pastorate of the Church toward the end of May. In hopes of persuading her not to do so, the members of both her Association and the Church passed several resolutions. The second of them read: "That while we feel that she has not met with the support which she had reason to expect, we venture to hope that she will reverse her decision, and remain with us."[7] She did so for one more month, but then in July she and her husband, Gilbert, left to spend the rest of the summer in Concord, New Hampshire.

Mrs. Eddy saw great danger in what she later described as "the mistake of believing in mental healing, claiming full faith in the divine Principle, and saying, 'I am a Christian Scientist,' while doing unto others what we would resist to the hilt if done unto ourselves."[8] This led her to investigate "the metaphysical mystery of error."[9] She knew evil to be an illusion, but also knew that unless its true nature was specifically uncovered, thought could be influenced unconsciously. Her next edition of *Science and Health* expanded the original sixteen pages on this subject into a forty-six page chapter entitled "Demonology." Her reasons for giving so much thought to this problem can be understood from what she would later add to her textbook:

> Every Christian Scientist, every conscientious teacher
> of the Science of Mind-healing, knows that human

will is not Christian Science, and he must recognize
this in order to defend himself from the influence of
human will. He feels morally obligated to open the
eyes of his students that they may perceive the nature
and methods of error of every sort, especially any
subtle degree of evil, deceived and deceiving.[10]

On their return in September, the Eddys moved back to
their house in Lynn, and Mrs. Eddy resumed her previous
activities of preaching and teaching. While those duties
took up most of her time, Mrs. Eddy's primary concern was
the revision of her textbook, *Science and Health*. She spent
all of her free moments working on it. In August 1881 it
was published in two volumes with a cross and crown
emblem on its covers for the first time.

The Third edition of *Science and Health* is particularly
notable for the addition of the chapter "Recapitulation."
Mrs. Eddy explained, "This chapter is from our class-book,
First edition, 1870."[11] The class-book had been privately
published in 1876 as *The Science of Man*. It remains the
basis of teaching Christian Science today. Even though the
Third edition of *Science and Health* was a significant
revision, its message and vision remained unchanged. She
revised the textbook "only to give a clearer and fuller
expression of its original meaning."[12]

As noted previously, Mrs. Eddy had felt that the
condition of her students' thought at that time called for a

more thorough elaboration of the mesmeric workings of evil, or the carnal mind, which she put into that chapter, "Demonology." She wrote: "Uncover a lie, and, snake-like, it turns to give the lie to you." Later, in the current edition of *Science and Health,* she phrased it, "Uncover error, and it turns the lie upon you."[13]

Two months after the Third edition appeared, a letter from eight of Mrs. Eddy's students was delivered to both her Association and the Church.[14] They accused their teacher of "temper, love of money, and the appearance of hypocrisy" and declared her unfit to lead them. What hurt Mrs. Eddy most was not the accusations, which were patently false; rather it was that some of her most intimate students had broken their oath to her and the Church: "if thy brother shall trespass against thee, go and tell him his fault between thee and him alone."[15] There had been no prior indication from the signers of any dissatisfaction.

Two weeks after this, on November 9, 1881, the students who remained loyal ordained their teacher as Pastor of the Church of Christ (Scientist). A week later they passed a set of resolutions, which Mrs. Eddy edited and approved, declaring her "to be the Chosen Messenger of God to bear His Truth to the Nations," and deploring the dissidents' "wickedness and abuse of her."[16] These resolutions were subsequently published in a Lynn newspaper.

An essential element of God's message to mankind is

divine healing, which was never far from Mrs. Eddy's thought. She told one of her secretaries in 1908:

> When I was in Lynn, those opposing me said
> that I had been a very good woman but now I had
> become very bad. There was one gentleman . . .
> who was a member of the Congregational Church
> who always stood up for me. He would say, "I do
> not understand her, but I know she is good."
>
> One day he appeared at my house with a
> message. He came with a crutch for there was
> trouble with his hip. As he stood before me leaning
> on his crutch I said to him, "Which do you lean on
> the more, that crutch or on God?" He looked at me
> and said, "On God," threw away his crutch, which
> fell against the door, and stood erect and free. . . .
>
> This gentleman left his crutch behind him and
> went from the house well.[17]

Healings that took place as a natural occurrence during Mrs. Eddy's sermons were often as notable. She recorded one such incident in an article she wrote a few years later for the "mind-body" magazine, *Mind in Nature:*

> On March 15, during my sermon, a sick man was
> healed. This man had been assisted into the church
> by two men, a crutch and cane, but he walked out

of it erect and strong, with cane and crutch under
his arm. I was not acquainted with the gentleman,
was not even aware of his presence.[18]

In fulfilling her capacity as Pastor, Mary Baker Eddy
demonstrated the nothingness of sickness and sin by
revealing the omnipotence of divine good. It's not
surprising that healing was often the result.

CHAPTER 9

Launching out deeper
(1882–1885)

THE THIRD WEEK IN JANUARY 1882 arrived cold, gray, and rainy. In the Eddy household in Lynn, Massachusetts, however, there was little time to notice the weather. Mary and Gilbert were preparing for an extended trip to the country's capital, Washington, D.C., and there was much to be done. The Church and Mrs. Eddy's students needed guidance and encouragement. Arrangements had to be made for their Sunday sermon in the absence of Mrs. Eddy, their recently ordained pastor. The students would need to work together. She counseled two of them:

> Let the church work together and not separate.
> Let each who can, take a part, and be not weary in
> well doing and God will help you. . . .
> I would recommend that your Sunday service
> be holden alternatively in Boston at your rooms
> and in Charlestown and you and Mrs. Whiting,
> Miss Bartlett, and Mrs. Poor's name be registered
> alphabetically to take care of the services.[1]

> This I beg that you "love one another even as I
> have loved you." That no root of bitterness springs up
> among you. That no pride comes up or vain inquiry
> "who shall be greatest," but remember I have made
> myself the servant that I might lead others to Christ.[2]

The Eddys spent ten weeks in Washington, charmed by its beauty, and fully occupied in a vibrant, crowded schedule of activity. She taught and lectured; he devoted much of his time to studying copyright law. Toward the middle of March, enthusiasm sparkling through her words, Mrs. Eddy wrote a Boston student:

> I have had parlor lectures for two evenings.
> About fifty have listened to me and expressed
> themselves as pleased. Editors, Colonels, teachers,
> one clergyman, etc. . . . . This is the most beautiful
> city I was ever in.[3]

Two weeks earlier she had written:

> I have worked harder here than ever! Fourteen
> consecutive evenings I have lectured three hours
> every night besides what else I am about. Go to bed
> at 12, rise at 6, and *work*.[4]

The "what else" she was about included healing. Mr. and Mrs. Eddy went one Sunday to the church the President normally attended. They were introduced to the minister, who

Photo: W. S. Warren

Mrs. Eddy in 1882. She made the purple velveteen
dress she is wearing for speaking engagements.

asked if he might call on them and was warmly welcomed to do so. The minister spent the better part of an afternoon listening to Mrs. Eddy's explanation of Biblical truths. As the supper hour approached, he was invited to stay. He told them he was not able to eat solid food but would enjoy their company. Doctors had diagnosed stomach cancer and limited him to a liquid diet. Mary's heart went out in compassion to the man. In 1901, Mrs. Eddy recounted the minister's healing:

> I said to him briefly, that this was an excellent opportunity to put to test our talk of the afternoon. He replied by saying that he hardly could consent to test the doctrine for the sake of killing himself. However, I voiced the Truth and asserted his ability to eat in comfort. He went with us to the table, soon forgot himself and his false fears and partook heartily of the salads, meats and pastry. At the conclusion of the dinner he said, "What have I done? Will I survive?" We assured him there was no danger. He felt no harm and never after was again troubled.[5]

If the time in Washington seemed overflowing with activity, the return to New England on April 4 was no less so. The next Sunday Mrs. Eddy took her place in the pulpit in the Church's rooms at Hawthorne Hall. She later told a student,

> Preached yesterday to a large audience . . . from the text "What I do thou knowest not now but shall know hereafter." Spoke mostly of Jesus'

healing that was not understood now but shall be
and his Christ-character will *then* be understood. I
wish you could see the wild enthusiasm here over
this blessed Truth.

The reception was indeed a splendid affair.
There was a crown of flowers and on the word
Truth a large cross with the word Love, another bed
of flowers on green leaves with the motto Welcome.
This was over the door. The company was so large
it took an hour to shake hands. This was my entry
into Jerusalem. Will it be followed with the cross?[6]

At the end of April the Eddys leased a brownstone on
Columbus Avenue in Boston, providing a new home, not
just for themselves, but also for the Massachusetts
Metaphysical College.[7] But the brightness of this spring
was greatly darkened by Gilbert's death on the third of
June. This was especially hard for Mary, a very bitter blow.
She went to Vermont to a student's family home to regain
her peace; only that student and one other accompanied
her. She felt an urgent need for healing—and the healing
came. Toward the end of July, she delivered an address at
the Methodist church in Barton, on the subject that was
ever in her heart and on her tongue: Christian healing. The
minister called the next day, and they spent the morning
talking about her lecture. On returning home Mrs. Eddy
wrote in her Bible: "Aug. 6th 1882 . . . opened to Isaiah
54."[8] One of the many comforting verses she read was,
"thou . . . shalt not remember the reproach of thy

widowhood any more." By the end of October she could tell a student, "The ship of science is again walking the wave, rising above the billows, bidding defiance to the flood-gates of error, for God is at the helm."[9]

The next few years were to see a focus on publication and outreach. "I have so much writing on hand now, something I have not spoken of to the students," Mrs. Eddy confided in a letter.[10] When the Christian Scientists' first magazine, the *Journal of Christian Science,* appeared in April 1883, she served as its Editor and provided much of its content. The work, though stimulating, was arduous. She had little leisure, working seven days a week, and resting solely in the love of the work and the love of God. Much to her delight, the leading religious papers in Boston sent her courtesy copies of theirs in exchange for her *Journal.* For more than a year she had also been revising her textbook, *Science and Health.* She made a significant addition to it by including in this Sixth edition a section titled "Key to the Scriptures," and it was published in September 1883. Originally Mrs. Eddy had intended to put this "Key" into her Second edition, which appeared in 1878, but serious problems with the printer and other circumstances prevented this. The "Key" consisted of metaphysical interpretations of many Bible names and terms, which today can be found in the textbook's Glossary. Twenty-three of these terms and interpretations first appeared in the more than 600 pages of notes on the book of Genesis that Mrs. Eddy had made between 1866 and 1869.[11] Echoes from these notes appear throughout today's textbook, as seen in the following two examples:

Heaven was happiness and not a locality but was the atmosphere of a principle where all was harmony.[12]

and

This truth stands at the threshold of your thoughts a guest so new and strange that we know

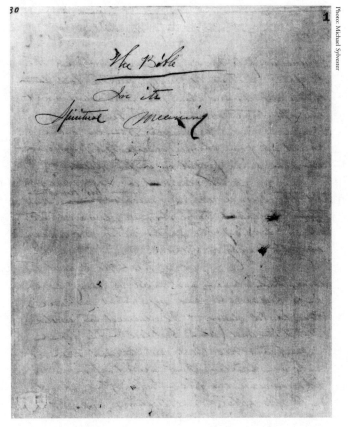

The cover of Mrs. Eddy's manuscript on the book of Genesis

> it must knock loudly and long before you open
> unto it—and yet once passed the iron portal of
> beliefs which close against it where truth sups with
> understanding and ever thereafter will you say of it,
> We have entertained angels unawares.[13]

Christian Science was indeed knocking loudly at the threshold of the public's thought. The newspapers and churches were more and more raising questions and making criticisms of this new denomination. It would eventually cause Mrs. Eddy, a year and a half after the publication of the textbook's Sixth edition, to issue two pamphlets—"Historical Sketch of Metaphysical Healing" and "Defense of Christian Science."[14]

Even with the continual demands of writing, publishing, and preaching, Mrs. Eddy still found time to teach classes and counsel her students. In 1884 she even made a trip to Chicago. Writing to a student after her return, she explained:

> I went in May to Chicago at the imperative
> call of people there and my own sense of the need.
> This great work had been started, but my students
> needed me to give it a right foundation and
> impulse in that city of ceaseless enterprise. So I
> went, and in three weeks taught a class of 25 pupils,
> lectured in Music Hall to a *full* house, got 20
> subscriptions for my Journal, sold about thirty
> copies of Science and Health etc. . . .

A lady educated in a convent a Catholic was
healed mind and body by a few minutes conversation with me in Chicago. She changed her whole
course of life and her letter to me since my return
alludes to it.[15]

Because she was no longer in the public practice, the
question had arisen "Has Mrs. Eddy lost her power to
heal?" She answered this in the June *Journal.* Her reply
began, "Has the sun forgotten to shine, and the planets to
revolve around it?"[16] Her students had no doubt about her
healing abilities. Clara Choate went to Mrs. Eddy one
night, asking her to come and help her four-year-old, who
was ill. She had tried to heal him herself, but with no
results. Mrs. Eddy came and prayed at his bedside for a few
minutes. Suddenly the little boy turned and began kicking
the wall next to his bed as hard as he could. Mrs. Eddy sat
quietly without saying a word. He continued until he was
tired, then he turned in bed again and fell asleep: he was
healed. Later, Mrs. Choate asked her teacher at a meeting
of students how she had treated her son. Mrs. Eddy replied:

The only thought that I had was "Warren
Choate, your mother governs here with the Truth."
Mrs. Choate, you don't govern that child
morally when he is well, so you can't heal him when
he is ill. You have done all that could be done
except that you had neglected to handle the moral

> question, and this must be handled in every case
> whether it be an adult or a small child. You never
> make him mind, and if you give him a command
> you don't insist upon his carrying it out.[17]

The student who related this account went on to comment, "This lesson was brought home forcibly to us in the Association because we would never have considered that the moral question should be handled in the case of a child."[18]

Mrs. Eddy saw beneath the surface of things, and expected the same of her students. She was instant and loving both in her rebuke of the wrong method and in her explanation of the right way to heal. In answer to one student who had said he had been foiled by a case, Mrs. Eddy alluded to Jesus' words to Simon: "Launch out deeper, Anchor yourself to God."[19] In a note to another she wrote, "Are you ready to help? You say yes, but why don't you help me if you are willing and can handle this? All you say is inconsistent unless you *do* as *you say.* I healed a case of softening of the brain in a minute, three weeks ago, but I didn't say I would do it—and then desert the sufferer."[20] And to another, "Let our lives make the difference between a false and a true Mind healer."[21] It was because she *lived* what she taught and because she "let this mind be in [her], which was also in Christ Jesus,"[22] that Mrs. Eddy was able instantly to heal a minister in Washington, D.C., a woman in Chicago, and a little boy in Boston. She constantly launched out deeper, and anchored herself to God. There is no other way to be a Christian Scientist.

CHAPTER 10

Defender of the Cause
(1885–1887)

THE MENTAL ATMOSPHERE in Boston's Tremont Temple
on March 16, 1885, would likely have been daunting to
most speakers trying to explain what must have seemed a
very different way of being a Christian. The thoughts of the
nearly three thousand attendants ranged from benignly
curious to highly skeptical to openly hostile. But Mary Baker
Eddy stood before them all in order to defend her "child,"
the Cause of Christian Science. At a previous Monday Noon
Lecture, the then quite prominent Reverend Joseph Cook
had harshly criticized this relatively new face on Boston's
religious scene. Not only did the new faith promise healings
after the manner of Jesus, it spoke in a new language that
contradicted a number of traditionally and, consequently,
firmly held doctrines. Even worse, it was led by a woman!

Mrs. Eddy had been allowed only ten minutes in which
to reply to the Reverend Mr. Cook's criticism. She began:

> As the time so kindly allotted me is insufficient for
> even a synopsis of Christian Science, I shall confine
> myself to questions and answers.[1]

She posed and answered the following questions: "Am I a spiritualist? I am not, and never was. . . . Do I believe in a personal God? I believe in God as the Supreme Being. . . . Do I believe in the atonement of Christ? I do. . . . How is the healing done in Christian Science? This answer includes too much to give you any conclusive idea in a brief explanation. I can name some means by which it is not done. It is not one mind acting upon another mind; it is not the transference of human images of thought to other minds. . . . It is Christ come to destroy the power of the flesh; it is Truth over error. . . . Is there a personal man? The Scriptures inform us that man was made in the image and likeness of God. . . ."[2]

That day, Mrs. Eddy's students gave away 800 copies of her pamphlet "Defense of Christian Science." The following month, she wrote to her students in Chicago requesting that they publicly refute lies in the press about her and Christian Science. In a meeting of her students in Boston on May 6, the minutes record that "Mrs. E. Hopkins made a very satisfactory report for the Com. on Publication. Several Papers had been replied to. She had been able to get an article into the Boston Herald as had also Mrs. Hale." The minutes of this meeting continue:

> The President [Mrs. Eddy] stated that she was
> proud of the literary capacity of her students.
> Articles for the press should be arranged judiciously.
> There is a great work to be done with the Clergy.
> They have got to be talked with lovingly. In this

spirit call upon them to recall their assertions that
are false.[3]

It's interesting to note that she concluded her remarks to
her students: "Now if you want to be healers, be honest."
Always, healing had a part in every effort Mrs. Eddy put
forth. At a meeting of her students the previous February,
she had told them:

> . . . the grand secret of all your success is in your
> Christianity. Just in proportion as mortal sense is
> hushed, just in that proportion will healing be done.
>
> Some say "we are doing all we can." Stop the
> utterance. *Do more.* God is making the extreme trial
> an occasion for your good. Such moments are the
> most glorious of all experience, because God's hand
> is stretched out over them.
>
> We have God on our side to meet *all* questions,
> and I have never found an hour when He would
> not deliver me.[4]

Mrs. Eddy's ability to hush mortal sense was certainly
evidenced on a shopping excursion she made with a
student to look at carpets in a Boston rug emporium:

> A gentlemanly and kindly man waited upon them.
> The women could not help noticing that his face was
> partially bandaged. After just a few moments, Mrs.
> Eddy seemed to lose all interest in the purpose of their

errand. . . . "Come Julia, let us not look further to-day.
We can come again." On the second or third day after,
Miss Bartlett returned alone to the store. The same
salesman advanced to serve her. The bandage was no
longer on his face. Very earnestly the man asked her
who might the lady be who had come with her on the
previous occasion. Then, in a reverent and awe-struck
voice, he said, looking intently at Miss Bartlett, "I can't
explain it, but that lady had something to do with a
very wonderful thing which has happened to me."
Then he told her that not long after she and her
companion had left the store on the earlier visit, his
face, which had been scarred, began rapidly to heal;
and, looking, she saw it was perfectly clear. The
affliction had been cancer.[5]

At the end of 1884, a Boston University professor had
made a rather sarcastic public offer of one thousand dollars
if Mrs. Eddy or one of her students could reset a hip or
ankle dislocation without physical manipulation, and two
thousand dollars to restore the sight of one born blind. This
challenge was brought up at the next monthly meeting of
her students' association. Several spoke of their recent
practice: healings of pneumonia, a sprained wrist,
diphtheria, and opium addiction. Pleased with these
reports, Mrs. Eddy told them, "the higher grew the affection
of Jesus, the grander grew his demonstration. Affections
teach us the way to liberty. We sail into the great, glorious
sea of possibilities through the storm and not the calm."[6]

The Massachusetts Metaphysical College on
Columbus Avenue in Boston, where Mrs. Eddy lived and taught

The next month, February 1885, Mrs. Eddy responded to the professor through the pages of her *Journal of Christian Science*. With characteristic kindness she replied: "Will the gentleman accept my thanks due to his generosity; for if I should accept his bid on Christianity he would lose his money. Why? Because I performed more difficult tasks fifteen years ago. At present I am in another department of Christian work, where 'there shall no sign be given them,' for they shall be instructed in the principle of Christian Science that furnishes its own proof."[7]

From 1885 through 1887 Mrs. Eddy taught a total of seventeen classes: eight Primary, seven Normal, and two others.[8] In addition to her teaching, throughout 1885 she was working on a major revision of her book *Science and Health with Key to the Scriptures,* striving to make ever clearer the science of Christian healing. At the end of July she engaged a Unitarian, the Reverend James Henry Wiggin, as an editorial assistant to help her.[9] At that time students had no way of easily locating ideas or subjects in *Science and Health,* except to rely on their memory or personal notes. They were utilizing it and the Bible as their textbooks. Bible concordances and reference books were worn thin from constant use; but there was nothing to so assist the students with their teacher's book. Mrs. Eddy met the need with an index, which the Reverend Mr. Wiggin prepared for the new edition under her direction.

The first printing of the Sixteenth edition, published in February 1886, sold out in ninety days, and the second printing was half spoken for even before it arrived from the printer, University Press. Mrs. Eddy marketed her book through bookstores and booksellers. She had been doing this for a number of years. Now, dozens of new inquiries came, and purchasing agents bought *Science and Health* in bulk. Students were selling the book, too. To one she wrote: "How important that this book that God dictated should be our only standard, especially now that so many are trying to raise false standards in the name of C[hristian] S[cience]. Let us as loyal adherents draw up nearer to the book that has the *divine* signet upon it and hold this one banner aloft. Then we shall put to flight the aliens."[10]

The "aliens" were, for the most part, a number of disaffected students who had left Christian Science and were attempting to build up their own "mind-cure" schools. Mind-cure was a generic name for any number of mental healing theories that had sprung up suddenly and flourished for a time in the mid-1880s. They all had one very significant feature in common—none of them saw the need for pure Christianity as the sole basis of healing. Regardless of the unique aspects of each, and for all their differences, they were simply various forms of mentally directed will-power, or mesmerism. The problem was that they claimed to stand under the umbrella of Christian Science, hoping thereby to gain acceptance and respectability.

Mrs. Eddy saw the great danger in this. For her, mesmerism was the very antipode of her discovery and she referred to it as animal magnetism. In order to counter mind-curists' misleading efforts to teach what decidedly was not *Christian* healing, she requested her loyal students who had been trained to teach Christian Science to establish formal "Institutes" for teaching and healing and sponsoring church services in their own cities around the country. And she told them, ". . . be careful and put Christians to the head

Photo: H. G. Smith

Mrs. Eddy in 1886

of your College, *old tried* Christians that shall control its management."[11] This was before Christian Science churches had begun regularly organizing in local communities. Lecturing was also a method Mrs. Eddy felt could do a great deal to offset the claims of the mind-curists. She asked a few students who had shown particular promise to prepare themselves for public speaking, even suggesting that professional tutoring would help.

For the questioning public, Mrs. Eddy also chose to differentiate Christian Science more clearly through pamphlets. She revised and expanded "Defense of Christian Science," giving it the new title "Christian Science: No and Yes." She wrote a new pamphlet, "Rudiments and Rules of Divine Science." Her students' association provided the funds to publish the Reverend Mr. Wiggin's "Christian Science and the Bible." And she herself paid for the publication of Hanover P. Smith's "Writings and Genius of the Founder of Christian Science." Hanover had been Mrs. Eddy's student since 1880. He first became interested in Christian Science at nineteen when she healed him. He had been born deaf and mute.[12]

William Gill was another student Mrs. Eddy healed. Before coming into Christian Science he had been a minister and, partly because of this background, she had made him Editor of the *Journal.* Unfortunately, he lasted only four months before going astray and joining the mind-curists. However, before he left at the end of 1886 she healed him of an injured foot. More than ten years later Mrs. Eddy referred to this in a letter to a student:

Oh! I was glad to hear that you, at least, demonstrated *Christian* Healing. When I united the joint
of Gill's toe—in a minute—and he said why could
not your students have done this? I made an excuse
as best I could. . . .

My students are doing more for, and against,
C.S. than any others can do. They are the greatest
sinners on earth when they injure it; and doing
more good than all others when they do the best
they know how.

Here I must leave it; but the fruits of my awful
experience in preparing the hearts of men to receive
Chris[tian] Scie[nce], is *patience* in tribulation, hope,
and *faith,*—before these graces of the Spirit evil *must
fall.* May you, my *faithful dear one* be strengthened
and uplifted by the cross of others—by seeing sin
and so avoiding it in your own dear self.[13]

Christian healing—this is what distinguished Christian
Science and Mrs. Eddy from the mind-curists, who
prescribed less demanding paths without the Christian
cross to bear. It is also what separated her from most of the
theologians of that day, because, in order to heal as Jesus
did, one needs to believe and understand that God does
not know evil, and therefore one must treat evil as an
illusion of the carnal mind. Mrs. Eddy taught that to the
degree the purity of the divine Mind was reflected in the
students' minds, to that degree they would find success in
healing.

CHAPTER 11

"Those who watch and love"
(1888–1889)

WHEN GEORGE GLOVER, Mary Baker Eddy's son, wrote that he was coming to Boston to spend the winter of 1887–88 with his mother—and his wife and three children were coming as well—the news came at an especially busy time for Mrs. Eddy. Her days and weeks were filled with teaching classes on Christian Science, meeting with her students' association in the chapel of Tremont Temple, regularly writing for *The Christian Science Journal*,[1] maintaining a constant and growing correspondence with students, and serving as Pastor to her Church. Nevertheless, she welcomed her son and his family. Mrs. Eddy loved her grandchildren, and she enjoyed introducing them to the members of her Church.

Children were one of her heart's delights. Mrs. Eddy loved their receptivity to good, and they loved her in return. There were two occasions in the overly crowded months that began 1888 when children and church would combine to lighten an otherwise heavy calendar. The first of these was reported in the March *Journal:*

Chickering Hall was crowded Feb. 26, for a
service which has long been desired by many of the
members of the church. . . . twenty-nine children,
including a few babes, were led to the platform, and
placed in semicircles. Rev. Mrs. Eddy then moved
about slowly among them. From each she received a
card on which was written the child's name. Raising
her hands over each in turn, she then repeated the
name, and very slowly and emphatically pronounced
this blessing: "May the baptism of Christ with the
Holy Spirit cleanse you from sin, sickness, and
death." No water was used in the rite, but it was
nevertheless impressive. . . .

The short address which followed, by Mrs.
Eddy, was on "Names and Baptism." In the Bible
we read that names were changed . . . but these
indicated changes of character and career, not of
name only. The baptism of the Christian should be
a baptism into Spirit, and should represent "the
answer of a good conscience toward God," as says
Peter in his First Epistle. . . .[2]

Mrs. Eddy's grandchildren were among those christened. This
was the only formal occasion of christening in the Church.

Easter Sunday found them all at a Chickering Hall
decorated with lilies. The service that first of April was
largely a concert by the Sunday School children. No fewer
than eighteen hymns and anthems cheered both Pastor and

congregation, the fresh young voices often in harmony, sometimes not quite on key. Halfway through, twelve young ladies each answered a question, responding with a passage from *Science and Health with Key to the Scriptures.* The Pastor's grandchildren, Edward, Evelyn, and Mary Glover were among the singers.[3] The following day Mrs. Eddy wrote to Capt. Joseph Eastaman and his wife, who had directed the concert:

> I have no words to tell you how much I enjoyed the beautiful occasion that you got up for Easter Sunday.
>
> The whole was a perfect *success,* even the *little* mistakes of the "darlings" were *beautiful*—and my "April fool" finished the symbols of the day. You ask why did you not finish up the singing and your part of reading Hymns?
>
> I answer, Because I got so absorbed by the children's entertainment that I *forgot* it, and that was the *April's fool,* and the compliment to you Mrs. Eastaman.[4]

Mrs. Eddy's joy in and love for children had a decidedly healing effect on them, too. The daughter of one of Mrs. Eddy's students was twice quickly healed by Mrs. Eddy. First was an instantaneous healing of inherited lung trouble and chronic coughing.[5] The mother, Emma Thompson, was attending one of Mrs. Eddy's classes at the time. The second healing occurred during a subsequent visit when the young girl, Abigail, and her mother were in Boston. Abigail later recounted:

> . . . I was stricken down suddenly and confined to my bed with a most distressing hip trouble. . . . Finally the pain became so intense that my dear courageous mother found herself overwhelmed with discouragement and fear, . . . she hastened at five o'clock in the morning to Mrs. Eddy's home. Mr. Frye met her at the door. . . . Mrs. Eddy heard them talking and . . . listened to the conversation in the hall below. . . .
>
> [Later Mrs. Eddy told Mrs. Thompson] "when I heard your conversation I said to myself, it is time for Mother to step in on this case and save that child, and hurrying back to my room I dropped into a chair and immediately reached out to God for the healing."
>
> So quick was the response that when my mother returned to me a few minutes later, even before reaching the bedside, she was greeted with the cheery ring of my voice calling to her the welcome message, "Mother I am better"—and soon we both realized with overwhelming joy that I was not only better, but completely healed.
>
> Through the many years that have followed I have never spent another day in bed, and from the

depths of a grateful heart I give the entire credit for
my abounding health to the completeness and
permanency of our Leader's realization of the
healing power of God.[6]

When Mrs. Eddy was preaching in Boston two years
earlier, another mother, Mrs. Mary Dunbar, had been
reaching out for healing:

> . . . Mrs. Dunbar resolved to go and hear her. Mrs.
> Dunbar's only child, a daughter then about four or
> five years of age, never had walked. She could creep
> on her hands and knees but below her knees the
> bone had never hardened, but was like cartilage, so
> that her feet dangled and were useless. Mrs. Dunbar
> tried to interest members of her family and friends
> to go with her to hear Mrs. Eddy preach, but as no
> one seemed willing to go she decided to go alone.
> She did go one Sunday afternoon and sat in the
> audience. Mrs. Eddy did not know she was there by
> anything Mrs. Dunbar said or did.
>
> On her return home her family were waiting for
> her with curiosity. They asked her if she had actu-
> ally seen Mrs. Eddy and what she looked like. Mrs.
> Dunbar replied that she had seen her but did not
> know what she looked like. They then asked her
> what Mrs. Eddy wore, and Mrs. Dunbar replied, "I
> do not know." They inquired what Mrs. Eddy had

said and again Mrs. Dunbar replied, "I do not
know." In jest they then asked her what she *did*
know. To this Mrs. Dunbar replied, "I know I have
found the Truth. I know I have found that for
which I have always sought."

The sleeping room of little Ethel Dunbar
adjoined her mother's bedroom on the second floor
of their home. Ethel had never been able to get in
and out of bed as other children of her age could do.
The following morning, before Mrs. Dunbar was up,
Ethel climbed out of bed and ran across the floor to
her mother, perfectly normal. She was healed.[7]

It was not at all uncommon for healings to result from
Mrs. Eddy's public speaking. A young woman from
Germany, Bertha Reinke, who had come to America to
study medicine and also hoped to find a cure for her own
physical problems, came to hear Mrs. Eddy speak; she came
out of curiosity, because it was unheard of in her country
for a woman to preach. She had never heard of Christian
Science and had not known of its focus on healing before
she attended the service:

Human energy and will power alone had
enabled me to come to this lecture and while I was
waiting for the "Lady Preacher" to appear, it seemed
as if I could not endure my mental and physical
condition much longer.

Then something wonderful happened. Escorted by a gentleman the "Lady Preacher" appeared on the stage. For a few moments she gazed silently over the audience. I felt an atmosphere such as I had not known before. She spoke with a gentle, low but very clear voice. As I was not accustomed to hear an address in English, and as I sat so far from the stage, the words themselves were not understood. But as I listened I experienced an inexpressible feeling of relief, and the pains and misery, with which I had gone to this lecture hall, had fallen away from me.

Not knowing to whom I had been listening, I asked an usher for the name of the "Lady Preacher." In utter astonishment he looked at me and answered, "Why, that was Mrs. Eddy!"—Mrs. Eddy?! I had never heard the name before—I left the hall free and well.[8]

One of the most outstanding examples of the healing effect of Mrs. Eddy's public speaking occurred when she traveled to Chicago and spoke at the Central Music Hall to an audience of about four thousand, a little less than a quarter of whom were students of Christian Science. She chose as her text the first verse of the ninety-first Psalm and the address that followed, "Science and the Senses," was given extemporaneously, as she had had no idea she was expected to speak until she arrived at the hall.[9] *The Boston Evening Traveller* described what happened at the end of the address:

When she had finished, the scenes that
followed will long be remembered by those who
saw them. The people were in the presence of the
woman whose book had healed them, and they
knew it. Up came the crowds to her side, begging
for one hand-clasp, one look, one memorial of her,
whose name was a power and a sacred thing in
their homes. Those whom she had never seen
before—invalids raised up by her book, *Science
and Health;* each attempted to hurriedly tell the
wonderful story. A mother who failed to get near
held high her babe to look on her helper. Others
touched the dress of their benefactor, not so
much as asking for more. An aged woman,
trembling with palsy, lifted her shaking hands
at Mrs. Eddy's feet, crying, "Help, help!" and the
cry was answered. Many such people were known
to go away healed.[10]

Some of the other healings involved rheumatism,
paralysis, diabetes. One in particular was noted by several
people. A woman in the front row had come in with great
difficulty on crutches. At the conclusion of the talk, she
arose and spoke to Mrs. Eddy, who leaned over the
platform to reply. Immediately the woman laid down her
crutches and walked out healed and free.[11]

A year later, Mrs. Eddy taught a class in which she told
her pupils:

Why do you give long treatments? Because you don't give them on the right side. . . . It's the power of the living God we want. If the voice of God were heard all would be healed. You are so buried in the life of the senses! That's what makes long treatments. It's spiritual want that prevents healing. It is knowing that your life is hid in Christ that gives power. There is a belief of lethargy where mind is attached to personality,—When you realize Truth, Love, you heal. . . .

When a student doesn't heal it's his own fault. I am out of patience at hearing a student ask his patient to work when the patient is up to the ears in the waves. Don't ask anything of your patient. Show him your Science and when he is healed he will work.[12]

Mrs. Eddy expected her students to heal as she did. To one who had told her of a quick healing, she wrote, "Your consciousness of Truth healed instantaneously. Thus you see it is our fault not to be more filled with the realization of God, good and so reflect this true consciousness. Your cases of cure were so satisfactory I want to publish them in the June No. of our Journal."[13]

Mrs. Eddy's standards were very high. When students fell short, she was not shy about correcting them. Unfortunately, there were those who did not have either the humility or maturity to see that she was not rebuking

Photo: W. Shaw Warren

Mrs. Eddy at 67

them personally—she was rebuking the errors that prevented them from doing as they should. Before she had left for Chicago, Mrs. Eddy had requested that her students' association hold a meeting while she was away to resolve a disagreement that had arisen at their previous meeting. At this special meeting, a number of outspoken students who objected to their teacher's methods and actions withdrew from the association and influenced others to do likewise. In all, thirty-six left without allowing Mrs. Eddy the opportunity to meet with them face to face to respond to their accusations.

Mrs. Eddy expressed her feelings about this rebellion in a letter to two of her Chicago students, John and Ellen Linscott:

> It is to "kill the 'heir' that the inheritance may be ours" for which they are at work. But my greatest regret is that as in the parable when the Lord took away the inheritance from the wicked stewards and gave it unto others—because of this motive and means, so will it, must it, be with them. Oh, if they only knew that the heir gained the inheritance by helping every one else up instead of pulling them down, to rise over other errors, then would they be wiser and understand how to gain and retain this inheritance.[14]

Even so, Mrs. Eddy continued to love them. Several weeks later she tenderly invited two of those who had influenced others against her to come to church: "I shall preach next Sunday and I hope you will be there to learn more of the way to heaven the joys that are imperishable. I never felt my Father so near as now. May God bless you and save you from sin is the prayer of your Pastor and Teacher."[15] Love was the only way Mrs. Eddy knew to respond to hate or settle disagreements. A number of years after this she would write a poem entitled "Love." It's a beautiful lesson on healing disputes. She first points out, "The arrow that doth wound the dove / Darts not from those who watch and love," and she ends with

> . . . Love alone is Life;
> And life most sweet, as heart to heart
> Speaks kindly when we meet and part.[16]

In the autumn of 1888, Mrs. Eddy expressed much of her love through teaching others how to heal by spiritual means alone. In the middle of a class in September, after finishing a lesson one day, she healed an insane woman who had been brought to her by the woman's brother. The woman had fallen on the floor screaming, as she believed she was being crushed by a giant serpent. Clara Shannon, a member of the class, witnessed this healing. She later recounted:

> Our Leader looked upwards, as if she had seen
> the face of an angel in her communion with God.
> In a moment, she said to the woman, "Has it
> gone?" but there was no reply. Mrs. Eddy repeated
> her question, but the woman still seemed not to
> hear it. Then she spoke with authority and asked,
> "Has it *gone?*" and the poor woman looked up, and
> her whole body was shaken and quivering as she
> answered, "Yes!" I watched the changes of
> expression that came over [the woman's] face,

from fear to peace and joy. And, oh! the love that
was expressed in our Leader's face as she looked
down on her, stretched both arms and lifted her up,
saying, "Get up, darling!" Then our dear Teacher
put that needy one's head on her shoulder and
patted her face, as she lovingly talked the truth to
her. Mrs. Eddy then went out of the room and
talked to the brother, who took her home, and then
she asked me to come and have supper with her,
and to sing to her. During the evening she turned
to me and said, "You saw what happened to that
lady today? Well! She will never be insane in this
world again." And she has not been.[17]

In November, Mrs. Eddy wrote a student, "We are
gaining in the onward march slowly, but surely, through
the clouds of selfishness out into the light of universal love.
God speed the dawn. Our cause has had a great propulsion
from my late large classes. Over fifty members have gone
into our C. S. Association since the stampede out of it."[18]

What also resulted from the experience with the
rebellious members was a heightened awareness of the great
need to alert students of Christian Science to the influence
of animal magnetism. In her textbook, *Science and Health,*
Mrs. Eddy defines animal magnetism as "the false belief
that mind is in matter, and is both evil and good; that evil
is as real as good and more powerful. This belief has not
one quality of Truth."[19] The problem of animal magnetism

is not one of overcoming a real power, but of not being influenced by the false suggestion that matter or brain or human methods have power.

The minutes of Mrs. Eddy's students' association for November 7, 1888, record:

> Our Teacher . . . gave a synopsis of the history
> of animal magnetism from its first appearance to
> the present time. . . .
>
> She also instructed her students how to detect
> its touch, and named its antidote which is love.
> "Love," said our Teacher, "will meet and destroy
> every claim of error," and urged her hearers to rise
> into its atmosphere and thereby win victories over
> sin. Her words, always so encouraging and
> instructive, were especially so today.[20]

In a letter the following month, Mrs. Eddy wrote, "I consider the most important point in teaching today is the proper instruction on handling this basic error, Animal Magnetism. . . . I have warned all my students of this need."[21]

Mrs. Eddy would teach only one more class in Boston. A few days after her March 1889 class ended, she wrote a friend that she did not want to teach anymore, but wanted the Bible and her textbook, *Science and Health with Key to the Scriptures,* to serve as teacher.[22] Just prior to this class, she had met with her students' association and impressed upon them "the great need of constant and careful study of

Mrs. Eddy bought the house with the tower
—385 Commonwealth—in 1888 and lived there until 1889.

the Scriptures in connection with *Science and Health* to enable us to follow our Master [Christ Jesus]."[23] These two books formed one foundation on which rested the demonstration of Christianly scientific healing.

During this period, Mrs. Eddy was also taking steps to forward her Cause, this Christian movement of spiritual healing, outside of Boston and the United States. She wrote students about promoting her textbook in Europe, especially in England. She also requested her followers to start organizing churches in towns where Christian Science healing was being publicly practiced. Boston, though, was to remain the center of operations. She wrote the Editor of the *Journal,* "As I have said before Boston is to be the headquarters of Christian Science. God has made it so."[24]

In some respects, Mrs. Eddy was pleased with the progress her Cause was making. In May 1889, she wrote a friend, "My students are doing wonderful works at healing. Their letters surprise me with their records."[25] Shortly after this, Mrs. Eddy felt she should refocus her own efforts. She wanted uninterrupted time to revise *Science and Health.* Word had reached her that some Christian Scientists were using written formulas in their healing work. She strongly warned against this, writing one student:

> Tell every one whom you know of doing this, that it is as far from scientific as it would be to give or order drugs. The written direction, beyond a general scientific rule for practice which is already given in Science and Health, confines the practice to mortal mind and is nothing more or less than human directions, mind cure, and will produce the effect only of animal magnetism.[26]

Mrs. Eddy was also concerned about the loss of Christian fellowship among her students. In August 1889 she wrote a friend, "I do not approve of all that is done by my students. When they take sides against each other it almost prostrates me. O! when will this Spirit of Truth and Love prevail throughout the ranks of those who profess to be Christian Scientists? I reprove, rebuke, exhort with a depth of love that has no soundings, but the harvest has not come." She ends the letter, "Do remember the influence that is exerted mentally to prejudice my students against one another and by which they misjudge."[27]

Because they continued to "misjudge," Mrs. Eddy dissolved her students' association and suspended the formal organization of the Church in Boston. As she wrote to Laura Sargent at the end of 1889, "This was after ten years of internal feuds caused always not by the main body, but by two or three members that mesmerism used to do as the Bible says, one sinner destroyeth much good."[28]

Mrs. Eddy requested her students in Boston to continue to conduct church services, but as a voluntary association that acted under the commandment to love one another, rather than under congregational rules.[29] She announced her retirement[30] to the Field and moved back to her home state of New Hampshire. She not only wanted quiet time in which to work on a major revision of her textbook, she was also praying and listening for God's guidance as to what final form the Church of Christ, Scientist, should take so that divine Love and Christian healing would fill it to the exclusion of all else.

At the close of the year she sent a message to the Christian Science Field, describing good healing as "instantaneous cure." The "way" to this accomplishment, she told them, was marked by three milestones: self-knowledge, humility, and love.[31]

CHAPTER 12

Impelled by Love
(1890–1892)

THE DAWN OF 1890 found Mary Baker Eddy at one of the most significant crossroads in her life. Before leaving Boston, Massachusetts, for Concord, New Hampshire, Mrs. Eddy had resigned as Pastor of her Church; had given the responsibility for publishing *The Christian Science Journal* to a "Publication committee" of her students; and had closed the Massachusetts Metaphysical College, of which she was President and teacher. Under her direction a Board of Directors was appointed and made responsible for maintaining church services in Boston, including the employment of another pastor who would preach in strict accord with the teachings of Christian Science.

Having thus cleared the decks, Mrs. Eddy devoted herself to revising her book. Her purpose was not to add new ideas, but rather to elucidate and illuminate more thoroughly the divinely inspired concepts that had been there from the first writing. When the Fiftieth edition of

Science and Health was issued in January 1891, a number of highly significant changes by the author were to be found: there was a new arrangement of chapters, having several new chapter titles; marginal headings had been incorporated for the first time; Scriptural quotations had replaced literary ones at the beginning of each chapter; the previous thirty-eight-page index had grown to seventy-one pages; throughout the book, portions of text had been shifted and forty pages of new material had been added; and almost every page showed evidence of some rewriting. Of this new edition Mrs. Eddy wrote two of her students, "I made it a special point . . . to so systematize the statement of Science as to compel the *scholar* to see it is demonstrably true, and *can be* understood on the basis of proof."[1]

The Discoverer of Christian Science did not write *Science and Health* from a theoretical basis. While all of its concepts had first come to her as divine revelation, she hadn't begun the book until she had first proved its practicality by healing others through scientific, Christian prayer. Perhaps to emphasize this point, she added to the new edition, "Working out the rules of Science in practice, the author has restored health in cases of both acute and chronic disease, and in their severest forms. Secretions have been changed, the structure has been renewed, shortened limbs have been elongated, cicatrized joints have been made supple, and carious bones have been restored to healthy conditions."[2]

In regard to the "shortened limbs," it is very possible that Mrs. Eddy could have been thinking of a healing that occurred a year or so before she left Boston. The man who was healed related his experience to a Christian Scientist in Los Angeles in 1903:

> About eighteen years ago, while living in Boston, I fell from the third story of a building on which I was working, to the pavement. My leg was broken in three places. I was taken to a hospital, where they tried to help me. They said that the leg was so bad that it would have to be amputated. I said, "No, I would rather die." They permitted it to heal as best it might, and as a result I had to wear an iron shoe eight or nine inches high. I was called to Mrs. Eddy's home on Commonwealth Avenue, in Boston, to do some light work. Mrs. Eddy came into the room where I was busy, and observing my condition, kindly remarked, "I suppose you expect to get out of this some time." I answered, "No; all that can be done for me has been done, and I can now manage to get around with a cane." Mrs. Eddy said, "Sit down and I will treat you." When she finished the treatment she

said, "You go home and take off that iron shoe,
and give your leg a chance to straighten out." I
went home and did as I was told, and now I am so
well that, so far as I know, one leg is as good as the
other.[3]

Mrs. Eddy healed the same way she loved God: it was simply in her nature and had been from childhood. Nothing was more important to her than doing God's will, which she perceived through daily prayer. She was continually urging her students to lean more on God instead of turning to her for advice, sometimes referring them, in her letters, to Proverbs 3: 5, 6 in the Bible:

Trust in the Lord with all thine heart; and lean
not unto thine own understanding.
In all thy ways acknowledge him, and he shall
direct thy paths.

But this by no means meant she had stopped caring for them. Quite the contrary, Mrs. Eddy felt toward her pupils as a mother feels for her own children. As she wrote to one of them: "God has given me new lessons and I too must 'be about my Father's business.' Do not think it is for lack of love, but only a conviction of duty that makes me desire to be isolated from society."[4]

It is the great need for loving one another that most clearly dominates Mrs. Eddy's correspondence during this period. A beautiful example of this can be seen in her words to one pupil:

> Oh may this Easter Sunday carry you my prayer
> . . ."Little children love one another" . . . you must
> love *all.* No matter if they persecute you even, you
> must love all. But you must love especially the
> brethren. You must meet with them, cheer them, in
> their labors, point the way of love to them and
> show them it by loving first, and waiting patiently
> for them to be in this great step by your side, loving
> each other and walking together. This is what the
> world must see before we can convince the world of
> the truths of Christian Science.[5]

When Christian Scientists in Chicago were at odds over the controversial pastor of their Church of Christ, Scientist, George Day,[6] Mrs. Eddy wrote to a Christian Science teacher[7] there of how she "had a great love for all of his good sayings and doings, and had forgiven and forgotten any things that he had uttered against me." She closed this letter:

> O do show me how great is your love for God
> by forgiving, yea more, by loving all mankind and

for once I ask it show yourself the best Christian of
the two by taking the *first* step towards recon-
ciliation. Will you do this dear? My heart bleeds
with this name among men—that we are *not*
brethren. I would humble myself in the dust to have
this otherwise.[8]

The week before, Mrs. Eddy had heard that Mr. Day was
ill and had sent him "a letter calculated to heal him."[9] Two
days after writing the Chicago teacher, Mrs. Eddy learned
that her letter to Mr. Day had accomplished its purpose.

In writing to another student about the relationship of
divine Love to healing, Mrs. Eddy said:

The healing will grow more easy and be more
immediate as you realize that God, Good, *is all* and
Good is *Love.* You must gain Love, and lose the
false sense called love. You must feel the Love that
never faileth,—that perfect sense of divine power
that makes healing no longer power but grace.
Then you will have the Love that casts out fear and
when fear is gone doubt is gone and your work is
done. Why? Because it never was *undone.*[10]

In the spring of 1891, Captain Joseph S. Eastaman, one
of the Board of Directors of the voluntary Boston church,

witnessed a demonstration of this healing "grace" in action. He told his experience to one who later recounted it for posterity:

> Captain Eastaman had an appointment with Mrs. Eddy. . . . He arrived at her home at the appointed time, was met at the door by Mrs. Eddy's secretary Calvin Frye who ushered him into the reception room, then went up the stairs to inform Mrs. Eddy that the Captain had arrived. As he started to return down the stairs he suddenly pitched head first to the foot of the stairs, apparently with a broken neck caused by the fall.
>
> Mrs. Eddy, hearing the noise, came to the head of the stairs and said what is the matter? then she noticed Mr. Frye lying on the floor. She said, "Calvin get up on your feet." She said again, "Calvin get up at once." The third time she said calmly, "Calvin arise immediately you are all right." Mr. Frye arose at once, looked up at Mrs. Eddy who was coming down the stairs, and then walked into another room. Captain Eastaman had his interview with Mrs. Eddy and then left to take the train back to Boston. Captain Eastaman was positive that he had witnessed a demonstration over the claim of accidental death.[11]

Calvin Frye's diaries show that his daily work for Mrs. Eddy went on completely uninterrupted and unhampered by this incident. About four months later, another student, David A. Easton, visited Mrs. Eddy in her home. He told her he was dying of consumption. A week later, he wrote her:

> I am healed. I realized it the next day after I saw you. . . . When I called on you I seemed to be in a swift current of mortal thought, that I could not resist and that was carrying me down, down. Your few but vigorous words seemed to lift me out of that current. I feel like a new man.[12]

In her reply Mrs. Eddy wrote, "I felt it when I held your hand and God touched you. I told you I could do nothing for you, but I knew that moment of God's power. Oh tell your wife to let you this time go preach the gospel of healing. Remember this duty yourself when the hour comes."[13] A year and a half later Mrs. Eddy would ask the Board of Directors to call him to serve as pastor of The First Church of Christ, Scientist, in Boston.

When Mrs. Eddy reorganized the Boston church in the summer of 1892, she changed it from a local church to what would become an international one. More importantly, she would gradually replace the former congregational government and its member involvement with a church governed by divinely inspired laws.[14] She had purposely caused the previous organization to dissolve because of continual internal congregational disputes caused by a few members. Her ideal of church government was one supported by the members' love for one another.

In the March 1892 issue of the *Journal,* Mrs. Eddy wrote of church organization in the same terms she used to describe marriage: "If our Church is organized, it is to meet the demand, 'suffer it to be so now.' The real Christian compact is love for another. This bond is wholly spiritual and inviolate."[15] The prosperity and progress of the organization rests on the love felt and expressed by its members for each other.

In order to support this concept best, Mrs. Eddy was inspired to have her reorganized church governed by Rules which she wrote—Rules based on the law of God. If the members obeyed these Rules, their human opinions would have no place and consequently could not inhibit their love for one another.

On September 1, 1892, Mrs. Eddy established The First Church of Christ, Scientist, through a Deed of Trust which created The Christian Science Board of Directors to administer the Church in accordance with the Rules she had written. Each of these Rules, or By-Laws, was divinely inspired to meet the need not only of the moment, but of the future as well.[16]

In October, Mrs. Eddy wrote to a student:

> My task the past summer, to breast the storm of
> blind guides, and deliver the people and establish
> Christ's Church in Boston, has been beyond
> description. But I was enabled to accomplish it.
> This new form of Church government is a light
> set upon a hill.[17]

This "light" is produced by the flame of divine Love, the
power and grace that exist for the healing of mankind,
individually and collectively—the same power and grace
that underlie all of Mary Baker Eddy's healing works.

CHAPTER 13

The demand for more grace
(1893–1895)

IT BECAME MARY BAKER EDDY'S PRACTICE, after she moved to Pleasant View, her home in Concord, New Hampshire, to take daily carriage rides through the town and surrounding region. These drives usually lasted no more than an hour and provided a break in a very demanding work schedule. Sometimes she would stop at the Western Union telegraph office to send a message to her church workers in Boston. On those occasions Henry Morrison, the office manager, usually came out to her carriage. One afternoon, while he was talking with Mrs. Eddy, she asked if he was "feeling as well as usual." He told her of a chronic stomach problem. After their conversation he never again had trouble with his stomach, nor with severe colds that he had been subject to.[1]

At another time when Mrs. Eddy was watching the approach of a storm, she noticed a man on crutches enter her gate. She sent word to offer him shelter and food. After eating, he stayed in the carriage house until the rain had stopped. A few months later when some members of the Pleasant View household were going to Concord, a workman who was breaking stone on the road stopped their carriage. He asked if they remembered him. When none did, he told them that he was the one to whom they had given shelter. He went on to say that while waiting for the storm to pass he had fallen asleep, and upon waking, "I rose and walked without my crutches, and have never needed them since." He couldn't understand it. When told about this on their return, Mrs. Eddy recalled the man and acknowledged she had prayed about the situation.[2]

And when telephone wires were being put up in Concord, a young lineman working in front of Pleasant View was hit in the eye by a wire. He was brought into the house, and Mrs. Eddy talked with him. The next day he was back at work, completely healed.[3]

Healing was central to Mrs. Eddy's nature. She was continually counseling her students in their practice of Christian Science. To one she wrote:

> The healing of my students changes its stages as
> they learn from experience. It starts a marvel of
> power and then becomes a marvel of *grace*. The
> latter is gained by the spiritualization of practice
> which acts on the moral more than the physical
> degree of healing, but is sure to produce the latter
> which never relapses. More of the spirit than letter

is required to reach this Christ-stage of healing
sickness and sin. This dear one, is what I want you
to attain.[4]

To encourage "more of the spirit than letter," Mrs. Eddy
spent much of 1893 working with James Gilman, an artist
from Vermont, on illustrating a poem she had written early
in the year. In this poem, titled *Christ and Christmas,* she
wanted to convey her feelings about Soul's expression of the
Christ and Christian Science and their representatives, but
not human personalities. In an article in *The Christian
Science Journal* she wrote:

> I never looked upon my ideal of the face of Jesus, but
> the one in my work approximates it.
> . . . Pictures are parts of one's ideal, but this ideal is not
> one's personality,—note this. When looking behind the
> veil of the temple he that perceives a semblance be-
> tween the thinker and his expressed thought, cannot
> blame him for it, but must credit himself.[5]

It was important to Mrs. Eddy that not only Christian
Scientists but the public in general have a correct concept
of who she was as the Discoverer and Founder of
Christian Science. To this end she prepared an address to
be given at the World Parliament of Religions, which was
being held in conjunction with the 1893 Chicago World's

Fair. The Editor of the *Journal,* Judge Septimus J. Hanna, delivered Mrs. Eddy's address, but, unfortunately, afterward allowed the press to have the manuscript against Mrs. Eddy's prior instructions. The next day the newspapers reported that it was the Editor's address and named him the leader of Christian Science. Mrs. Eddy was greatly disappointed: a rare opportunity had been lost through disobedience. As she wrote to one of her Chicago workers several weeks later:

> For the world to understand me in my true light, and life, would do more for our Cause than aught else could. This I learn from the fact that the enemy tries harder to hide these two things from the world than to win any other points. Also Jesus' life and character in their first appearing were treated in like manner. And I regret to see that loyal students are not more awake to this great demand in their measures to meet the enemies tactics.[6]

(By "the enemy" Mrs. Eddy was referring to the "carnal mind" St. Paul speaks of in Romans 8:7.)

She also saw the demand for Christian Scientists to be awake to the need for readily practicing Science at all times: "Oh how I wish all of my students were awake and demonstrating as they ought the divine Love pouring out upon us such miracles of favor. Today a runaway horse with

N. B. Fear the world to understand me in my true light and life; would do more for your cause than anything else could. This I learn from the fact that the enemy tries harder to hide these two things from the world than to win any other points... Also Jesus' life and character on their first appearing were attacked in like manner. And be glad to see that loyal students are now more awake to this great demand in their measures to meet the enemy's tactics. Again with love M.B.E.

a sleigh dangling behind him was making gallops towards my sleigh—but when I turned and looked him in the face he turned away from the sleigh and rushed by us—and turned just as if reined by a driver."[7]

In 1894 Mrs. Eddy's predominant concern was the completion of the construction of the Original Edifice of The Mother Church. She had been constantly encouraging the Church's Board of Directors to finish the building before the end of the year. But as the months passed, this appeared less and less likely. Mistakes and delays seemed to be more the order of the day than uncommon occurrences. A railway strike, recalcitrant contractors, and continual postponements had to be overcome. By the beginning of September only one exterior wall had been completed. The

Directors—Joseph Armstrong, Stephen Chase, William B. Johnson, Ira O. Knapp—had little or no experience with such a large building project, but they kept going forward because Mrs. Eddy constantly turned them to divine Mind.

Earlier in the year Mrs. Eddy had written one of her students, "Am glad that the demand for more grace to meet the emergencies of this hour is being realized by many of my students. Our prayer in stone, our monumental church, that is to be built in Boston will tend greatly to unify our numbers. May God give us the true *substance* of this type of Love."[8]

By December, things looked hopeless: the bell tower was unfinished; the auditorium, filled with scaffolding, still had

The Mother Church under construction in November 1894

no balcony or pews; and the walls and ceiling had yet to be plastered. At this point "lack" was the overriding problem: lack of laborers, lack of supplies, lack of time. However, when an incident of lack appeared in Mrs. Eddy's own town of Concord at the same time, she showed clearly how it was to be overcome.

There had been no rain in the Concord area throughout November. The farmer who delivered Pleasant View's milk told the cook that his well was empty and his cows were beginning to go dry. When Mrs. Eddy was told about this, she smiled and said, "Oh! if he only knew, Love fills that well."[9] The next day when the farmer came, he was overjoyed to tell the cook that that morning he had found his well full of water. And what was amazing to him was that there had been no rain to fill it. Mrs. Eddy wrote to the Board of Directors on December 10, telling them about this experience. The challenges faced in building the church were met and overcome. Love had filled the void.

The first church service was held in the new edifice on Sunday, December 30. It was also the first Christian Science service where the pastor was not a preacher delivering a sermon, but two books from which a Reader read a Bible Lesson. On December 19 Mrs. Eddy had instructed the Board:

> The Bible and "Science and Health with Key to the Scriptures" shall henceforth be the Pastor of the Mother Church. This will tend to spiritualize thought. Personal preaching has more or less of

2748

Pleasant View.
Concord. N.H. Dec. 19, 1894.

Christian Science Directors.
My beloved Students,
The day is well nigh won. You will soon rest on your arms. Thank God you have been valiant soldiers—loyal to the heart's core. "Who is so great a God as our God".
Present no contribution beyond Dedication day.

2748 P.2

When you know the amount
requisite and have re-
ceived it for finishing
the church building —
close all contributions
and give public notice
thereof.
Hold your services in
the Mother church, Dec. 30,
1894. and dedicate this church
Jan. 6th. The Bible and
"Science and Health with Key
To the Scriptures" shall hence-
forth be the Pastor of the
Mother church. This will tend
to spiritualize thought. Personal
al preaching has more or less of
human views grafted into it.
Whereas this word contains only
the living health giving Truth.
With love mother,

Mary Baker Eddy.

human views grafted into it. Whereas the pure
Word contains only the living health giving Truth.[10]

The Mother Church was dedicated on January 6, 1895.
One who attended that service has written:

> When I went home after the dedication of The
> Mother Church I manifested a belief of a severe
> bronchial trouble which seemed very tenacious.
> During this time I was called back to Mrs. Eddy's
> home for an interview. While there, no manifesta-
> tion of the trouble appeared, and when taking my
> leave she accompanied me to the door, and putting
> her hand on my arm she said, "That is not in your
> body, but in consciousness, and you can put it out."
> I returned home, but the healing was not in evi-
> dence for a few days, when it suddenly disappeared.
> When I returned to stay in Mrs. Eddy's home she
> suddenly asked me, "How long was it before you
> were free? I only ask the question because I wanted
> to see how long mesmerism could seem to hold my
> work. You were healed when you left here, but you
> did not know it."[11]

To keep the members of her Church awake and alert, Mrs.
Eddy had been establishing church duties and Rules as the
need arose for them. Those that were first adopted also
supported and confirmed the main points of the September 1,

1892, Deed of Trust, which had served to reorganize the Church. In March 1895, Mrs. Eddy requested that all these Rules be put together in a *Church Manual.* She later wrote to the committee given this task: "Let the Manual be brief and gotten out *soon.* There is a great call for it so that the By-Laws shall be read by all its members."[12] Mrs. Eddy expected members to be healers. A number of years after the *Manual* was first published, she wrote:

> This Church is impartial, its rules apply not to one member only, but to one and all equally. Of this I am sure, that each Rule and By-Law in this Manual will increase the spirituality of him who obeys it, invigorate his capacity to heal the sick, to comfort such as mourn, and to awaken the sinner.[13]

The Mother Church was designed so that healing would permeate all of its activities. To emphasize this in the midweek church meeting, Mrs. Eddy requested changes in the conduct of this service, which up to that time had been a continuation of Bible Lessons from the Sunday service.[14] On January 15, 1895, she sent the following notice to be read at the next meeting:

> My dear Students: Make broader your bounds for blessing the people. Have Friday evening meetings to benefit the people. Learn to forget what you should not remember viz. self, and live for the good you do.

The Mother Church

Conduct your meetings by repeating and demonstrating practical Christian Science. Tell what this
Science does for yourself and will do for others. Speak
from experience of its Founder—noting her self sacrifice
as the way in Christian Science. Be *meek*, let your
mottoes for this meeting be, Who shall be least and
servant and "Little children love one another."
Affectionately yours, Mary Baker Eddy.[15]

Meekness was a quality Mrs. Eddy especially valued. She taught that it is essential in the healing practice. It was certainly evident in her own healing work; it is one of the defining qualities of the Leader of Christian Science, together with her purity, fearlessness, honesty, wisdom, unselfed love, and absolute faith in God. With these as her foundation stones, she built a Church that offers mankind the Science, or divine laws, of Christian healing. In her understanding and demonstration, this divine Science is the Comforter promised by Jesus.[16] Her own estimation and recognition of what God had done for mankind through her can be seen in a comment she made to some visitors to Pleasant View one day: "As Mary Baker Eddy, I am the weakest of mortals, but as the Discoverer and Founder of Christian Science, I am the bone and sinew of the world."[17]

CHAPTER 14

The Founder at work
(1896–1898)

MARY BAKER EDDY BEGAN 1896 by delivering a communion address in her own Church in Boston, Massachusetts—The Mother Church, The First Church of Christ, Scientist. In her talk she turned thought away from the persecution of Jesus of Nazareth to his demonstration of divine, infinite Love, forgiving his enemies, which enabled him to overcome the cross and the grave.[1] As often occurred on such occasions, one of those who heard her speak was healed:

> This man had been a pronounced invalid for years and had grown so irritable that his family could scarcely live with him. He was unable to walk without support. . . . he was visiting in Boston not far from the Christian Science Church there. Sunday morning, hearing the chimes, he asked to what church they belonged. On being informed that it was the Christian Science Church, and that the worshipers in that church claimed to heal the sick, he went to the service. He said he had not been there long when a woman came in who was

announced as Mrs. Eddy, and she gave a talk. She
had not talked long, until all of a sudden he felt
that he was healed. He did not miss his canes until
after he reached the house of his friend. The next
day he bought *Science and Health,* a book written
by the same Mrs. Eddy who spoke in the church.
Since then he has been an ardent student of that
book. [An old friend said of this man], "I don't
believe even he realizes the transformation that has
taken place in him. I assure you I never saw so great
a change in any person."[2]

A week after the service, Mrs. Eddy wrote to one of her
students, "Oh let us love our dear enemies and show them in
our own lives even as we try to—the way to Heaven. . . . The
communion was very sweet on Sunday and impressive. I felt
sure I did some healing and have since heard of a few cases."[3]

One of the other healings had happened before the
service as Mrs. Eddy was entering the church. She passed a
man on crutches in the street and nodded to him, smiling.
He later wrote of the experience:

When I returned into our home, both Mother and
sister noticed a change in me—I had noticed it immediately for I was stronger and could walk so much
better on my way to the house—the next day or two
the neighbors and my friends noticed the change—Dr.
Marr said he had never known of such a quick come-
back [from typhoid fever] and was surprised.[4]

Mrs. Eddy was continually counseling her students on the need for more effective healing. At the end of January she wrote to one student, "To know there is but *one* God, one Cause, one effect, one Mind, heals instantly. Have but One God, and your reflection of Him does the healing."[5] The following day she wrote to another, "Love is the only and all of attainments in spiritual growth. Without it, healing is not done and cannot be either morally or physically. Every advanced step will show you this until the victory is won and you possess no other consciousness but *Love* divine."[6] In the February issue of *The Christian Science Journal,* in reply to the question as to whether she would teach again, Mrs. Eddy said in part, "The hour has struck for Christian Scientists to do their own work; to appreciate the signs of the times; to demonstrate self-knowledge and self-government; and to demonstrate, as this period demands, over all sin, disease, and death."[7]

The needs of the world beyond the United States were also drawing Mrs. Eddy's attention during this period. She sent one of her students, Julia Field-King, who had previously established a Christian Science church in St. Louis, Missouri, to London, England, to build up a church there specifically through healing and teaching. She also began to consider the need to translate *Science and Health with Key to the Scriptures* into French and German.

As the weather warmed in the late spring, Mrs. Eddy became acquainted with a sixteen-year-old girl who lived on a neighboring farm in Concord, New Hampshire. Her family had emigrated from England three years before This girl, Minnie Ford, had spent most of the previous winter (1895–1896) in the hospital with tuberculosis. Homesick, she returned to her family's farm against the judgment of doctors who did not expect her to recover. As a result of Mrs. Eddy's daily carriage drive, the two met and she invited the teenager to visit her. They soon became friends. Minnie later recounted one occasion when she accompanied Mrs. Eddy on a walk:

> [Mrs. Eddy] invited me to go with her to
> feed the gold fish in the fountain. She called
> them to her by saying "come to Mother," and to
> my surprise they came instantly and took the food
> out of her hand. She looked at me and smiled,
> she was so sweet. During this time my illness
> was entirely forgotten and the first thing I knew
> I was well.[8]

Later in the summer, Mrs. Eddy asked Minnie's parents if their daughter could join her household staff to help with the cooking and cleaning. They said no, feeling she was too young. Of this decision Minnie wrote, "As I look back over the years I feel my parents and I were most ungrateful, she had saved my life, and her dear face will be in my memory always."[9]

What drew most of Mrs. Eddy's thought during the latter half of 1896 was the preparation of her book *Miscellaneous Writings, 1883–1896.* It was published the following February and comprised almost all of her contributions to

Photo: Thomas Marr & Sons

Pleasant View, Mrs. Eddy's home in Concord, New Hampshire

the *Journal,* which she had started fourteen years earlier as publisher and editor. In the March 1897 *Journal,* Mrs. Eddy announced that all Christian Science teaching by her students would stop for one year. Her notice read, in part:

> "Miscellaneous Writings" is calculated to prepare the minds of all true thinkers to understand the Christian Science Text-book more correctly than a student can.
>
> The Bible, Science and Health with Key to the Scriptures, and my other published works, are the only proper instructors for this hour. It shall be the duty of all Christian Scientists to circulate and to sell as many of these books as they can.[10]

At the end of January, Mrs. Eddy had written to one of her most promising students, James Neal, telling him she wanted to give him a copy of her new book. This letter also speaks eloquently of his recent decision to devote his life to the healing practice of Christian Science. She wrote:

> Your letter is my best New Year's gift. I had felt for some time the fitness you possessed for healing, I knew it when you were a member of my College class. It looked a waste to have you in a counting room. Now, thank God, I have at least one student in Boston that promises to be a Healer such as I have long waited and hoped to see. Oh may the Love that looks on you and all guide your every thought and act up to the impersonal, spiritual model that is the only ideal—and constitutes the only scientific Healer.
>
> To this glorious end I ask you to still press on, and have no other ambition or aim. A real scientific *Healer* is the highest position attainable in this sphere of being. Its altitude is far above a Teacher or preacher; it includes all that is divinely high and holy. Darling James, leave behind all else and strive for this great achievement. Mother sighs to see how much her students need this attainment and longs to live to see one Christian Scientist attain it. Your aid to reach this goal is *spiritualization*. To achieve this you must have *one God*, one affection, one way, one Mind. Society, flattery, popularity are tempta-

tions in your pursuit of growth spiritual. Avoid
them as much as in you lies. Pray daily, never miss
praying, no matter how often: "Lead me not into
temptation,"—scientifically rendered,—Lead me
not to lose sight of strict purity, clean pure
thoughts; let all my thoughts and aims be high,
unselfish, charitable, meek,—*spiritually minded.*
With this altitude of thought your mind is losing
materiality and gaining spirituality and this is the
state of mind that *heals* the *sick.* My new book will
do you much good. Do not purchase one, Mother
wants to give you one. I welcome you into the
sanctum of my fold. God bless you.[11]

Seven months later she wrote him again:

Now dear one, watch that worldliness and the
natural mortal love of human applause or any
possible pride or vanity creep not into your
thought, for these are among the thieves that would
steal into the good man's house and spoil his
goods—take away the riches of purer and higher
thoughts—which weigh in God's scale helping you
to heal the sick and reform the sinner. To this end
pray to divine Love daily; for if the good man
watch, his house will not be broken open.[12]

The student who had been sent to London was also
successful in her mission, and First Church of Christ,

Scientist, London, was dedicated on November 7, 1897.[13] Mrs. Eddy had sent $1,000 to the Christian Scientists there to help them purchase a church edifice.

Eighteen ninety-eight proved to be a landmark year for the Cause of Christian Science and its healing activities.[14] In January, Mrs. Eddy established the Church's Board of Lectureship and reorganized The Christian Science Publishing Society, which had been an independent corporation, and made it a part of The Mother Church. In February, she established the Church's Board of Education. In April, she provided the twenty-six subjects for the weekly Bible Lessons. In May, she changed the testimony meeting from Friday evening to Wednesday. In September, she established the *Christian Science Weekly,* which she renamed *Christian Science Sentinel* four months later. In November, Mrs. Eddy taught her last class, to which she invited seventy students. And in December, she established the Church's Committee on Publication. At the end of 1898, she wrote to a lecturer whom she had appointed, "I have wrought day and night this year to make way for our church and a systematic order of action in the departments of C[hristian] S[cience]."[15]

Earlier in the year, in February, Mrs. Eddy had addressed a meeting of Church members in Concord. Her talk focused on the Ninety-first Psalm, which she considered one of the foundation stones of the Christian Science religion.[16] She said that this Psalm "contains more practical theological and pathological truth than any other collection of the same number of words in human language except the Sermon on the Mount of the great Galilean and hillside Teacher."[17] She went on to say that the first verse of this psalm emphasizes an essential point of Christian attainment—dwelling "in the secret place of the most High":

> But what is the sacred secret of the Almighty? So far as experience reaches and Truth has unfolded its immortal idea through spiritual sense, this secret is spiritual *Love*, whereon David has based all Christianity, all healing, all salvation. This Holy of holies is indeed to human sense a secret for it involves God's own nature. The bodily senses are shut out from it. Eye hath not seen it, ear hath not heard it, neither do the human affections abide in the sanctum of Spirit, even though they are oft touched by its holy influence, rebuked, chastened, uplifted, purified by spiritual Love. The sole habitat of this secret place is infinite, and infinity is a secret to the finite senses. In fact Spirit, Divine Love destroys all fear, pain, sorrow, and sin.
>
> Because the senses of Spirit are spiritual and Divine they dwell in the understanding, abide in the secret of Infinity and demonstrate Life, Truth, and Love. How then can human sense or intellect attain the secret of Spirit or Divine Love? By turning away from the false evidence or material sense testimony and listening to the teachings of Spirit.
>
> This solid secret, this substance enduring, this place wherein if a man dwell he can never lose the

true sense of God, of Life, and Love is not even
sought by the five material senses and is found only
by "My Spirit saith the Lord."
1. The secret place of the Most High is spiritual Love.
2. The way thereunto is Christ Truth, but the way
   to find this Way is:
   1. The knowledge of God.
   2. The understanding of God.[18]

It was this spiritual Love that gave Mrs. Eddy her ability
to heal so quickly, to meet challenges of whatever nature with
such authority. One day she was talking with two students in
her home in Concord. One of them later recounted:

> While she was giving us some instruction of work
> to be done, there came a very heavy thunder storm.
> Mrs. Eddy stepped to the window. It made me so still
> for I felt the divine presence as she spoke with God
> and immediately the storm ceased and a double
> rainbow was over the home at Pleasant View.[19]

The book of Genesis in the Bible says that God gives man
dominion "over all the earth." So that this age may be able
to demonstrate that dominion through Christian healing,
Mrs. Eddy shared the revelation she received from divine
Mind in her book *Science and Health*. After that, God led her
to found a Church based on that revelation and to structure
The First Church of Christ, Scientist, in such a way that its
activities could bring about "the healing of the nations."[20]

CHAPTER 15

The "wedding garment" of divine Love
(1899–1901)

At the beginning of 1899, Mary Baker Eddy received a letter from a student she had taught eleven years earlier. He wrote that he had served as Reader in his branch Church of Christ, Scientist, and recounted how much time and effort since his class instruction in Christian Science from her had been devoted to healing—and how he was "still working for that great Prize to be able to have on the wedding garment."[1] He also hoped to be taught further by her. In reply Mrs. Eddy wrote about that "wedding garment":

> It is first the desire above all else to be Christ-
> like, to be tender, merciful, forgetting self and
> caring for others' salvation. To be temperate,
> humble, pure, whereby appetite and passions cease
> to claim your attention and you are not discouraged
> to wait on God. To wait for the *tests* of your sincere
> longing to be good, and seek through daily prayer
> for Divine teaching. If you continue to ask you will
> receive,—provided you comply with what you must
> do for yourself in order to be thus blessed. Reading,

or listening to my teaching the truths of C[hristian]
S[cience] will not do for you what this earnest
seeking and *knowing* and *following* can do for
you. . . . Be of good cheer, you cannot *seek* without
finding.[2]

The *wedding garment* is a term Jesus had used in a
parable about those invited by a king to his son's wedding
to which "many are called, but few are chosen."[3] In her
Message to The Mother Church for 1900, Mrs. Eddy wrote:
"To-day you have come to Love's feast, and you kneel at its
altar. May you have on a wedding garment new and old,
and the touch of the hem of this garment heal the sick and
the sinner!"[4] Mrs. Eddy was speaking out of her own
experience. A number of years earlier she had told her
students' association: "One of the best cures I ever
performed was, apparently, under the most adverse
circumstances. I had spent one year of incessant toil upon
the [manuscript] of my book, *Science and Health,* and put
it into the hands of a printer for publication, who, I found,
had allowed it to be taken from his possession, and I was
thus obliged to return, in the sackcloth of disappointment,
without it. A student soon called desiring me to assist in a
case that was dying. I put on the wedding garments at once
and healed the case in twenty minutes."[5]

Mrs. Eddy's "desire above all else to be Christ-like" was
constant. Her healing ability remained undiminished
throughout her life. Clara Shannon, a cherished worker in
Mrs. Eddy's Pleasant View home during the late 1890s, was

living proof of this. At one point Clara became severely ill with diphtheria and went to stay with nearby friends so as not to burden Mrs. Eddy. Mr. and Mrs. Ezra M. Buswell helped her to bed and began to pray earnestly. Clara's condition, however, continued to worsen until it appeared that death was imminent. At this point Mrs. Eddy arrived at the Buswells in her carriage. Upon learning of the situation, she told Mr. Buswell to go tell Clara that she need not be afraid, divine Love was with her, and that she, Mrs. Eddy, was praying for her. The effect was immediate, and the suffering ceased. Clara then fell asleep and the next morning arose, dressed, had breakfast, and walked back to Pleasant View completely healed.[6] Not many months after this, Mrs. Eddy healed another household worker, her cook, Lydia B. Hall, of the same illness.[7] But Mrs. Eddy's thought was not confined just to her own home. She was deeply involved in the activities of her Concord, New Hampshire, community, of her son and his family, who lived in South Dakota, and especially of her Church in Boston, Massachusetts.

For her son, Mrs. Eddy had a new house built and gave it to him as a Christmas present. She also oversaw and paid for the private schooling of her grandchildren. In Concord, New Hampshire, she made a gift of shoes to all of the impoverished children of the city. She also initiated the paving of Concord streets and contributed financially to this endeavor. In connection with this latter benevolence, a remarkable incident occurred. A student wrote Mrs. Eddy a number of years after the fact:

There was a splendid testimony given last
evening at First Church [Chicago]. A man who said
he was formerly an actor, was ill, despondent, discouraged, without a God, and most forlorn in the
world; drifted into a [Christian Science] lecture one
night; listened, was interested, afterwards wrote the
Lecturer, and upon hearing that he might find the
true God, secured the textbook [*Science and Health*],
and notwithstanding he was just then offered a good
position, he declined that and went to Concord
instead, took a job on the road then building out
Pleasant Street, where he could see you pass every
day in your carriage, and altho[ugh] it was pretty
rough work for an actor, unaccustomed to the uses
of pick and shovel, he actually enjoyed his work, was
healed, soundly converted, has known God ever
since, and would not take anything in exchange for
what he has learned thro[ugh] your teachings.[8]

At the top of this letter Mrs. Eddy wrote in her own hand,
"Case of healing by me on street, person unknown." Such an
incident was not at all uncommon. On another occasion
during this period, Marie Chalmers Ford, who was fairly new
to Christian Science and had been visiting her brother in New
Hampshire, came to Concord before returning to her home
in Ohio. She wrote Mrs. Eddy about what had happened:

As the time for my departure [from my
brother's] drew near I became so ill that I could

scarcely walk without great suffering, and it seemed
as though I would not be able to go alone, if at all.
All the time I was holding to this one sentence in
Science and Health, page 494, "Divine Love always
has met and always will meet every human need,"
and I found myself on the train for Concord. When
I reached there I went directly to Christian Science
Hall [a combination church and Reading Room]
and was told that in a short time your carriage
would pass. I sat down in one of the windows to
read, but my suffering was still so intense that I
could scarcely see the pages. Very soon someone
came to me quietly and said that your carriage was
coming. Of course I expected you only to drive
past, but instead you drove up and stopped almost
directly in front of where I sat in the open window.
Someone from the Rooms went out to your
carriage and you talked with them several minutes.
Many times during those few minutes you glanced
up at the window where I sat and looked straight
into my eyes. You drove away and I arose from my
chair perfectly healed. There was not the slightest
sense of pain or suffering left, and I had not been
free from pain night or day for almost a week.[9]

On the front of this letter's envelope, Mrs. Eddy wrote,
"case of my healing."

In June 1899, Mrs. Eddy traveled to Boston to address
the Annual Meeting of The Mother Church.[10] That year it

was being held in Tremont Temple because of the large number of members attending. Mrs. Eddy told her listeners that the special demand of the hour was "the fulfilment of divine Love in our lives. . . ." She went on to say, "Divine Love has strengthened the hand and encouraged the heart of every member. . . . Divine Love hath opened the gate Beautiful to us, where we may see God and live. . . . Divine Love will also rebuke and destroy disease, and destroy the belief of life in matter. . . . Divine Love is our only physician, and never loses a case. It binds up the broken-

MRS. EDDY ADDRESSING THE CHRISTIAN SCIENCE CONVENTION IN TREMONT TEMPLE.

An 1899 drawing published in the *Boston Record*

hearted; heals the poor body, whose whole head is sick and
whose whole heart is faint. . . ." As was usual when Mrs.
Eddy spoke publicly, healings occurred. One of these was
published in the *Christian Science Sentinel:*

> I awoke on the morning of that day with a sense
> of suffering so severe that it was a great effort to get
> up. I could eat no breakfast, and after working
> [praying] an hour, was relieved, but by no means
> free. Ordinarily I should have thought it the part of
> wisdom to remain quiet, but so great was the desire
> to be present at the meeting and hear our Leader,
> that I arose, dressed, and went to the Temple, feeling
> that I should hear the needed word of healing and
> strength from her lips. Nor was I disappointed.
> While Mrs. Eddy was speaking, the pain lessened,
> and then I forgot it completely until later, during
> the services, I realized that all sense of discord had
> vanished. Not only this, but for many months
> afterwards I was better and stronger, did better
> healing work for my patients, and experienced an
> unusual degree of spiritual and mental freedom.[11]

A year after this address Mrs. Eddy wrote this to one of
her students: "Our churches spring up spontaneously from
the soil of healing—but I know that a healer needs all her
time to do her best in caring for patients. It is an absorbing
subject to lift the mind above pain, disease, and death and
when I practiced I could not attend to aught else."[12]

Beginning in August 1899, however, a great deal of Mrs. Eddy's attention was focused where she would not have chosen. Josephine Woodbury, a former pupil, brought a libel suit against her. Mrs. Eddy knew the accusations against her to be foundationless, and over the next two years she was deeply involved in her own legal defense. She continually counseled her attorneys on how to proceed, and issued specific instructions throughout this period to those she had asked to pray about the case. One of the more preposterous allegations Mrs. Woodbury made at the time, was that the Discoverer of Christian Science had never healed anyone. As a result of the evidence presented, the suit was decided in Mrs. Eddy's favor. While this suit was going on she had been inspired to write the poem "Satisfied," which begins:

> It matters not,
> What be thy lot,
> So Love doth guide;
> For storm or shine—
> Pure peace is thine—
> Whate'er betide.[13]

Mrs. Eddy counseled others, including her own son, against instigating legal suits. To one student, in August 1900, she wrote:

> I have heard what pains me; I long to hear your
> legal quibble is settled amicably. You know the

scripture saith brother must not go to law with
brother and that before unbelievers. Forgive, be
unselfish, meek and Christlike or you cannot be a
Christian Scientist.[14]

In January 1901, Mrs. Eddy brought about a significant
adjustment in the government of The Mother Church
when she made The Christian Science Board of Directors
solely responsible for the transaction of the Church's
business. Up until this time, a select group of "First
Members" also had limited responsibilities, though Mrs.
Eddy had been gradually diminishing even these duties. A
few years previously she had written a letter that was read
at a church business meeting, admonishing, "When, if ever
will all the members of this church, even while under the
rod, behave themselves as Christian Scientists and not have
to be put into straight jackets to keep them from quarreling
in the sackcloth of this solemn hour?"[15] In June 1901, Mrs.
Eddy wrote to a student, "Wisdom is one third of
C[hristian] S[cience], the other two thirds is *Love*."[16]

Once, after reviewing a Christian Science lecture, Mrs.
Eddy wrote to its author, ". . . it lacked that appeal of Love
that touches the heart. Dear one, cultivate this tender
emotion, have a cell less in the brain and a fibre more in the
heart in yourself and it will do much for your lectures and
in healing the sick."[17]

At the end of April 1901, Mrs. Eddy granted a rare
interview to a newspaper reporter, Joseph I. C. Clark.[18]
When asked, "On what is Christian Science based?" she

replied, "I can tell you on what I based my conception of religion and on which, so far as in me rests, I have laid its foundation in Christian Science: The Ten Commandments, The Ninety-First Psalm, The Sermon on the Mount, The Revelation of St. John the Divine."

Mrs. Eddy learned from the Bible how to wear divine Love's "wedding garment." Her "desire above all else to be Christ-like" enabled her to heal as Jesus had. And she worked to see that this desire predominated in all the activities of her Church.

CHAPTER 16

"The Cause needs healers"
(1902–1904)

MARY BAKER EDDY WROTE of *Science and Health with Key to the Scriptures:* "The textbook of Christian Science maintains primitive Christianity, shows how to demonstrate it, and throughout is logical in premise and in conclusion. Can Scientists adhere to it, establish their practice of healing on its basis, become successful healers and models of good morals, and yet the book itself be absurd and unscientific? Is not the tree known by its fruit?"[1]

As evidenced by her correspondence, Mrs. Eddy was especially concerned about the need for more effective Christian healing. To this end she was continually working to make clearer her textbook on the Science of Christ-healing. At the end of January 1902, the 226th edition of *Science and Health* was issued. Readers familiar with the book could immediately see it was a major revision. Mrs. Eddy, assisted by two of her students, Edward A. Kimball and William P. McKenzie, had spent months working on it. She significantly rearranged the chapters, putting them

Photo: Michael Sylvester

The 226th Edition of *Science and Health,* a major revision

in the order that they have today, and she added a new final chapter, "Fruitage," a compilation of healings from the pages of *The Christian Science Journal* and the *Christian Science Sentinel.* What ties these healings together is that they were all accomplished solely through the reading of *Science and Health.* Mrs. Eddy also reviewed the marginal headings in the book and rewrote some of them.[2] And she told Kimball and McKenzie to make sure that all Scriptural quotations in the book were according to the King James Version. Another new feature she added was line numbering, in anticipation of a concordance that was then being prepared. As a consequence, an index that had been a part of the book since 1886 was not included.

whatever contradicts its divine Principle is false

232 SCIENCE AND HEALTH.

1 Him was not anything made that was made," — can triumph over sin, sickness, and death.

3   Many theories relative to God and man, neither make man harmonious nor God lovable. The beliefs we com-

Denials of di- monly entertain about happiness and life
6 **vine power.** afford no scathless and permanent evidence of either. Security for the claims of harmonious and eternal Being is found only in divine Science.

9   Scripture informs us that "with God all things are possible," — all good is possible to Spirit, — but our prevalent theories practically deny this, and make heal-
12 ing possible only through matter. These theories must be untrue, for the Scripture is true. Christianity is not false; but religions which contradict its principle are
15 false. *only that divine P*

   In our age Christianity is again demonstrating the power of divine Principle, as it did nineteen hundred
18 years ago, by healing the sick and triumphing over death. Jesus never taught that drugs, food, air, and exercise could make a man healthy, or that they could destroy
21 human life; nor did he illustrate these errors by his practice. He referred man's harmony to Mind, not matter, and never tried to make of none effect the sen-
24 tence of God, which sealed His condemnation of sin, sickness, and death. *The*

   In the sacred sanctuary of Truth are voices of solemn
27 import, but we heed them not. It is only when the sup-

Signs posed pleasures and pains of sense pass away
following. in our lives, that we find unquestionable signs
30 of the burial of error and the resurrection to spiritual life.

   There is no place nor opportunity in Science for error

Teaching and practice The

A page of the 226th edition with Mrs. Eddy's corrections

Mrs. Eddy devoted herself throughout 1902 to reading through the new revision page by page.[3] As a result, she corrected and standardized the capitalization of words relating to God, removed repetitious sentences and paragraphs, and added a little new material. In a letter to Albert F. Conant, who was compiling the Concordance, Mrs. Eddy wrote in the spring of 1903:

> My "last changes of Science and Health" may continue so long as I read the book! but I will stop now and you may finish the Concordance immediately. Owing to the fact that the book should unfold in proportion as my thought grasps the spiritual idea more clearly so as to voice it more simply and thus settle many queries—I wished I had not commenced a Concordance, but had had an Index attached to S.&H.[4]

Her reason for not returning the index to her book at that time was due to copyright considerations, on which her attorney had advised her.

Revising *Science and Health* was just one of many continuing assignments Mrs. Eddy gave herself. As she wrote to a friend, "My whole time is employed in the work for humanity."[5] To two students who had given her a copy of Wycliffe's translation of the New Testament, she wrote:

> To-day it is a marvel to me that God chose me for this mission, and that my life-work was the

theme of ancient prophecy and I the scribe of His
infinite way of Salvation! O may He keep me at the
feet of Christ, cleansing the human understanding
and bathing it with my tears; wiping it with the hairs
of my head, the shreds of my understanding that
God *"numbered"* to make men wise unto salvation.[6]

Mrs. Eddy saw salvation as the scientific understanding
and demonstration of God's supremacy, which heals sin
and sickness. Time and again during this period, she was
writing to her followers of the great need for more quick,
effective healing work. She wrote to Alfred Baker, a former
doctor turned Christian Scientist:

> The sick need you and you can do great good
> by healing. The Cause needs healers a million times
> more than teachers. The best healer is the best
> Scientist and will take the place that God has for
> all to take.[7]

To the Editor of the *Journal* and *Sentinel:*

> I started this great work and *woke the people* by
> demonstration, not words but works. Our peri-
> odicals must have more Testimonials in them. . . .
> Healing is the best sermon, healing is the best
> lecture, and the entire demonstration of C[hristian]
> S[cience]. The sinner and sick healed are our best
> witnesses.[8]

To a Boston student:

> . . . I retain my conviction that the greatest need
> that our Cause has is *better healers*. Those of
> experience, Christian character, and ability are more
> needed, much more, to fill this appointment in
> proof of C.S. than to build up churches.[9]

To a Christian Science practitioner:

> Unless we have *better healers*, and more of this
> work than any other, is done, our Cause will not
> "stand and having done all stand."
> *Demonstration* is the whole of Christian Science,
> nothing else proves it, nothing else will save it and
> continue it with us. God has said this—and Christ
> Jesus has proved it.[10]

And to a teacher of Christian Science:

> . . . healing the sick and reforming the sinner
> demonstrate Christian Science, and nothing else
> *can, does.*
> Beloved child, will you not address yourself to
> gaining this height of holiness? Nothing is so much
> needed for your own happiness and distinguishment,
> and for the success of our Cause, and for the glory of
> leading on and up the human race, as this one dem-
> onstration. By it I got the attention of the world, my

words and writings, sermons and students, or
adherents, could not, did not, do it. But my wonderful *healing* did it. I had hoped that you would
have followed in these footsteps. Dear, dear Augusta,
begin today. Leave all for this.[11]

Mrs. Eddy's healing work was still "wonderful," as a
worker in her home recounted. A circus performer with an
eye injury, whom Mrs. Eddy had seen at the 1901 New
Hampshire State Fair, later paid a visit to her:

One day, a man whom she had seen jump
from a great height called to see her. He had on
dark goggles. She asked him if he were not afraid
when he took that leap. He explained to her that if
he were to become afraid the jump was too high,
he would be killed. After talking to him in a most
heavenly way for some time, one could see by the
expression of his face how enlightened he was
mentally. Then she began again, and talked to him
about his lack of fear, he still asserting that he had
no fear when jumping—he knew he could do it.
She said to him, "Why not apply the same rule to
your eyes?" One, he told her had been destroyed
through an accident, the other was all right, but he
wore the dark goggles to hide the bad eye. They
were sitting in the library and as she talked to him
I could see and feel that his fear was removed, and
his thought was full of hope and joy, although he

did not then realise the blessing he had received. A
day or two afterwards the cabman who drove him
to the station reported there that he had two perfect
eyes when he reached the station.[12]

At the end of June 1903, Mrs. Eddy invited those who had
attended The Mother Church's Annual Meeting in Boston to
visit her home in New Hampshire. About ten thousand came
to Concord and heard her speak briefly from the balcony of
her Pleasant View home. A number of healings occurred at
this gathering: a man was healed of smoking, a woman of
exhaustion, and a boy who was crippled was healed. Another
wonderful healing happened during Mrs. Eddy's carriage
drive after her talk. An account of this appears in the
reminiscences of Lottie Clark, a Christian Science nurse:

> . . . I was in a seven passenger car going to Hyde
> Park, Boston to a [Christian Science] lecture. Soon
> after we started the woman in the front seat turned
> around and said she wished to tell us of a woman
> who lived in Concord, New Hampshire. This
> Concord woman was paralyzed on one side, she had
> not a penny in the world, and her home was so
> unhappy she felt she could no longer live in it. So she
> decided to leave home and never return. As she left
> her yard she looked up the street and saw a large
> concourse of people. Out of curiosity she followed
> them, they were the ten thousand on their way to
> Pleasant View. When they arrived this woman was on

the outskirts of the crowd, so far away that she did
not even hear the sound of Mrs. Eddy's voice when
she spoke. When Mrs. Eddy turned around and
returned to the house[, to] this woman['s] helplessness,
hopelessness, and despair was added this fresh
disappointment at not hearing what she knew must
have been a very important message to have attracted
that size crowd. She turned around with tears flowing
freely down her face to return to Concord. As she
walked along she came to a vacant lot, she crossed
this lot to the street on the other side, and there she
stood weeping bitterly, her face drenched with tears
when she saw a team of horses coming. She stood idly
watching them and as they approached she recognized
the woman in the carriage to be the same one who
had spoken from the balcony, so she waited to see her
at close range. As the carriage passed Mrs. Eddy
leaned forward and looked at her. No word was
spoken, but the woman was instantly healed. She
returned to her home and found the home condition
healed. This was the end of the story. We all sat
spellbound and overwhelmed at the wonderful
healings of Mrs. Eddy. All was quiet for a while, then
the woman who sat beside me spoke up and said very
quietly, "And I was that woman, and I have lived
happily in my home ever since." Then she added,
"Never before nor since have I seen the love and
compassion in any human face that I saw in Mrs.
Eddy's when she leaned forward and looked at me."[13]

In 1903, Mrs. Eddy in her study at
Pleasant View with Pamelia Leonard,
Lida Fitzpatrick, and John Lathrop

As Mrs. Eddy wrote to one of her students a year later, "Faith in and the spiritual understanding of the allness of divine Love heals. . . . Work and wait, watch and pray till you know the allness of God, and in that understanding you will gain the desired result, the "secret place", when you can *abide* under the assurance spiritual, of His support."[14]

At the time Mrs. Eddy spoke from her balcony, she had been at work three months on revising the *Manual of The Mother Church*. She finished this at the end of July, and it was issued on September 5, 1903. The Twenty-ninth edition of the *Church Manual* contained seventeen new By-Laws, amendments to 122 existing ones, and the deletion of twenty old Rules. Mrs. Eddy also revised the Church "Tenets" and "Historical Sketch." One of the new By-Laws she added was "Healing Better than Teaching:"

> Healing the sick and the sinner with truth,
> demonstrates what we affirm of Christian Science,
> and nothing can substitute this demonstration.
> Neither the Teacher in the Board of Education nor
> a member of this Church shall teach the Normal
> course in Christian Science for three consecutive
> years, dating from August 1st, 1903. I recommend,
> that, during this interval, each member shall strive
> to demonstrate by his or her practice, that Christian
> Science heals the sick quickly, and wholly; thus
> proving this Science to be all that we claim for it.

A week after its publication, she provided an article entitled "Mental Digestion" for the *Christian Science Sentinel* about this new *Manual.* She ended this article with an extraordinary statement: "Of this I am sure, that each Rule and By-law in this Manual will increase the spirituality of him who obeys it, invigorate his capacity to heal the sick, to comfort such as mourn, and to awaken the sinner."[15] In Mrs. Eddy's eyes, the *Manual* was much more than a compilation of Rules to operate her Church in an orderly manner. She also intended it to be a guidebook that, when understood and obeyed, would make its students better Christian healers. Like *Science and Health,* the *Manual* was to be applied to all aspects of one's daily life.

In 1904 Mrs. Eddy twice wrote to her Church's Board of Directors about the great importance of better healing work by Christian Scientists. In May she told them:

> I have just saved the life of one of my students and treated him only once. The demonstration of what I have taught them heals the sick. It absolutely disgusts me to hear them babble the letter and after that fail in proving what they say! It is high time that they stop talking Science or do prove their words true.[16]

And in August she wrote:

> As I understand it, God has His cause demonstrated in healing the sick. . . . Explain to those

who write, that less teaching and more healing is
best for our Cause, and for the students; fewer
reports of new churches and more testimonials of
our cures, argue more for the progress of Christian
Science.[17]

Nothing was more important to Mrs. Eddy than doing
God's will. To her, healing was the highest activity anyone
could aspire to, and she devoted herself through her books
and her Church to do all that could be done to promote
and extend this activity to all mankind.

CHAPTER 17

The cross
(1905–1907)

BY 1905 MARY BAKER EDDY had become a national figure. Her church, The First Church of Christ, Scientist, in Boston, Massachusetts, was prospering far beyond the world's expectations. Consequently the media of that day were focusing more and more of their attention on her as Founder and Leader of the Christian Science movement. A good deal of this interest was not friendly. But no matter what confronted her, Christian healing remained at the forefront of her thought.

On May 25, 1905, Mrs. Eddy wrote to one of her longtime students:

> What I need for help in my life-labor more
> than all else on earth is a—*healer* such as I [was]
> when practising. . . . Gain that *one point*, [be] an
> instantaneous healer of all manner of diseases.
> I [was] that, and you should be. Our great Master
> was that and called upon his followers to do likewise.
> You can be this and must be in order to be a
> Christian Scientist. Now address yourself to this

duty of yours, watch, pray, labor, and have *faith!*—
Know that you can be what God demands you
to be and now are—His image and likeness—
reflecting God, the one and only Healer, reflecting
God, Life, Truth, Love.[1]

Four months earlier, Mrs. Eddy had demonstrated
exactly what she meant in this letter. In a reminiscence,
George Kinter, a worker in Mrs. Eddy's home during this
period, recounts what happened "late one winter night of
January or February in the year 1905." Mrs. Eddy had
called several times for her longtime personal secretary,
Calvin Frye, but without response. She then summoned
Mr. Kinter to see why Calvin had not come. Upon entering
Frye's bedroom, George found him slumped in a chair:
"Mr. Frye had passed on—he had no pulse, he was stone
cold—and rigid." When informed of this, Mrs. Eddy came
immediately to the bedroom and "began at once to treat
him. . . . [She] continuously denied the error and declared
the Truth with such vehemence and eloquence for a full
hour, as I never had heard on any other occasion. . . . I
remember quite well many of her utterances and actions":

> Calvin, wake up and be the man God made!
> You are not dead and you know it! How often have
> you proved there is no death! Calvin, all is Life!
> Life!! Undying Life. Say, God is my Life. . . .
> Declare—I can help myself. . . . Rouse yourself.
> Shake off this night-mare of false, human belief and

of fear. Don't let error mesmerize you into a state of
believing Satan's lies about man made in God's
image and likeness! Your life-work is not done. I
need you. Our great blessed Cause needs you.

Life is as deathless as God Himself for Life is God,
and you are His spiritual offspring. Calvin, there is no
death, for the Christian Christ Jesus has abolished
death and this treatment is not reversed by error.

After an hour, Calvin moved a little and then spoke in very
low tones: "Don't call me back. Let me go, I am so tired." To
which Mrs. Eddy replied, "Oh, Yes,—We shall persist in
calling you back, for you have not been away. You have only
been dreaming and now that you have awakened out of that
dreamy sleep, you are not tired. . . . Thank the dear God,
who is Mind, is omnipresent good, you do not concede any
claim of the material senses." By the time another half-hour
had gone by, Calvin had completely recovered. The rest of
the night was peaceful, and Mr. Frye was at his post the next
morning, doing his usual work for Mrs. Eddy.[2]

A month after this experience, Mrs. Eddy received a
letter from a Mary Crane Gray, who had just been introduced to Christian Science. Her husband had become
insane after losing a considerable fortune through bad
financial investments, and the doctors had said he was
incurable, recommending he be put in an asylum. Instead,
Mrs. Gray wrote to Mrs. Eddy, begging her to heal her
husband: "I poured out my heart's anguish in a ten paged
letter to Mrs. Eddy. I did not know that she was not taking

cases of healing at that time. The third day after the mailing of that letter, my husband arose healed." He had no memory of being ill. His wife told him what she had done in writing to Mrs. Eddy. He told her, "I will seek employment at once."[3]

Mrs. Eddy no longer had a public healing practice because she was devoting all her time to helping humanity through her work as Leader of the Cause of Christian Science. And she knew that in order to succeed in this role, she must continue to grow spiritually. She told a newspaper journalist in June 1905, "All that I ask of the world now is that it grant me time, time to assimilate myself to God."[4]

As Leader, Mrs. Eddy was continually urging her followers to leave all for Christ. In her message "Choose Ye" to The First Church of Christ, Scientist, in Boston (written for the dedication of its grand Extension to the Original Edifice built more than a decade earlier), Mrs. Eddy reminded Christian Scientists of the Scripture, "He that taketh not his cross, and followeth after me, is not worthy of me."[5] And then she wrote, "On this basis, how many are following the Way-shower? We follow Truth only as we follow truly, meekly, patiently, spiritually, blessing saint and sinner with the leaven of divine Love which woman has put into Christendom and medicine."[6] For Mrs. Eddy, this "leaven of divine Love" was Christian healing. As she had written to the First Reader of The Mother Church, "Is not healing the sick the highest and best thing done in the field? Yes, it is: our great Master made it thus."[7] And to a Christian Science lecturer she wrote:

Now I name a need that is above all others to
ensure the perpetuity of the present success of
Christian Science and its continued advancement,
namely a higher and more practical *healing*. A
definite immediate cure is the demonstration of
what you promulgate in theory, and theory as to
religion or philosophy without practice is worse
than nothing for it disappoints the seeker of it and
destroys the evidence of its truth, making the
situation more hopeless, than even ignorance.[8]

The Mother Church and Extension in 1910

Mrs. Eddy did not limit healing to praying for sick men and women alone. In May 1906, a Christian Scientist in the Philippines wrote to her about treating animals and received the following reply:

> . . . heal the animals as well as mankind. When
> I [was] in practice I healed them and found them
> responsive to Truth in every instance. God gave
> man "dominion over the beasts" and we have no
> authority for supposing that He ever recalled that
> gift or took away from man his rightful spiritual
> heritage.[9]

And three days after sending that letter, Mrs. Eddy wrote to the Board of Directors of The Mother Church regarding the need to pray about destructive weather conditions:

> . . . consider this my proposition—that you require
> some of the best C[hristian] Scientists in Boston
> and vicinity to pray once each day that no thought
> of earthquake, tornado, or destructive lightening
> enter thought to harm it, but that He who reigns in
> the heavens and watches over the earth saves from
> all harm.[10]

A year and a half later, on September 24, 1907, Mrs. Eddy wrote in her notebook that when she prayed, "Terrific clouds all over the sky changed instantaneously by me and a gentle rain and *rainbow* appeared."[11]

Photo: Calvin Frye

Mrs. Eddy in her study at Pleasant View

Since the early 1870s when she had first written *Science and Health,* her textbook of Christian healing, Mrs. Eddy had been continually at work on making it clearer for readers to understand. Six major revisions had been the result of her efforts, the last one occurring in 1902. In October 1906, she wrote to a helper, "It becomes necessary to publish a new edition of S&H because of the *over worne* [printing] plates. I have given much thought day and night to revise this book so as to make its meaning clearer to the reader who knows not Christian Science."[12] For the next eight months she devoted herself to this task, and when she was finished she added to the book's Preface, "Until June 10, 1907, [the author] had never read this book throughout consecutively in order to elucidate her idealism."[13] Certainly, Mrs. Eddy had read through her book before, but this was the first time she had done so solely for the purpose of "elucidat[ing] her idealism."

Science and Health had been the outcome of God's revelation of His nature and laws to Mrs. Eddy. Over the years the book has proved its divine origin in its ability to heal those "honest seekers for Truth"[14] who read it. In November 1907, Mrs. Eddy had read a newspaper interview with the founder of the Salvation Army, General William Booth. The article reported that his health had failed. This caused Mrs. Eddy to write to a Christian Scientist in England, instructing him "to find a way" to present her book to the General, adding that "now is the time to heal this man of faith."[15]

In the middle of her work of revising *Science and Health* came one of the most severe challenges Mrs. Eddy ever faced.

What began as sensational, competitive journalism between *McClure's Magazine* and a major newspaper, the *New York World,* culminated in a legal suit brought in her name by her "Next Friends" against certain members of her household and officers of her Church. These "friends" were her son George, one of his daughters, a nephew and a cousin of Mrs. Eddy's, along with her estranged adopted son. As "Next Friends" they claimed she was mentally incompetent and being taken advantage of by those around her.

Mrs. Eddy's metaphysical approach to this suit can be seen in the directions given to one she had asked to pray about this case: "She wanted the belief of 'lawsuit' handled with absolute metaphysics. I was not to outline what the verdict would be but to know that Truth would prevail and that divine Mind would direct the verdict—which it certainly did."[16] After Mrs. Eddy was interviewed by a court-appointed group of "Masters,"[17] the suit was dismissed.

An especially interesting sidelight of this experience was Mrs. Eddy's healing of a newspaper reporter who had throat cancer and could no longer talk. This reporter had come to find scandal, and left completely healed. In his later years, he turned to Christian Science and felt "he owed a debt of gratitude to Mrs. Eddy for his healing. . . ."[18]

In the same month in which the "Next Friends" suit ended, Mrs. Eddy invited the Countess of Dunmore, a Christian Scientist from England who was in America with her two daughters at the time, to visit her. One of the daughters, Lady Victoria Murray, later recounted:

My last visit to Pleasant View was in [October] 1907 with my mother and sister after the passing on of my father. . . . Nothing could exceed the kindness and sympathy shown to us at that time, especially to my mother who was suffering severely from the sense of loss. Mrs. Eddy, "moved with compassion," tenderly assuaged my mother's grief, lifting her to a higher recognition of Life, then turning to me, she asked if I had any questions. "Yes," I replied, "I would like to know how *you* heal the sick." Leaning back in her chair she smilingly said, "I will tell you. I heal the same way today as I did when I commenced. My original way was instantaneous. The students did not understand any more than an English scholar could understand a foreign language without learning it. They therefore put it into their language. The argument used in healing is simply tuning-up. If your violin is in tune, it is unnecessary to tune it up. Keep your violin in tune." This last sentence was repeated quite imperatively and much emphasized.[19]

No matter what the material world threw at her feet—disease, storms, insanity, death, or a legal attack that threatened everything she had worked to establish—Mary Baker Eddy treated them all as occasions for healing. To her they were opportunities to show the world that God is an ever-present Father-Mother, an unfailing Physician, and a perfect Judge.

CHAPTER 18

Crowned by Love
(1908–1910)

ON THE AFTERNOON OF JANUARY 26, 1908, Mary Baker
Eddy left her home of fifteen and a half years in Concord,
New Hampshire, and moved to Chestnut Hill, a suburb of
Boston, Massachusetts. That morning Mrs. Eddy had
turned to her Bible, as was her daily custom, and it opened
to First Corinthians, chapter 9. After reading verses 10
through 14 to her household, she gave what John Lathrop
described as a "grand talk" on "healing the sick [being] the
only test of a Christian Scientist."[1] When Mr. Lathrop left
Mrs. Eddy's service a month later, she told him, "Give all
your time to the healing. *Perfect* yourself in this."[2]

Nothing was more important to Mrs. Eddy than Christian
Scientists' devotion to the practice of Christian healing. To
encourage and support this devotion of thought and action
was the underlying purpose of her efforts to establish the
Cause of Christian Science, which is to save the world from
sin and sickness. Earlier in January, a letter to Mrs. Eddy
from another former household worker had appeared in the
Christian Science Sentinel. It began, *"My Beloved Teacher:—*
Just a word to express my love and deep sense of gratitude to

you for all you have done and are doing for mankind."[3] Over the previous forty-two years Mrs. Eddy had devoted her life entirely to sharing with her fellowman the revelation she had received from God. In this revelation, she discovered

> . . . the Christ Science or divine laws of Life, Truth, and Love, and named my discovery Christian Science. God had been graciously preparing me during many years for the reception of this final revelation of the absolute divine Principle of scientific mental healing.[4]

And further on in *Science and Health*, Mrs. Eddy writes,

> God selects for the highest service one who has grown into such a fitness for it as renders any abuse of the mission an impossibility. The All-wise does not bestow His highest trusts upon the unworthy. When He commissions a messenger, it is one who is spiritually near Himself.[5]

On the basis of the "final revelation" and on her own life experience in the healing practice, Mrs. Eddy had written *Science and Health*. Using this book and the Bible as her only textbooks, she personally taught Christian Science to several thousand students. She went on to serve as pastor of the first Church of Christ, Scientist, which she established with the help of her students; founded the Massachusetts Metaphysical College, serving as its President and Teacher;

was the first publisher and Editor of *The Christian Science Journal;* and reorganized her original church into The Mother Church, The First Church of Christ, Scientist, in Boston, Massachusetts, creating for it a government founded on divinely inspired Rules and By-Laws. All this was done in order to give to mankind an understanding of God that enables one to heal the ills of the world, through prayer based on the laws of God.

It was natural for Mrs. Eddy to expect that any situation which suggested a denial of God's ever-present goodness could be healed through Christianly scientific prayer. And she applied it even to the minor annoyances of the day. After moving to her new home in Massachusetts, one of her secretaries later recounted:

> [Mrs. Eddy] noticed that one of the trees on her place did not appear to thrive, but was drooping and showing every evidence of dying. She learned that the superintendent of her grounds proposed to cut the tree down and remove it. Immediately she sent word to him to do nothing of the kind, but to do what he could for the tree in his way, while she took the question up according to Christian Science. In a remarkably short time the tree began to grow and thrive, and today [in 1926] it occupies a place on her grounds.[6]

For Mrs. Eddy, no problem was too small or too big for Christian Science healing. When she took up residence in

Chestnut Hill, her thought turned more than ever to reaching the world with this practical, healing truth. In the April 11, 1908, *Sentinel* she issued a statement on "War," which began, "For many years I have prayed daily that there be no more war. . . ." Her message concludes by pointing out the need for arbitrating disagreements between nations and the necessity for arming navies to prevent war and preserve peace.[7] A copy of this *Sentinel* was sent to the President of the United States, Theodore Roosevelt, by a Christian Scientist. He responded with a personal note that said, "That is interesting and important. I wish that all other religious leaders showed as much good sense."[8]

A few weeks after this, the editor of the *Minneapolis Daily News* requested a statement on what Christian Science could do for universal fellowship. Mrs. Eddy replied:

> Christian Science can and does produce
> universal fellowship as a sequence of divine Love.
> It explains Love, it lives Love, it demonstrates
> Love. The human material so-called senses do not
> perceive this fact until they are controlled by divine
> Love, hence the Scripture: "Be still and know that
> I am God."[9]

Impelled by divine Love, Mrs. Eddy was led at this time to establish a daily newspaper. As early as 1878, she had publicly declared an interest in having a newspaper at her disposal "to right the wrongs and answer the untruths."[10]

THE WHITE HOUSE
WASHINGTON

From Chestnot Hill Files.

9772

Personal.

April 20, 1908.

My dear Mr. Davis:

I have your letter of the 18th instant, with en-
closure. That is interesting and important. I wish
that all other religious leaders showed as much
good sense.

With regard, believe me,

Sincerely yours,

Theodore Roosevelt

Mr. Hayne Davis,
381 Central Park West,
New York, N.Y.

Hayne Davis sent President Roosevelt
the Sentinel for April 11, 1908, which
contained Mrs. Eddy's stand on
Armament and Arbitration. This is
President Roosevelt's reply.
2195

The letter from Theodore Roosevelt commenting on Mrs. Eddy's statement about war that had been published in the *Christian Science Sentinel*.

This desire was part of her motive for starting the *Journal* in 1883, the weekly *Sentinel* in 1898, and the German *Der Herold der Christian Science* in 1903. In the summer of 1908, she called on the Board of Directors of The Mother Church and the Board of Trustees of The Christian Science Publishing Society to start *The Christian Science Monitor.*

Mrs. Eddy wanted a newspaper for the home, but she expected it to have a healing effect on the world. She said it is "to spread undivided the Science that operates unspent."[11] In this she was paraphrasing a line from Alexander Pope's 1733 poem "An Essay on Man," which speaks of the "MIND of ALL" that "spreads undivided, operates unspent."[12] For Mrs. Eddy, this "MIND" was nothing less than the one omnipotent God, who is divine Love meeting all mankind's needs. And "a newspaper edited and published by the Christian Scientists"[13] could be a healing manifestation of that divine Mind. On the morning of November 25, 1908, the day the *Monitor*'s first issue was published, Mrs. Eddy opened her Bible to Song of Solomon 8:6, 7. These verses speak of the strength and power of love to withstand the forces of the material world.

It was so important to Mrs. Eddy that Christian Scientists express divine Love in *practical* ways. For the Communion service of The Mother Church on June 14, 1908, she instructed that the sermon be on the subject of "Works," especially as illustrated in John 15:2: "Every branch in me that beareth not fruit he taketh away: and every branch that beareth fruit, he purgeth it, that it may bring forth more fruit."[14] Two days before this service was held, Mrs. Eddy wrote:

Faith without works is the most subtle lie apparent.
It satisfies the student with a lie—it gives them
peace in error, and they never can be Christian
Scientists without that faith which is known and
proved by works. Words are often impositions and
faith without works is dead and plucked up by the
roots, it is not faith but is a deceiving lie, lulling the
conscience and preventing demonstration.[15]

And if the demonstration of healing does not instantly
appear, what then? The patient may require practical care
while the metaphysical treatment continues until the
healing is accomplished.

On November 16, 1908, Mrs. Eddy requested The
Christian Science Board of Directors to adopt a new Church
By-Law which established the requirements of a Christian
Science nurse, "A member of The Mother Church who
represents himself or herself as a Christian Science nurse shall
be one who has a demonstrable knowledge of Christian
Science practice, who thoroughly understands the practical
wisdom necessary in a sick room, and who can take proper
care of the sick."[16]

While such nurses may be needed in cases where healing
was not immediate, this did not mean that Mrs. Eddy
expected her students to be less than radical in their
reliance on God for healing. In July 1909, she wrote to
Alfred Farlow, who was serving as the Church's Manager of
Committees on Publication and had had a minor accident:
"If you use a crutch you are not depending on Christian

Science. Choose ye this day whom you will serve. . . . Now take God's side. You *can walk* without a crutch, do *it*."[17] The next day, Mr. Farlow replied, "I have not used the crutch during the time since I received your first letter. This morning I am wonderfully improved and will spend the day at home. I can now see how the crutch has hindered me. I have neglected working for myself because I could get around on the crutch and have the time for other work."[18] Mrs. Eddy had her secretary respond, "Mrs. Eddy says that what she tells a student to do absolutely, she expects them to do it, but not before they can do it *scientifically* and then it can't hurt them, and they cannot suffer from it."[19] She expected Christian Scientists, when confronted with physical challenges, to pray—relying solely on God to "resolve things into thoughts, and exchange the objects of sense for the ideas of Soul."[20] This was certainly how she worked for herself. Less than a week after her correspondence with Mr. Farlow, Mrs. Eddy told one of her secretaries:

> Our thought must be scientific in all things,
> even the littlest of any. One time my hair was
> coming out in handfuls and I could not stop it
> until I thought God will protect,—"the very hairs
> of your head are numbered,"—then it stopped.[21]

One of the things that most concerned Mrs. Eddy was the danger to Christian Scientists of becoming complacent.

In August 1909 she wrote Alfred Farlow to "stir the dry bones all over the field, to more words, actions and demonstrations in Christian Science. I am weary waiting for the impulse of Christian Science to become more active all over our field. Get somebody—and more than one—to ring out the first arousal. 'Awake thou that sleepest, and arise from the dead, and Christ shall give thee light.' "[22] Two days after sending this letter, she completed her own work on the manuscript of *The First Church of Christ, Scientist, and Miscellany.* It was a collection of articles, notices, and letters that had appeared in print since the 1897 publication of her first compilation of similar pieces in *Miscellaneous Writings.*

Six months before Mrs. Eddy had moved from Concord, New Hampshire, Arthur Brisbane, a New York journalist, interviewed her. He later recounted to friends, ". . . it was my privilege to discover one of the keenest intellects I had ever encountered and the most gentle and sweet woman I had ever met. Her very presence was restful to me. During our conversation I mentioned this, telling her how very tired I was. She then asked me if I would like to have a Christian Science treatment and I told her I would. All I can say is that it was a most unbelievably beautiful experience . . . that treatment proved to me the great need in the world today for Christian Science."[23]

Without the proof of healing, there is no Christian Science. Healing that results from leaning on God alone through prayer, from denying that which is ungodlike and affirming the perfection, omnipotence, and omnipresence of the one divine Principle, Love, and man as this One's perfect spiritual manifestation: this is healing as the outcome of divine law prayerfully realized. And the practice of healing must extend beyond oneself. The crown of divine Love comes in the unselfed living for others. Mrs. Eddy had written to a student a number of years earlier, ". . . you never can be a practical Christian Scientist without healing the sick and sinner besides yourself. It is too selfish for us to be working for ourselves and not others as well. God does not bless it."[24]

Feeling God's blessing was a vital element for those healed by Mrs. Eddy. Miss Elsie Bergquist, a Christian Scientist, has left the following account of an incident related by her father, who was not a student of Christian Science at the time:

> During the year 1909 he was working on a building in Chestnut Hill, not far from Mrs. Eddy's home. One day, feeling very tired, he left work early and decided to go to see the architecture of Mrs. Eddy's home. As he approached, Mrs. Eddy's carriage came out of the drive way. She smiled upon him and he felt so uplifted that he could have run along side of the carriage for miles. Of course he did not do this, but he forgot to look at the architecture of the house and started to walk. He walked all the way to Boston [more than 5 miles] without fatigue and did not feel tired again for a week.

My father told the members of his church
about the spiritual uplift that he received from
Mrs. Eddy, how he had felt that the Spirit of the
Lord had descended upon him. . . .[25]

Untiring in her work for mankind in the name of Christian Science, Mrs. Eddy, through her prayer and private correspondence, remained active in guiding the Cause up to the time of her passing on December 3, 1910. Calvin Frye, Laura Sargent, Adam Dickey, Irving Tomlinson, and William and Ella Rathvon were with Mrs. Eddy on that Saturday evening.[26] The last thing she said to them was, "I have all in divine Love, that is all I need."[27] Earlier in the year she had written to one of her students who had just lost her husband:

Your dear husband has not passed away from
you in spirit; he never died, only to your sense; he
lives and loves and is immortal. Let this comfort
you dear one, and you will find rest in banishing
the sense of death, in cherishing the sense of life
and not death. Your dear husband is as truly living
to-day as he ever lived, and you can find rest and
peace in this true sense of Life.

Mind not matter is our Life, and we can rejoice
in knowing that Mind never dies. Sin and a false
sense of life is all that dies. Immortality and
blessedness never die, hence we should banish this
false sense, it is not real.[28]

There was never a more loving or practical Christian Scientist than Mary Baker Eddy. Her lifetime of healing testifies to this. The Discoverer and Founder of Christian Science continues to lead mankind to the comfort of divine Science through the healing activities of her Church, and, most of all, through her writings, chief of which is *Science and Health*. To understand Mrs. Eddy in her true light, however, depends on gaining a practical understanding of the divine revelation in that book to such a degree that one can heal as she did.

PART TWO

*More Healing Works
of
Mary Baker Eddy*

More Healing Works of
Mary Baker Eddy

TURNING TO GOD in healing prayer with compassion for all was as natural to Mary Baker Eddy as a plant's turning to the light. There are numerous accounts of Mrs. Eddy's healing works, in addition to those already related, in the collections of the Church History department of The First Church of Christ, Scientist. Some are in her letters to others, some are in her words as recorded by those who heard her speak, others come from relatives of those healed, or from those healed themselves. Although it has not been possible to verify some of the healings, all of these healings are consistent with her character and work and the accounts are from reliable sources.

The accounts of healing in this section—many not published before—are quoted directly from the original documents. Sometimes for fuller details there are accounts of the same healing from two different writers.

The healings recounted in this book do not constitute all of the published accounts of Mrs. Eddy's healings. More can be found in Mrs. Eddy's own writings and in other biographies of her, especially Sibyl Wilbur's *The Life of Mary Baker Eddy*, Irving Tomlinson's *Twelve Years with Mary Baker Eddy*, and Clifford P. Smith's *Historical Sketches*.

Niece healed of enteritis (1867)

Miss Ellen C. Pilsbury, of Sanbornton Bridge, now Tilton, N.H., after typhoid fever, was suffering from what her physicians called enteritis of the severest form. Her case was given up by her medical physician, and she was lying at the point of death, when Mrs. Glover (afterwards Mrs. Eddy) visited her. In a few moments after she entered the room and stood by her bedside, [Ellen] recognized her aunt, and said, "I am glad to see you, aunty." In about ten minutes more, Mrs. Glover told her to "rise from her bed and walk." She rose and walked seven times across her room, then sat down in a chair. For two weeks before this, we had not entered her room without stepping lightly. Her bowels were so tender, she felt the jar, and it increased her sufferings. She could only be moved on a sheet from bed to bed. When she walked across the room at Mrs. Glover's bidding, she told her to stamp her foot strongly upon the floor, and she did so without suffering from it. The next day she was dressed, and went down to the table; and the fourth day went a journey of about a hundred miles in the [train] cars. Elizabeth P. Baker [Mrs. Eddy's stepmother] (*Science and Health,* Third edition, pages 152–153)

～

(Martha Rand Baker, Mrs. Eddy's sister-in-law, to Addie Towns Arnold)

I have never had an opportunity to tell this story for no one was interested in Christian Science here, and as a son's wife, I have not wanted to take sides either way. When we found Ellen did not have a chance to live, we wrote Mary about it, and she came to us at once. We went to Ellen's room, and Mary sat beside her bed. Ellen had not known any of us for several days, but in a short time she looked up and said, "I am glad to see you, Auntie." Mary soon told her to rise and walk. We were horrified at this, and stood spell-bound. She rose, however, and walked seven times across her room, and then sat down. The next day she was dressed, and went down to the table. On the fourth day Mary took her home to [Taunton] with her. (Arnold reminiscences)

Internal tumor healed (1867–1874)
(*Mrs. Eddy in* Science and Health)
A lady having an internal tumor, and greatly fearing a surgical operation, called on us. We conducted her case according to the [S]cience here stated, never touched her person, or used a drug, or an instrument; and the tumor was wholly removed within one or two days. We refer to this case to prove the [divine] Principle. (*Science and Health,* First edition, page 117)

Man yellow with disease healed (1867–1874)
(*Mrs. Eddy to Lida Fitzpatrick*)
I used to heal with a word. I have seen a man yellow because of disease and the next moment I looked at him and his color was right; [he] was healed.
I knew no more how it was done than a baby; only it was done every time, I never failed, almost always in one treatment, never more than three. Now God is showing me how, and I am showing you. (Fitzpatrick reminiscences)

Heals friend of invalidism caused by hip trouble (1868)
(Mrs. Eddy in a letter to Sarah Bagley)

I had at Lynn a sweet visit, stopped at Mr. Winslow's. When I went there Mrs. Winslow was very lame and sick, had not walked up stairs naturally for years and given up trying to go out at all. I stopped two days and when I came away she walked to the Depot with me almost a mile. They were one and all urgent for me to stay there this winter, but I am not of their opinion. I don't want society, and what's more I won't have it; I detest the hollow heartedness of aristocracy, I loathe the hypocrisy of available friendship or in common parlance "such as pays." Mr. W. is a father to me, he attended to all my business, went through from one Depot to the other with me and set me right for here. (Church History document L08306)

～

. . . Mrs. Winslow had been for sixteen years in an invalid chair, and Mrs. Patterson [as Mrs. Eddy was then known], who occasionally spent an afternoon with her, desired to heal her.

"If you make Abbie walk," said Charles Winslow, "I will not only believe your theory, but I will reward you liberally. I think I would give a thousand dollars to see her able to walk."

"The demonstration of the principle is enough reward," said Mrs. Patterson. "I know she can walk. You go to business and leave us alone together."

"But I want to see you perform your cure, Mary," said Charles Winslow, half mirthfully. "Indeed, I won't interfere."

"You want to see me perform a cure," cried Mary Baker, with a flash of her clear eyes. "But I am not going to do anything. Why don't you understand that God will do the work if Mrs. Winslow will let Him? Leave off making light of what is a serious matter. Your wife will walk."

And Mrs. Winslow did walk, walked along the ocean beach with Mary Baker and around her own garden in the beautiful autumn of that year. She who had not taken a step for sixteen years arose and walked, not once but many times. (Sibyl Wilbur, *The Life of Mary Baker Eddy,* pages 143–144.)

Woman in agony, given up by the doctors, healed
(1868–1879)
(Mrs. Eddy to Irving C. Tomlinson)

A student in Lynn had a patient who to every appearance was [a] very serious case. Before coming to Christian Science a counsel of physicians had pronounced the case hopeless, then my student was appealed to. He treated the patient for some days when I was called in. I found the sick one in great agony. The face was purple and the head was rolling from side to side. In fifteen minutes after my arrival the pain had departed, the face had assumed a normal color and the patient was at ease. When a member of the household who had gone out on an errand for the invalid returned, he found her up and about her work. (Historical File: Tomlinson notes)

Little lame boy healed (1868–1888)

While living with Mrs. Eddy at Pleasant View, she told many wonderful things, proving more and more the power of her healing work through Christian Science.

. . . she told us of the case of a child who was born helpless. While out walking one day, Mrs. Eddy observed a small boy drawing another and younger child in a little cart. She inquired of the older boy what was the matter with the little fellow. He replied: "He is my brother and he has never walked." Mrs. Eddy looked into the sweet face and beautiful blue eyes of the little boy lying flat on his back in the cart, his legs dangling over the edge, limp and helpless. In relating the incident, she said the sense of the perfect child of God was so clear to her that the boy slid out of the cart and went running down the street, saying: "See me yun (run)!" He reached his home, which was nearby, crying out: "Mamma, see me yun! See me yun!" (Julia E. Prescott reminiscences)

Severely crippled man healed (1870)
(Mrs. Eddy to Lida Fitzpatrick)

I was at a house [Mrs. Charles Slade's] and the woman came running into the room as white as ashes, and said a cripple was at the door and he looked so dreadful she slammed the door in his face. I went to the window, and there was—well it was too dreadful to describe; his feet did not touch the earth at all; he walked with crutches. I gave him through the window all I had in my pocket—a dollar bill—and he took it in his teeth. He went to the next house and frightened the woman there, but she did not slam the door in his face. He asked her to let him lie down a few minutes; she let him go into a bedroom and lie down. He fell sound asleep, and when he wakened up was perfectly well. Sometime afterward, the woman who was kind to him, was in a store and this man came rushing up to her and said, "Yes, you are the one, but where is the other woman?" Then he told her he was the one who was healed by me. The papers are writing up my history; the history of my ancestry; writing lies. My history is a holy one. (Fitzpatrick reminiscences)

～

Later, on being asked by her students as to how she healed him, Mrs. Eddy simply said, "When I looked on that man, my heart gushed with unspeakable pity and prayer." (Judge Septimus J. Hanna, *The Granite Monthly,* October 1896)

Dead child restored (1870–1872)
(Mrs. Eddy to Henry Robinson)
One little child was put into my hands. I did not come soon enough. Utterly helpless, utterly prostrated, and the doctors said he was gone. The little arms hung down, and it looked limp as a corpse, no appearance of life. I could not feel the pulse. The mother was crying and said "He is dead; you have come too late." I said, "Go out a little while." She did and that little creature rose right up, yawned and rubbed his eyes. I set him down. He walked to the door and his mother took him. (Historical File: Henry Robinson)

~

Mrs. Eddy told me she was called to treat a child. When she went in, the mother was holding it and thought it had passed on. Mrs. Eddy said, "Let me take the babe." She did and the mother went into the next room. In about ten minutes she put the child down and it walked toward the door. Mrs. Eddy opened the door and when the mother saw the child walking (it had never walked before) she screamed and the babe sat down, and Mrs. Eddy said, "I saw I had another patient on my hands." (Victoria H. Sargent reminiscences)

Chronic invalid healed (1870–1874)
(Jenny Coffin to Mrs. Eddy)

Your wonderful science is proved to me. I was a helpless sufferer six long years, confined to my bed, unable to sit up one hour in the long, long twenty-four. All I know of my cure is this; the day you received my letter I felt a change pass over me, I sat up the whole afternoon, went to the table with my family at supper, and have been growing better every day since; I call myself well. Jenny R. Coffin. (*Science and Health,* First edition, page 352)

Chronic liver complaint and convulsions healed (1870–1874)
(Mrs. Eddy in Science and Health*)*

A case of convulsions produced by indigestion came under our observation; they said she had chronic liver complaint, and was then suffering from obstruction and bilious colic. We cured her in a few minutes. She had said, "I must vomit my food or die," and immediately afterwards said, "My food is all gone, and I should like something to eat." Contending persistently against error and disease, you destroy them with Truth. (*Science and Health*, Third edition, page 203)

Broken foot healed (1870–1874)
(*Mrs. Eddy in* Science and Health)
   Mr. R. O. Badgely, of Cincinnati, Ohio, wrote: "My painful and swelled foot was restored at once on your receipt of my letter, and that very day I put on my boot and walked several miles." He had previously written me: "A stick of timber fell from a building on my foot, crushing the bones. Cannot you help me? I am sitting in great pain, with my foot in a bath."
   I never believed in taking certificates or presenting testimonials of cures; and usually, when healing, have said to the individual, "Go, tell no man." I have never made a specialty of healing, but labored, in every way that God directed, to introduce metaphysical treatment. I offer a few testimonials, simply to support my statements about Christian Science. (*Science and Health,* Twentieth edition, page 199)

Assassin thwarted (1872–1879)
   [Mrs. Eddy] also told of being in her room and having the impression that someone was coming to shoot her, and her first thought was to close and lock the door, but she left

it open, and a man entered her room and pointed a revolver at her and she said to him, "You cannot shoot," and his arm became as if paralyzed; his revolver dropped to the floor and he said using an oath, "I came to kill you." At that he left the room. (James Brierly reminiscences)

~

My mother [Annie Rogers Michael] told me that once as Mrs. Eddy sat at her desk she felt a sense of something wrong and turned and looked behind her. A man had entered the room and closed the door behind him. In his hand was a weapon pointed at Mrs. Eddy. She said, "You cannot do this wicked thing." The man's arm fell helpless at his side and the weapon on the floor. He said, "Well, I came to do it but I can't," and he left the room. (Julia Michael Johnston reminiscences)

Little girl restored (1872–1879)

A lady residing in Reading who had lived in Lynn, Mass. for a number of years, told me that one morning while shopping on Market St., Lynn, she saw an Italian woman run out from a side street, and crying, "My little girl is dead, help me!" Almost immediately another woman came around a corner and spoke to this Italian woman, stepped into her house and healed the little child. This lady was Mary Baker Eddy. In broken English the Italian woman began to express, in her emotional nature, her gratitude, saying, "O that lady must be a saint, she has healed my child."

Afterward I asked the lady who witnessed this healing of the child, "Did you become a Christian Scientist?" She answered, "No," and added, "My husband and I were members of a Congregational Church. Many of our friends attended that church also. Moreover, Christian Science was not popular. It was even ridiculed."

Later, however, her husband and she became Scientists. (Lewis Prescott reminiscences)

Child with fever healed (1873)
(Charles Green to Alfred Farlow)

34 years ago. Spring or early fall; drizzling rainy day. Mrs. Eddy came to my house, and wanted to know if she could rent a room. We told her that we had no rooms to rent. She said she knew that, but desired to get in that locality [Lynn], but my wife told her we had no room to rent, and then said, "You will have to excuse me, I have a sick child." Mrs. Eddy asked if she might see the child. We had quite a little chat with Mrs. Eddy, I think, before she saw the child. She went in and saw the little girl, Josephine, three and one-half or four years old. She had been very sick with brain fever. I had gone away for a few days, but was called back suddenly because she was so much worse. She rallied, and we thought was some better. Mrs. Eddy went into the room and stood at the bedside. She took the little girl's hand and spoke with her in a low voice. In about twenty minutes or half an hour she said let me dress the child. We could not understand, but let her do so. Then she said, let me take the child out. We protested on account of

it being such a rainy day, but we could not resist her. We had confidence in that woman. She took the child across the street and back. Although we were afraid, the child was all right the next day. The Doctor came the next morning, but could not understand it. The child came along all right. (Charles Green statement; Historical File: Alfred Farlow)

～

(Mrs. Eddy writing years later)

When at Lynn one morning I was impressed to call at the house of Mr. Green residing on Sagamore St. . . . I found the child in what is called brain fever, her physician of the regular school had given her up. I sat by her side a few moments then called for her child's clothes. She was dressed & went out with me into the street. It rained, we walked a few blocks and returned to the house. She called for something to eat, ate heartily and that night slept alone in her room. In the morning her parents were assured of her perfect recovery. (Document A10193)

Rheumatism healed (1873–1879)

I have heard both my grandmother and my father, John Cluff, speak of Mrs. Eddy healing my father in his youth of what seemed to be a case of rheumatism.

Mrs. Eddy (who was fond of my father), not seeing him about as usual one morning when she called at my grandmother's, inquired concerning him, wanting to know what was the matter, whereupon my grandmother told her that John was upstairs with what she thought was rheumatism, and that he was unable to get out of bed. Mrs. Eddy then went upstairs and found John with one leg doubled back on his body. Despite his protest that he could not move it and get up, Mrs. Eddy firmly insisted that he could get up and walk. My father related that he did get right up and hobbled downstairs, mostly on one foot and with the aid of the banister, but after walking about a little, the leg straightened out to its normal position and he found himself free. (Alice Cluff French reminiscences)

Painless childbirth demonstrated (1874)

I take pleasure in giving to the public one instance out of many of Mrs. Glover-Eddy's skill in metaphysical healing. At the birth of my youngest child, eight years old, I thought my approaching confinement was several weeks premature, and sent her a message to that effect. Without seeing me, she returned answer the proper time had come, and she would be with me immediately. Slight labor pains had commenced before she arrived; she stopped them immediately, and requested me to call a midwife, but to keep him below stairs until after the birth. When the doctor arrived, and while he remained in a lower room, she came to my bedside. I asked her how I should lie. She answered, "It makes no difference how you lie," and simply said, "Now let the child be born," and immediately the birth took place without a single pain. The doctor was then called into the room to receive the child, and saw I had no pain whatever. My sister, Dorcas B. Rawson, of Lynn, was present when my babe was born, and will testify to the facts as I have stated them. I confess my own astonishment. I did not expect so much, even from Mrs. Eddy, especially as I had suffered before very severely in childbirth. The M.D. covered me with extra bed-clothes, charged me to be very careful about taking cold, and to keep quiet, then left. I think he was alarmed at my having no labor pains, but before he went out I had an ague coming on. When the door closed behind him, Mrs. Eddy threw off the extra bedding, and said, "It is nothing but the fear the doctor has produced that causes these chills," and they left me at once. She told me to sit up when I chose, and as long as I chose, and to eat whatever I wanted. My babe was born about two o'clock in the morning, and the following evening I sat up several hours. I ate whatever the family did; had a boiled dinner of meat and vegetables the second day, made no difference in my diet, except to drink gruel between meals, and never experienced the least inconvenience from it. I dressed myself the second day, and the third day felt unwilling to lie down, and in one week was about the house, well, running up and down stairs and attending to domestic duties. For several years I had been troubled by prolapsus uteri, which disappeared entirely after Mrs. Eddy's wonderful demonstration of metaphysical science at the birth of my babe. Miranda R. Rice, Lynn, Mass. (*Science and Health,* Third edition, pages 134–135)

Fractured skull healed (1875–1880)

My personal acquaintance with Mrs. Eddy was very slight. I studied with her in the last Primary class of March 1889. While on a visit to Boston in the autumn of 1888 I was taken by a student of Mrs. Eddy's to call upon her and we spent the evening at her house.

I remember her speaking of a wonderful demonstration in the case of a workman, who, while repairing the roof of her house, fell to the pavement below and fractured his skull—within a short time the man returned to his work, healed.

On taking leave of me that evening she took my hand in hers and said, "Put your hand in God's hand, let Him lead you," words never to be forgotten, a priceless admonition. (Marguerite Sym reminiscences)

Man run over by a heavy wagon restored (1875–1880)

[Mrs. Eddy] spoke more than once of a man who was run over at Lynn. She said she saw the accident from her window, and it seemed to sicken her. He was carried into the house and she was called down to see if she could do anything for him. She turned her back on him and lifted her thought to God, and the first thing she knew he was standing behind her, speaking as if he were awakening from a dream. He was healed instantly. (Adelaide Still reminiscences)

∼

Story of a man run over by a heavy wagon; [Mrs. Glover] saw the accident. He was run over the bowels, was bleeding from mouth and nose. They carried him in a house for dead. Attempted an autopsy, but someone demanded Mrs. Glover. She healed him instantly, he put his hands to his head and found he was all right. (Harriet L. Betts reminiscences)

Cancer healed (1875–1880)

(Ellen Brown Linscott to Mr. Carol Norton)

For several months, during the year 1883, I was one of four students besides her private secretary that resided in the Massachusetts Metaphysical College, Boston, with our teacher, Rev. Mary Baker G. Eddy. . . .

One day I was in Mrs. Eddy's private room assisting her in some small way, when the housemaid appeared and said a lady wished to see Mrs. Eddy. She was occupied at the time on some work for the Cause of too much importance to leave, even for a short time, so she asked me to see the visitor for her, etc. Going down to the reception room I met a very quiet, dignified woman, who at once impressed me as being a person of great sincerity and earnestness. I shall never forget the look of disappointment that came into her eyes and face when I said Mrs. Eddy was so occupied that she could not possibly see her. I felt very sorry indeed for her. In answer to my question, Have you ever met Mrs. Eddy? she replied, "Oh yes, she healed me of a dreadful disease several years ago, and as I am passing through Boston I thought I would like to see her, for she certainly saved my life. But for her I would not be here today." I was all attention, and immediately asked, "What did Mrs. Eddy heal you of?" She replied, "A dreadful cancer. It had developed to the point where it was liable to terminate fatally any time." Again I asked, "How many treatments did you have?" She replied, "Only one." In answer to the next question put by me, "Did the cancer disappear all at once while Mrs. Eddy was treating you?"

she replied, "No, not at once, but it began to dry up and to heal at once and never gave me any pain again. In a very short time all trace of it had entirely disappeared." When she said this her voice had dropped to a very low tone and her eyes were filled with tears—of gratitude no doubt. She left the college keenly disappointed at not seeing Mrs. Eddy. To quote her own words as nearly as I can recollect them, she said, "I wanted to see the woman that performed such a miracle once more and thank her. I never saw her but once, you know. Give her my love. I am pleased to have met you and hope we may meet again sometime. I leave Boston today and only stopped over to see Mrs. Eddy." (Ellen Brown Linscott, January 21, 1899, letter to Carol Norton: Linscott reminiscences)

∼

She [the woman] gave me to understand the claim of cancer was in the chest—a little above the breasts. (Ellen Brown Linscott, September 19, 1904, letter to Mrs. Eddy: Document 163Ch216)

Severe abdomen pain healed (1876–1877)

In about the year of 1876 or 1877, when Mrs. Eddy was living on Broad St., Lynn, I was living in Beverly, Mass., and was very ill with pain in the abdomen and the doctor had not been able to relieve me. Some one proposed that I go to Lynn to see the "medium" who healed without medicine. I said I did not care who it was if they could help me. So I went to Lynn to see her.

Mrs. Eddy opened the door herself and invited me in. I told her what seemed to be the matter, and she talked with me a few minutes and then said, "now we won't talk any more." She closed her eyes & sat with her hands in her lap for about ten minutes and then she said, "You will not have that trouble any more," and I said aren't you going to rub me—or do anything—and she said, "You are healed," and I was.

As I went back to the carriage I said to the friends that it was the queerest kind of healing I had ever heard of for she did not even look at my tongue or feel my pulse.

When I asked Mrs. Eddy how much I owed her, she said fifty cents, but I was healed and never had this pain again. (Alice Swasey Wool reminiscences)

Withered and paralyzed arm healed (1876–1879)

A carpenter came to our house, for some reason, who had his arm in a sling. Father asked him what the trouble was and he said that he had strained the ligaments and paralysis had set in. The arm was partly withered and all the physicians said that it would continue to wither. He said that he had been to the best physicians and hospitals there were. Father told him about Mrs. Eddy and asked him if he went to her to come and tell him the result. About a week later the carpenter came to the house to tell father that he was completely healed. (Mary Godfrey Parker reminiscences, September 1932)

The Mother Church already has my record, in Mr. Farlow's account, of the carpenter with a paralyzed arm who father sent to Mrs. Glover and whom she healed. I might add that when this man came to see Mrs. Glover she was too busy to come down to talk with him and just opened a window in her parlor room on the second floor and called down to him. Father never told me any details of this experience other than those I have related, but as far as I know this was the only conversation Mrs. Glover had with the man and he came away healed. (Mary Godfrey Parker reminiscences, December 1932)

Eye restored (1876–1882)

An engineer came to her whose eye had been put out by a hot cinder. Mrs. Eddy gave him a treatment and an eye was manifested, but it was smaller than the other and deficient. She looked at it and said, "Is it possible that my understanding of God is as little as that?" Again she treated him and the eye was *perfect.* (Edward E. Norwood reminiscences)

Diphtheria healed (1878–1881)

One of the most delightful and sacred memories I hold of my experiences in Christian Science, and its Discoverer and Founder, Rev. Mary Baker G. Eddy, is of her healing me of acute and severe diphtheria about 1881. I had once before been very ill with this malady, and was treated by a famous physician, some years previous to my knowing anything of Christian Science. This last attack was worse than the former. My neck was swollen badly, I could not swallow, had not eaten for twenty-four hours, had chills and fever, no sleep, and was unable to rise from my bed.

On this particular Sabbath afternoon, our Pastor Emeritus, Mrs. Eddy, called, and at once came into my room. How shall I describe it all! She seemed to float lightly and fearlessly to my bedside, calmly uplifted in demeanor, spiritually confident, unaffected, no professional airs,—just sweet, quiet, and soothingly graceful. To my joy she sat upon my bedside and kissed me. In a few minutes she told me I was healed. But what had come over me? The fever was gone, I felt perfectly natural,—no soreness of throat, all swelling had disappeared; I was hungry, and was chatting and laughing. I was free, and what a glorious, exalted freedom. Nature was again beautiful; divine Love had triumphed through His truth, as revealed and applied in Christian Science by our beloved Leader and Teacher, Mrs. Eddy, whose noble and unselfish example is a divine inspiration to all who are seeking and following after God's way,—in Spirit and in Truth. I also wish to say that she did this without money and without price. At that time she was preaching Sundays without a salary; I state this because the money thought has been brought to the fore so often. I would also add that I have never had any recurrence of throat trouble since then; for all of which blessings I am most deeply grateful to God, and to our beloved Leader, Rev. Mary Baker G. Eddy.

　　　　Mrs. Clara Elizabeth Choate, Boston, Mass. [The above testimony comes from one of my early students, who has had much practice, who has learned by experience, who has done much good.—Mary Baker Eddy.] (*Christian Science Sentinel*, May 12, 1906, page 586)

Neck cancer healed (1878–1883)
(Mrs. Eddy to Irving Tomlinson)

Once a man came to me with a cancer that had eaten into the neck and the jugular vein stood out. I turned from sense testimony, closed my eyes and lifted my thought to God in prayer. When I opened my eyes the man was perfectly restored, neck normal and natural. This is Christian Science healing. (Historical File: Tomlinson notes)

∼

(Mrs. Eddy in Unity of Good)

. . . When I have most clearly seen and most sensibly felt that the infinite recognizes no disease, this has not separated me from God, but has so bound me to Him as to enable me instantaneously to heal a cancer which had eaten its way to the jugular vein. (page 7)

Diseased bodily organs healed (1882)

In 1853, when a small child, Susie [M. Lang] moved with her parents from Boston to Lawrence [Massachusetts] where she attended public schools and graduated with honors from the Lawrence High School. She studied piano and organ after graduating, and became a talented musician. She served as organist in the Haverhill Street Methodist Church in Lawrence, which church her family attended at that time.

About the year 1878 she was afflicted with an illness which her family physician in Lawrence was unable to cure. Her parents took her to a private hospital and sanatorium in Boston, near Massachusetts Avenue, in the vicinity of Columbus Avenue—where Mrs. Eddy established her Massachusetts Metaphysical College. When Miss Lang entered this hospital she was suffering from one physical disability, but after lingering there for more than a year she was informed by her attending physician that every organ in her frail body was diseased; and she was given up to die. During the many months of her prolonged illness in the hospital she daily read and studied her Bible, confident of God's love and goodness. It was then that God came to her rescue, for "Man's extremity is God's opportunity." Miss Lang and her father, Alfred Lang, then became aware of Mrs. Eddy's system of Christian healing and of the Massachusetts Metaphysical College, close by at 569 Columbus Avenue. Her father went to call upon Mrs. Eddy to ask for Christian Science treatment for his daughter. Mrs. Eddy took the case and the result was marvelously successful. Miss Lang was perfectly and permanently healed. She thereafter devoted her life to this wonderful Truth, to the teaching and healing ministry of Christian Science which had so uplifted and saved her from the "last enemy" and made her well and strong again. (Albert Lang reminiscences; Historical File: Susie M. Lang)

Injuries from an accident healed (1882–1884)

[Mrs. Isaac Foss] was driving with a span of horses, runaway; she was thrown out. When she was taken up, they found she was internally injured, and her ankle was sprained. For years her only relief was under opiates, suffering dreadfully all the time. Mr. Choate was her healer. He was located somewhere in New Hampshire. Took his patients to his house. This lady was there. He did not seem to reach the case. One day he told her he was going to Boston to see Mrs. Eddy and he would ask her to treat this lady. It was about six o'clock when she felt a very strange sensation; she was so stirred they put her to bed. When she got up, she got up well. She is now keeping boarders and does her own work and is a well woman. (Elizabeth Moulton statement; Historical File: Alfred Farlow)

Rheumatism healed (1882–1885)

A student came to Mrs. Eddy with a case of rheumatism which he had been unable to heal. The patient was bedridden and deformed from the disease and seemed to give no response to the treatment. Mrs. Eddy told the student how to work on it, but still there was no improvement. Upon his telling her there was still no lifting of the error, Mrs. Eddy said, "Oh, Lord, let the door be opened," whereupon the door of the room in which they sat swung slowly open. She then told the student to go, the patient was healed, and so it proved. (Grace Greene Felch reminiscences)

Weak back and limbs healed (1883)
(Ellen Brown Linscott to Mrs. Eddy)

That same season [summer 1883] I was suffering from a belief of a very weak back—could only *crawl up* stairs & more than one flight of stairs alarmed me. You healed me of that instantaneously. I had been healed of various claims by reading Science & Health before I studied with you in March 1883. (Document 163CH214)

~

Mrs. Linscott also said, "From early girlhood I had an infirmity in the limbs that prevented me walking up stairs easily. One day at the College, I was going up to my room on the third floor, groaning and complaining, and as I reached the landing on the second floor said aloud, 'I know I'll never get up to the next floor.' Just as I said it, the door opened, and Mrs. Glover came out and heard me. She gave a sweep of her hand, and commanded, 'Run up those stairs! Run up those stairs!' I started running, and have been running up stairs ever since." (Edward E. Norwood reminiscences)

Fifteen-year invalid healed (1883)

Previous to the year 1883, I, Jennie E. Sawyer, had been an invalid for fifteen years; pronounced incurable as I had chronic and organic diseases that would not yield to medicine or treatment of any material nature; and on three separate occasions my life had been despaired of and I had faced death, but had rallied and continued suffering until a relapse into another hopeless and dangerous condition.

Thus, life had become an endless torture; physicians gave me no hope of recovery as medicine seemed to poison the system, so there came a time when they recommended only fresh air, pure water, and sunshine together with absolute quiet, as the only hope of relieving the body of constant suffering and pain, as there was no waking moment that I was not enduring pain, and life had become a grievous burden until my constant prayer was that I might die,— thinking thereby I should enter into eternal rest. Finally I was sent to a resort or Rest Cure where no medicine was given and patients were required to do nothing but lie out in the sunshine or shade, ride in row boats on artificial ponds, read, or remain idle as they chose; but at first I was too utterly weary to even avail myself of these privileges. It seemed an amazing thing that one could be so tired and utterly weary that even breathing exhausted them, and still I lived!

But gradually, after gaining a degree of strength, I was able to sit up a portion of the day and wear my clothes a few hours at a time, and avail myself of a few moments of boatriding or of lying out on the porch; but before I was able to rely on myself at all,—after about seven weeks,—a letter came from my husband informing me that several friends had been urging him to try a mental method of healing which included no medicine and no physical exertion on the part of the patient,—and even mentally they did not require the patient to accept it until relief came and they could better understand it.

He had not at first been favorably impressed as such a method was unknown, and he, having studied medicine to a degree,—being a Druggist and having practiced Dentistry; his thought was that medicine having failed there was nothing one could resort to; it was like having done everything then expecting nothing to heal one. We had tried diet and travel, baths and electricity, and many different doctors and their remedies and methods, and were trying at that time to gain strength sufficient to have an operation, hoping to gain help in certain directions but not promised any sure relief.

Some people from Boston were visiting friends of ours and had brought these vague statements as regard a method of healing they had heard about, but could give no definite idea of what it really was except that a lady in Boston, through what was supposed to be a silent prayer, was healing people. He finally purchased *Science and Health* by Mary Baker G. Eddy, relating to her own experience of years of invalidism, and of her method of healing, which he could not understand but which seemed more Christian and spiritual than the ordinary faith of the church; and he, knowing that I firmly believed that the only ease I obtained was from God, he suggested that we go to Boston and consult Mrs. Eddy.

The very thought of such a proposition caused a relapse, for in my condition a trip of that distance was a momentous undertaking;—as I had lived for several years under the impression that any unusual exertion would end my life, I preferred dying at home and was opposed to the idea of attempting such a journey, feeling I could not endure it nor hope to reach the journey's end alive.

But my husband through reading *Science and Health* had gained a thought that had deeply impressed him as wholly different from any other Christian faith; it seemed a practical, workable, demonstrable faith and he desired to meet the Author personally. I had not seen, nor was I able to read the book; I was too weak physically or mentally to read or remember anything very long; and so a month or two passed before arrangements could be made to move me or I could gain courage or strength to attempt such a journey. It required closing his dental office and discontinuing business during our absence;—but finally the trip was accomplished and we arrived in Boston one evening about the middle of December of 1883.

Dr. Sawyer, leaving me at the Hotel, called at once on Mrs. Eddy at 571 Columbus Avenue where her home and College were situated; he gained an appointment for me the following morning. On his return to the Hotel from this first call on Mrs. Eddy, I remember he said, "I don't know how you will be impressed; I don't know what you will think! She seemed very much of a lady, and very sincere in her faith and work in Christian Science; she talked of God and of man's relation to God in a manner we are not familiar with; her talk seemed sensible and convincing and very interesting, but very strange and unusual. She did not even inquire specially about your physical symptoms or condition, but in some way I feel there is help for you in it."

The following morning on seeing Mrs. Eddy, I felt favorably impressed with her sincerity and womanly, motherly kindness; there seemed no opposition in my thought of trying this method of healing. She did not apparently diagnose my case, nor did she act as though I were an invalid; there was no talk of sickness; it was a strange experience, for my appearance plainly showed that I was a constant sufferer, and after having exhausted all material means to expect by doing nothing I should be healed;—even at that very moment I was too weary to listen or to grasp hold on what she was saying, feeling I would liked to have stopped breathing to catch up on strength sufficient to go on living; and so during this call I was unable to consider or follow the line of thought she was bringing out; still, there was something attractive and alluring in the idea of gaining rest and health through abiding in God's omnipotence, in the sure confidence and trust that she presented as possible. . . .

The only hesitation I felt of being healed was the dread of an invalid's convalescent state:—of gradually, slowly, gaining a degree of strength, and then through some cause suffering a relapse; then again, gaining a hope of health and then dying—that was more appalling to me than to die at once. I said to Mrs. Eddy, "If I gain my health it will be such a slow process, and then I must sooner or later die, and I would rather go now, as I feel willing and ready to die." In those days a Christian who was reconciled to die had reached a state of mind most commendable; I realize the absurdity of it now, for my readiness to go was not so much because of my love and service to God as to free myself of suffering and pain; not wholly unselfish, although I was young and the world held many attractions. Mrs. Eddy assured me there would be no convalescent state if I were healed in Christian Science; and she also startled me by saying, "If you die you will awaken to the realization that you are not dead, and still have your problem to solve, for Life is from everlasting to everlasting."

Another fear that greatly troubled me was that this thought might be contrary to my Christian faith of the Congregational Church, or that it might separate me from my mother who had died a few years previously; also fearing it might be an anti-Christ of which we were warned in the Scriptures. I felt I must voice my convictions and fears before taking up this new faith. It was fortunate for me that Mrs. Eddy had been an invalid, also a member of an orthodox church, for she understood my nervousness and fears, and she showed the utmost consideration for all my doubts and misunderstanding.

The most astounding thing was that she did not physically diagnose my case, nor ask what the different physicians had thought my trouble was. She did not give me any treatment, but rather questioned my thought about God and mankind and Life; and finally she said, "I would advise you to sit in my class and let me teach you." That was the most astonishing thing; for I had not been able to remember three lines of anything I read for months! I was too tired to think; and the presence and conversation of people wearied me almost beyond endurance; and physicians had repeatedly told me there was nothing to build on, and had warned me that I was liable to die at any moment. But she paid not the slightest attention to the doctors' verdicts but answered, "Your husband is in good health, and together you might gain a thought that would heal you." At that time to imagine that a "thought gained" would heal incurable, hopeless organic disease, seemed almost an insane idea. Up to that time I had been unable to bear the weight of my clothes but a few hours each day; still she assured me, "You will be able to sit in this class; for as you learn your true relationship to God, you will forget these things that now trouble you."

. . . Thus, I entered Mrs. Eddy's Class with trepidation and involuntary fear; a confusion of thought possessed me, for it was like entering a new unknown realm of thought wherein I might lose my old sense of faith and die before arriving at this new realization of how to trust God fully and entirely. I feared letting go of my personal sense measurement of life which had held me so long in bondage.

Mrs. Eddy at this time was a woman past sixty years of age, a well preserved beautiful woman;—not so much because of her physical charm as because there was discernible an inward light or reflection of thought that shone through her countenance that was an entirely new expression of being; this had its own influence,—one felt drawn to a better Life just from being in her presence. This realization of Life that she possessed gave impulse to her every action, word and speech. She was prepossessing, attractive, and kind in her manner, and most considerate in guiding the thought of the members of this Class away from the discussions in relation to matter as the only tangible evidence of life.

She guided the argumentative beliefs wisely into an acceptance of infinite Mind's power and presence; and this became a time marked by an absolute change of consciousness as regard Life and its demand together with its motive, purpose, desire and aim; thereby changing the whole current of thought from a material mortal mind basis to a spiritual perception of man and the universe as reflecting God and His handiwork in the world; thereby enabling one to recognize God's everpresence, protection, and care in every way, at all times and under all circumstances. . . .

Our first Class was taught by Mrs. Eddy in her home and College at 571 Columbus Avenue in Boston, Massachusetts, beginning in December 1883. She gave us about three weeks of time; she told Dr. Sawyer and myself that we were the first students to have come from the West [Milwaukee] for instruction with her, and she formed this Class especially to accommodate us as we had come so great a distance. There were but twelve students in this Class and only three besides ourselves were paying students, as she had gathered these people together who had been asking for instruction. Thus she made up this Class during the Holiday season; and she had an intermission of a few days on my personal account, as the new thought stirred me to a feverish condition, trying to change the consciousness from a material personal sense of life and body to a recognition of the spiritual mentality of being.

Our faith and trust was so vague and uncertain compared with her grasping hold on God's promises, that it was literally like being born again; this learning to abide in the kingdom of Truth and Love seemed a mighty effort, and created a fever of fear and unrest and disquietude that she claimed it were better to discontinue her explanations for a few days until the balance was adjusted on the side of trust and assurance. I felt I could not discontinue or cease learning more, as I was not well enough established in the new way to treat or pray in Christian Science, and my former way of praying I could not go back to. She noticed my unrest and asked before the Class disbanded, "Mrs. Sawyer, do you ever stir yeast when it is rising?" I answered, "No, but what has that to do with this?" She answered, "God's hand is leading you, and I would not do more just now." I did not understand it, and could not repress my tears. She sent one of her older students to meet me as I went from the classroom alone, and he said, "Mrs. Eddy wants you to know that you are in the most favorable condition of mind of anyone in the Class." I said, "This is too serious a matter to say anything like that; I don't know what I am here for; I cannot grasp it, and I cannot go back to my old faith." He said comforting words that were wholly lost on me, and although I do not cry easily I went out sobbing.

I remember taking *Science and Health* and thinking I will read until I know where and what God is; and suddenly as I was reading in the chapter on "Footsteps of Truth," it dawned on me that I was reaching far out for God as though He were a long way off—unapproachable and difficult to find. And out of that darkness and bewilderment, an illumination of thought encircled me, and I felt and knew and realized God's everpresence. It was like a conversion—a remarkable experience of "God with us" at all times, under all circumstances. My eyes were open to the truth of Being, and from that day to the present time it has been a daily, hourly, realization that my eyes need not be holden but may at all times recognize the bountiful mercy, love, and care of our heavenly Father that the Christ-thought brings to our consciousness, if we but turn our faces God-ward and realize His everpresence. Mrs. Eddy made a private appointment for that evening and gave us many new ideas and comforting thoughts. We scarcely realized what a privilege we had in these private talks with her, but later on we learned to treasure the words given.

. . . at the end of the Class, when Mrs. Eddy asked Dr. Sawyer if he would go to different cities and establish the work under her directions, and teach the Science wherever he found receptive minds, he accepted the call although he knew it would array public thought against him. He closed a lucrative business and followed along the line of Christian Science endeavor, the remainder of his earth-life. Mrs. Eddy then asked me what I thought of it, and what I was going to do with the thought she had imparted to me. I answered, "I am filled with a wonderful Truth. I don't know what I am to do with it!" She said in a most convincing manner, "You are going to heal with it!" She seemed to foresee the future and felt that I would apply the knowledge gained to heal others whether present or absent. She assured me that I was practically healed of my infirmities and apparent disease—that had not quite dawned on me, and it seemed almost incredible to think there would be no return of those ailments.

I realized that to practice Christian Science would place me where I would be a target for severe criticism among my home friends and Church people, but I also realized that I had left my home and friends in a hopeless, dying condition that none could help; and my life had been prolonged and saved and my health restored and my faith renewed through and by this revelation of the Christ-healing taught by my Teacher, Mrs. Mary Baker G. Eddy,—and I could not do less than make a solemn compact with God to give my remaining days to His service; so I promised to do all in my power to help others to understand this blessed Truth of Christian Science.

We arrived home early in January 1884, and at once began the healing for whoever desired help. My first case was a young girl of about twenty years, born of a consumptive mother; she had never been strong, and at this time was suffering from inflammatory rheumatism, which rendered her right arm and hand useless. I began the treatment on Friday evening and did absent work until Monday morning, when she called and said, "See what I can do!" and she lifted a large heavy Atlas with her right hand! This girl had been afflicted with a double curvature of the spine from her birth; and through the treatment her back was straightened and healed in twenty-three days. . . .

I personally got the blessing, and took this healing so to heart that nothing could shake my faith in Christian Science healing. In all these years of having professed Christianity I had never before realized that an actual possession of a living faith in our God could or would bring such a blessing into one's experience! At first only the chronic and apparently incurable cases came for treatment; and for several months we worked without compensation, and as suffering was relieved for one they would tell another of benefit received. Thus in time a Practice was established and, in a lesser way, we were Pioneers of our Teacher's method of treating; hundreds of miles away from her, we were endeavoring to practice Christian Science.

Planting a new thought, especially if it be of a religious nature, is not wholly a thing of joy or happiness, except in one's own consciousness of right action. We had at once called on our own Minister and Physician feeling sure they would appreciate this spiritual Truth and rejoice in the recovery of health; but our minister and church friends immediately turned a cold shoulder on us and many would not even allow an explanation in any direction, fearing it was of a mesmeric nature and in some way they could be made to believe in it without desiring to do so. They felt we had been innocently led astray by Mrs. Eddy's thought, and even the friends who had urged Dr. Sawyer to take me to Boston for this healing, dropped us socially. They simply judged it must be wrong because no minister had ever in all his study of the Scriptures discovered any such rendering of thought. . . .

Our physician was more lenient and kind and had to admit I seemed well, but he warned me that the moment "that woman's thought"—meaning Mrs. Eddy's thought,— "was off from me" I would pass out, as it was but mesmeric effect. He emphatically said he knew my physical condition and I could not be healed! Both minister and physician watched my case for several years, but there was no relapse, and I have outlived most of these friends. . . .

It is now forty-seven years of continuous practice, and teaching of Christian Science; and it has been one glorious experience,—of endeavor to undo self and sense and thereby serve God, the Giver of every good and perfect gift. (Jennie E. Sawyer reminiscences)

Lightning storm dispersed (1883–1888)
(Mrs. Eddy to Irving Tomlinson)

We should have the same control over the weather that we have over our bodies. I remember when I was preaching that on one occasion the sky became black and a flash of lightning was so severe that the soloist fell in [a] faint. I declared "Let there be peace" and almost instantly the sun came forth. (Historical File: Tomlinson notes)

Adulterer healed (1883–1888)

Mrs. Eddy had in one of her classes a woman whose face evidently showed great resentment. Mrs. Eddy asked her what the trouble was and found that she had an unfaithful husband. Mrs. Eddy explained how Jesus healed Mary Magdalene and said we must have the same mind Jesus had. Mrs. Eddy told her, "You will have to have it or you will never heal a case." The woman said she didn't have that mind and what was more, she didn't want it. But she was healed before she got through class and upon arriving home, found the husband changed—healed. (Irving Tomlinson reminiscences)

Pet bird's broken leg healed (1883–1888)

Mrs. Eddy was very fond of pets, especially birds. . . . On one occasion she had a little canary named Benny, and every morning he waited until Mrs. Eddy came down into the room, and would then burst into a flood of song. When she went to the Association meeting in Chicago, during her week's absence Benny never sang, but the day that the telegram was received, notifying the household of her return, he suddenly again burst into song.

On one occasion another little bird named May was given her, and in her spare moments, Mrs. Eddy would allow the birds to hop freely about the room. One morning some one in moving a heavy arm-chair rolled it on one of May's tiny feet. Mrs. Eddy picked up the bird, whose broken foot was hanging by a shred of skin, and laid her gently back in the cage. A few moments later a lady visitor called and while conversing with Mrs. Eddy suddenly stopped and said: "What *is* the matter with that bird?" indicating Benny, who was singing and chirping, flying to May's cage and back to them, and making a great noise. Mrs. Eddy replied by asking the visitor to look in May's cage, when the lady said: "Why, this bird has a broken foot!" Mrs. Eddy said: "Benny is sympathizing with her, and wants to tell us about it. But never mind, come back in three days." The lady did return at that time, and was amazed and delighted to see little May perfectly well, hopping about her cage and singing joyously. (Eugenia M. Fosbery reminiscences)

Dead goldfish restored (1883–1888)

A teacher whom I knew many years ago went through a class with Mrs. Eddy. She told me an incident that took place during this class from which she learned a great lesson. One morning at the beginning of the class Mrs. Eddy sat silently with her head bowed down. The members of the class all began to wonder if they had done anything which merited rebuke. At last Mrs. Eddy looked up and said: "I have been very wicked. Last night I saw one of my gold fish floating on top of the water, and I said, my gold fish is dead! But this morning I am happy to say, it is all right." Then she smiled at them. (Caroline Foss Gyger reminiscences)

Spiritualist with gallstones healed (1884)
(Mrs. Eddy to Lida Fitzpatrick)

I lectured one time where the spiritualists tried to break up the meeting; they would jump up and contradict without being asked. A lady in the audience—and the audience was large—was taken with one of her attacks of gall stones; fell on the floor in excruciating pain; I said to the spiritualists present—now is your time to prove what your God will do for you; heal this woman. They jumped about and did what they could but she grew worse and worse; I stepped down from the platform, stood beside her a moment and the pain left; she arose and sat in her chair and was healed. (Fitzpatrick reminiscences)

～

(Mrs. Eddy to Irving Tomlinson)

When my students in Chicago sent for me to visit them and lecture I wrote them that I was so tied down with work that it seemed well nigh impossible. They urged so insistently that at last I yielded though it did not seem to be the leading of God, but I knew that the wrath of man would be made to praise God.

At that time the Spiritualists were almost in control of Chicago and unknown to my students they plotted to make of the lecture a failure. These Spiritualists planned to attend the lecture in a body and to attempt to break up the meeting by leaving while I was lecturing. The hall was crowded, people standing in the aisles and even on the windowsills to hear the lecture. In the midst of the lecture there was a crash and I saw that the leader of the Spiritualists had fallen on the floor. Several of the Spiritualists rushed to her and attempted their manipulations without avail. Stopping in my lecture I went to the fallen woman, spoke to her and she arose healed. (Historical File: Tomlinson notes)

Inflammatory rheumatism healed (1884–1885)

I am a printer by trade, having learned the trade in Skowhegan and serving first on the *Portland Express*. I afterwards came to Boston and worked on the *Boston Journal* for over thirty-four years, afterwards working on the *Boston Globe* and other papers. My last employment was as night watchman in the Christian Science Church, leaving there in 1912.

I was attacked by inflammatory rheumatism in my early thirties in such form that even the bedclothing proved to be burdensome and painful. I had heard about Mrs. Eddy's meetings in Hawthorne Hall on Park Street, near Brimstone Corner and at the worst stage of the belief I was taken there on a stretcher, accompanied by the then Mrs. Littlefield. After the service ended Mrs. Eddy came down from the platform and greeted the members of the meeting personally—it was a small group of about a dozen people—and when she came to me and shook my hand and spoke to me, I felt the healing and responded by telling her that I was healed. I walked out of the Hall rejoicing, and that belief never made itself real to me again. (Henry A. Littlefield reminiscences)

Journalist's fatigue healed (1885)

It was in my youthful days of journalism in Boston—in the eighties—that I became deeply interested in hearing of this remarkable woman [Mrs. Eddy] and ventured to write to her asking if I might have the privilege of a personal interview? A gracious reply came to me, naming an evening hour, on a given date. I recall that I was rather unusually fatigued that night, and upborne chiefly by the anticipation of meeting the eloquent speaker to whom I had listened more than once, and that I went up the steps to her door with feet that lagged, though my thought did not. Her most kind reception largely banished the fatigue, and I see before me now the slender figure, the luminous eyes, the faintly rose-flushed countenance; the simple, dainty grace of her gown, and the beauty of the hand that clasped mine. . . . From her conversation that evening I wrote a letter to "The Inter-Ocean," of Chicago,—very crudely and imperfectly interpreting the substance of what she said, I am sure; yet perhaps conveying something of the great truths she unfolded: and almost any matter referring to Mrs. Eddy and her work was read by the curious public and widely discussed. . . .

I have mentioned my state of fatigue, that evening, simply to record the striking sequence of that experience. It was a Saturday evening; I was then living in the Vendome: and after walking back to the hotel from Mrs. Eddy's home (then in Columbus Avenue) I was conscious of the most intense exhilaration and joyous energy. I felt as if I could walk any distance, indeed, almost as if I could fly through the air. The next morning, after listening to Phillips Brooks, in Trinity, I turned to some writing and was all the time conscious of that intense exhilaration of energy, that sense of joyous exaltation, of mind and body. My work seemed to fairly write itself, independently of my exertion. The sensation was so vivid that in the evening I mentioned to a friend that I had gone on, all day, in a sort of rapturous happiness, and she replied: "Why, that was the effect of Mrs. Eddy on you." That had not consciously occurred to me before. But it is true, as I look back and see this period in perspective, that this meeting with Mrs. Eddy made itself a very definite date in my life,—one of those milestones in the onward march which one only adequately recognizes in after years. As I read it now, I can but regard this as the unconscious influence of a highly exalted spirit on another, who was so fortunate, perhaps, as to be sensitive to the spiritual vibration. (Lilian Whiting reminiscences)

~

(Alfred Farlow to Mrs. Eddy)

I am sending you a book which Miss Lilian Whiting has requested me to hand you. You will probably remember her. She still relates the story of the wonderful benefits she received from you twenty years ago, or more, when she called upon you on Columbus Avenue. She was much fatigued—worn out with her work. She said that after her interview with you she went away entirely refreshed and invigorated. (Alfred Farlow letter to Mrs. Eddy, July 7, 1909; Chestnut Hill File)

Moral vices healed (1885–1888)
(Mrs. Eddy to Irving Tomlinson)

A gentleman who went to Boston and became a leading merchant, brought a parrot to me of which he was proud for his ability to talk. His first word was an oath. Said I to the gentleman, "Did you teach him that." He saw his mistake and said no. Then I said, "Could he ever have heard you use that word." Then I spoke to him of his influence for good or evil, and the silent influence of this conduct.

He afterward said that from that interview he was a changed man. He ceased his profanity, and forsook other vices, and lived a different life thereafter. (Historical File: Tomlinson notes)

Hacking cough healed (1886)

In the first class I was in, a woman from Georgia seemed to have a hacking cough. Mrs. Eddy called her by name and said, "Why do you blaspheme God that way?" She never coughed again.

[More than] a year later when Mrs. Eddy delivered her address in Central Music Hall [Chicago] I met this woman at the door and we knew each other. Almost the first thing she said was "Do you know I have never coughed since." (Ruth Ewing reminiscences)

Mrs. Eddy's estranged cousin healed (1886)

In one of our Leader's early classes (and as I recall my mother's Primary class), one morning soon after the session opened, Mrs. Eddy was called out of the room and did not return for over an hour. When she entered again she expressed regret for the delay, but said she felt they would realize its importance when she explained what had kept her. She then proceeded to tell them that at one time, early in her discovery of Christian Science, she passed through quite a period of misunderstanding with her family, and in her extremity turned as a last resort for sympathy and financial help to a favorite cousin, who, like the rest, disappointed her by rejecting her faith and refusing to give her assistance of any kind.

Our Leader said, "From that time on I relied absolutely upon God, and now, after all these years, this same cousin has become alarmed over a physical condition, and today came to me in tears to ask for healing. Under the circumstances I felt sure you would be willing to wait while I stopped long enough to heal her." (Abigail Dyer Thompson reminiscences)

Heart disease healed (1886–1887)

I came to New York [City] at the request of my dear Teacher, Mrs. Eddy. This was early in October of 1885. I had been in this city over a year when Mrs. Eddy sent for me to come to Boston to spend Sunday with her. I went Saturday night, reaching the college at 571 Columbus Avenue, where Mrs. Eddy then lived, at nine o'clock Sunday morning. She asked me no questions about my heart, although she told me nine years after that she had sent for me because of what one of her other students had said about me. One of them had called upon me in New York, and later had told Mrs. Eddy that I was in a very bad condition physically, that my heart constantly made a creaking noise, such as a gate would make when swinging on a rusty hinge. When it was time for dinner I accompanied Mrs. Eddy to the dining-room, which was in the basement of the house. On returning to the parlor she ran up the stairs like a young girl. I was ashamed not to make at least an effort to do the same, but for twenty four years I had never run upstairs. Perhaps once or twice a year, if it were absolutely necessary, I would make the effort, going up two or three steps at a time, then sitting down to rest. This time I did go as fast as she did, but when I reached the top step I was in a sorry plight. How I looked I cannot tell. I only knew that I was seized with one of my old attacks, when it seemed as though an iron hand gripped my heart and was squeezing the very life out of it. She gave me one glance, and then, without asking me a question, she spoke aloud to the error. We are told that when Jesus healed the sick, he spake as one having authority. On this occasion Mrs. Eddy also spoke as one having authority.

As I look back on that wonderful event, I do not remember that the thought came to me at the time that she was healing me, neither do I remember that I had any special faith. The only sense I had was of her wonderful power. A few months after, I was seized with another attack, but it lasted only a moment and went, never again to return. That was eighteen years ago, and during all these years of unceasing work in Christian Science, I have constantly and fearlessly run up and down long flights of stairs when it was necessary to do so, and with no ill results. The belief of hereditary heart disease is not only dead, but buried. (Laura Lathrop, "Healed by Mrs. Eddy," *Christian Science Sentinel,* December 24, 1904)

Overwhelming fear healed (1888)

In August 1888 or about that time in one of the [*Journals*] appeared a notice that Mrs. Eddy would teach a Class in September of that year. I made application and received a letter from Calvin Frye, Mrs. Eddy's Secretary, stating that my letter had been received and if I would fill out the Blanks that he enclosed, that if I was accepted I would be notified when to appear. I was accepted and the Class was taught by Mrs. Eddy at [the College] on Columbus Avenue, Boston.

This was a wonderful demonstration to be made in a year, for prior to April 1887 I had been an invalid for ten (10) years, so in the year and a half I had to acquire an entire new wardrobe, made several trips to Chicago in order to learn more of Christian Science and also demonstrate over the needful supply for Class Instruction; just the day before I was to leave for Boston the demonstration was fully made. Thus proving that God does supply all our needs when we are wholly trusting Him.

In teaching the Class Mrs. Eddy sat on a platform and my seat was just at her feet. When I entered the Class I was so impressed by Mrs. Eddy's understanding of people and everything, that I was filled with such awe that tears flowed freely. When Mrs. Eddy entered the room where the Class was assembled it seemed as if she always surveyed the Class and it seemed as if she was looking into each face and seemed as if she was mentally greeting each one and seeing only the real man of God's creating.

One day at the close of the Class I told Mrs. Eddy that I was so afraid, just full of fear, instantly came the question, "My dear, what are you afraid of?" and I told her I did not know just what the fear was; for an instant she stood still and then said, "You know, God is Love." I was healed and that sense of fear has never returned. (Cordelia Willey reminiscences)

Calvin Frye restored (1888–1889)

Our aunt [Julia Bartlett] was present . . . when Mr. Frye fell downstairs and broke his neck. After he was revived, the students questioned him earnestly as to what he had been doing while Mrs. Eddy was restoring him. He said that he had been in the pantry eating a piece of pie. He explained that he had started downstairs to go to the pantry for a piece of pie, and that, to his sense, he never stopped. (Muriel Holmes; Historical File: Julia Bartlett)

∽

Miss Bartlett said that while Mrs. Eddy was living at 385 Commonwealth Avenue, Boston, Mr. Calvin Frye suddenly passed on, and Mrs. Eddy raised him from the dead. Some time elapsed from the moment he passed on until Mrs. Eddy restored him to life. One of the students who witnessed this demonstration asked Mr. Frye what his experience was during the time that, to them he seemed to be dead. He replied that he was in the pantry eating pie. (Lottie Clark reminiscences)

Cyclone dispersed at Pleasant View (1895–1897)

At Pleasant View, dominion over weather, storms, etc., was just the same as over other seeming material conditions. After a prolonged drought, the inharmonious condition was met by our Leader's watching and praying, the effect being rain when there was not a cloud visible in the sky. At other times heavy, dark clouds appeared when there was no rain. Also Truth was demonstrated to quell storms.

During part of the year cyclones were sometimes experienced at Concord, and one day Miss Morgan came to me and said that the clouds were gathering and there was going to be a dreadful storm, and she called me to look through the windows of her room, which was at the end of the house, looking towards the stables. Above, I saw dark clouds which seemed to be coming towards us very rapidly, and as Mother [Mrs. Eddy] had told me whenever I saw a cyclone or storm coming up I must let her know, I went to her room immediately and told her. She rose, and went to the verandah at the back of the house. By that time, the clouds had reached overhead. She then went into the front vestibule and looked on that side of the house. . . . I ran downstairs to the front door, opened it and went outside, looked up and saw the clouds hanging over the house—very heavy, black clouds, and in the middle, right over the house there was a rift—they were dividing—part were going one way and the other part in the opposite direction. This seemed to be such a strange phenomenon. I went in, closed the door and went upstairs to Mother, on the verandah, and told her what I saw. I said, "The clouds are divided just overhead!" She said to me, "Clouds! What do you mean? *Are* there any clouds?" I said, "No, Mother!" She was looking up, and I could see by the expression on her face that she was not seeing clouds but was realising the Truth. I saw the black clouds turn to indigo, the indigo to light grey, the light grey turn to white fleecy clouds which dissolved and there were no more, and she said to me, "There are no clouds to hide God's face and there is nothing that can come between the light and us—it is divine Love's weather."

That was early in the evening; the wind had been blowing terrifically, and Mr. Frye and another gentleman were in the attic, trying to pull down a large American flag. It was

"Fete" day and a gentleman had sent this flag as a gift to Mrs. Eddy; it was very large, so she had it hoisted, and Mr. Frye and this friend were trying to pull it down, and the strength of the two men was not sufficient to pull down that flag but suddenly the wind subsided and the flag yielded.

The next morning, early, when the mail was delivered, the postman was amazed to see that nothing had been disturbed in the garden, as, from a short distance down the road, and in the town there had been a great deal of damage. The lesson I learned then, through that experience, has since helped me through many storms by sea and on land. (Clara Shannon reminiscences)

Man in state asylum healed (1895–1902)

I did meet our beloved Leader, Mary Baker Eddy in Concord one day at her home there. She asked me what work I did and I said, "I am a school teacher." She said, "that is a good work helping the children." "Yes," I said, "I enjoy it; as I like children!" I used to see her riding with her driver around Concord. I remember one day she was riding past the State Asylum, a young man stepped out on a narrow porch and he called to Mrs. Eddy, "Mrs. Eddy help me!" She answered, "Yes, I will!" and I heard later that he was perfectly healed! O, she surely was called of God to do such healing work! (Addie P. Forbes reminiscences)

～

Before going to Concord, Mrs. Eddy had set aside a certain time in her day for driving. She strictly adhered to this arrangement, planned as a refreshing interlude. As she drove along the valley she occasionally passed an insane asylum where an inmate watched her closely through the gate. Mrs. Eddy did not permit this sad picture to disturb her, but let her thought rest upon him with such understanding of his divine birthright that he was fully restored. (Julia Michael Johnston, *Mary Baker Eddy: Her Mission and Triumph,* pages 130–131)

Poverty overcome (1899)

I [saw Mrs. Eddy] once at a Jewelers on Main St. [Concord] . . . and met her several times and she always bowed, smiled and shook her hand in such a beautiful manner I simply cannot describe it. I also sat on the seventh row of seats from the front when she spoke in Tremont Temple, June 6, 1899. Just before this I had no home and not one cent of money but received such inspiration that it seems simply unbelievable how I was provided for. I went to Boston from Toronto, Ont. fully believing this time I would both see and hear her. I did not know she was going to be in Boston and have always given her the credit for this wonderful financial help and my instantaneous healing. (Walter Scott Day reminiscences)

Obsessive hatred healed (1900)

On page 16 of Mrs. Eddy's 1901 Message to The Mother Church, she says, or rather, asks this question: "Shall it be said of this century that its greatest discoverer is a woman to whom men go to mock, and go away to pray?"

In the fall of the year before Mrs. Eddy penned this message to her church, a shoe salesman of Hartford, Conn., who had for a long time hated Mrs. Eddy with an unreasoning and unprovoked hatred that amounted to insanity, went to Concord, N.H., and stood outside her gate to see her as she came out to take her drive. He had a vacation about that time, and he was in the neighborhood, so took advantage of this opportunity to satiate his hatred by looking upon the object of his cruel obsession.

This man was in Asheville, N.C., a year later, and told of this experience. He said when Mrs. Eddy's carriage passed him at the gate, our dear Leader bowed and smiled sweetly upon him. There was something different in this greeting from what he had expected, for, said he, he felt a flood of divine love such as he never dreamt existed on this earth. It quite unnerved him, and before he realized what he was doing, he crumpled up and wept like a child. On his way home he bought a copy of *Science and Health* by Mrs. Eddy, and began the study of it. He was healed of some ailment (I do not remember what it was), and he became a devoted Christian Scientist. (Elizabeth Earl Jones reminiscences)

Sprained ankle healed (1902)

Mrs. [Elizabeth] Norton said that she and her husband [Carol] were in Los Angeles, California, and upon leaving a trolley car she slipped and sprained her ankle very badly. She was helped into the hotel and up to her room.

The following morning the ankle was discolored and so badly swollen that she could not walk. Mr. Norton went downstairs to breakfast, stopping at the office for mail, and among the letters was one from our beloved Leader, Mary Baker Eddy. This letter was addressed to them both and was dated Christmas Eve. Mr. Norton came upstairs and said, "What do you think we have received as a Christmas gift?" Whereupon he handed the letter to Mrs. Norton. As she read it her eyes filled with tears and her heart overflowed with gratitude and love for our beloved one who had so greatly blessed the whole world with her unselfish love, and as she finished the letter and handed it back to her husband she discovered that the ankle had been entirely healed, and she was able to walk. (Historical File: Irving Tomlinson notes)

Mrs. Eddy's letter was dated Dec. 24th, 1902. The above is an accurate account of the healing. [signed] Elizabeth Norton. (Tomlinson notes)

[Mrs. Eddy's letter follows:]
Pleasant View, Concord, N.H.
Dec. 24, 1902

Beloved Student:

For your faithful labors, and your memory, through the pretty apples, of me—I thank you. My prayer is that our one Father mother Love hallow your life with His everpresence; and your way be the path of pleasantness— pure, holy, a beacon light to save the wrecks upon earth's syren shoals; to lure the wanderer, help the weak, and comfort the weary.

Mother sends her love to Mrs. Norton together with thanks for those sweet-eyed flowers that came from your "cottage by the sea." May this Xmas be a sweet benediction after your work is done or ready for renewal.

Tenderly thine mother
M. B. Eddy
(Document L04254)

Smoker healed (1903)

There was also a man named Strubble, I think the name was, from New York who was healed of smoking on this same occasion [when Mrs. Eddy spoke to a gathering of Christian Scientists from the balcony of her home]. He was a good Scientist but could not seem to overcome this particular belief. He was standing right opposite the gate at Pleasant View with a cigar in his mouth when Mrs. Eddy drove out in her carriage. He told me that as the carriage passed, she looked straight at him, and he took the cigar out of his mouth. That afternoon he lit another cigar and tried to smoke but found it made him sick. That was the last time he ever attempted to smoke, for his taste for tobacco had been completely destroyed. (John Salchow reminiscences)

⌒

[Wentworth Winslow's sister] spoke of the testimony of a noted actor which had appeared some time before in the periodicals and said that this same actor was still a slave to the tobacco habit when he was in Concord some time later, and that while there he was walking along the street one day with a big cigar in his mouth when our Leader passed in her carriage. She looked at him—he threw away the cigar and never had the least desire to smoke after that. He explained it by saying: "She saw the real man." (Caroline Getty reminiscences)

Calvin Frye revived again (1903)

It was my privilege to witness a healing at Pleasant View in 1903 which was the result of Mrs. Eddy's own understanding of the truth. I always felt that at the time Mrs. Eddy actually restored Calvin Frye to life. My sister was then serving in Mrs. Eddy's household as maid. I remember coming down the second floor hall on my way to Mr. Frye's room and seeing Maggie running out of his room very much agitated. She told me that Calvin Frye was dead, said she had taken hold of him and his flesh was cold and stiff. As I stepped forward I could see him through the open door crumpled up at his desk, his face hanging white and limp against his chest and his arms and hands inert. Just then Mrs. Eddy's voice came from her room. She was out of my line of vision, but from the sound of her voice I could tell just about where she was. Apparently she had not received any response to her ring for Mr. Frye and was leaving her room to find out why he did not answer. I heard her voice coming nearer. It was evident that she had entered Mr. Frye's room and was approaching him, though from the sound of her voice I am sure she did not come directly up to him but stood still in the center of the room. I heard her ask over and over again, "Calvin, do you hear me?" It seemed to me that this went on for five minutes with no response on his part or sign of life. Then I heard him say very faintly, "Yes, Mother, I hear you." I turned and left the hall at that, feeling sure that all was well and that I would not be needed. As my sister had left the hall, as far as I know I was the only one who witnessed this healing. (John Salchow reminiscences)

∼

I have heard of several restorations from the dead made by Mrs. Eddy, but as they were not given at even second hand, I refrain from quoting, except that Calvin Frye told me that Mrs. Eddy had restored him (in answer to my question). (Edward E. Norwood reminiscences)

Injuries from an accident healed (1904)

While Mrs. [Ella] Sweet was at Pleasant View the Concord church was in the process of building. Mrs. Eddy had said several times she wished my mother to see it. Some time, however, passed, when on a certain day she made arrangements to have Mr. Frye and Mr. Kinter accompany Mrs. Sweet to the church and show her through. She especially requested the two gentleman to look carefully after her.

During her walk through the unfinished building, as I understood, she stepped on a loose board or piece of wood, which flew up and struck her in the face leaving quite a wound, also her ankle was strained. Earnest work was done by all three. They returned home and each went to his room to continue work.

In a brief time my mother's bell rang summoning her to Mrs. Eddy's study. She responded, taking a chair a little behind or to the side of Mrs. Eddy, hoping the difficulty might not be noticed. Mrs. Eddy remarked, "Mrs. Sweet why do you sit there, come where I can see you." She then asked to know what had happened and if help was being given. She wanted to know how mother was working for herself. Mother said she was handling the false claim of accidents. Mrs. Eddy replied, "That will not meet the case. Animal magnetism is trying to separate you from me and I need you." She talked a little and complete healing followed. (Clara Sweet Brady reminiscences)

Illness healed (1905)

One day when Mrs. Eddy was taking her daily drive, she passed an old acquaintance on the street. He could scarcely walk with a cane, but her sense of God and perfect man was so strong that he was healed. This was his statement in a letter following the incident, and which I heard our Leader read: "I have been very ill lately and have suffered a great deal, but was entirely healed the day you passed me on the street. I am grateful to God." (Julia Prescott reminiscences)

Severe throat condition healed (1907)
(Adela Rogers St. Johns to Irving Tomlinson)

When I had the pleasure of calling on you with Miss Allen last August, you asked me to write you details of a healing which I told you about at that time, and that is the occasion for this letter.

The story was told to me originally by Louis Weadock, who in 1906 was the star reporter of the New York Herald.

In that capacity, he was sent to Concord, with many other newspapermen, to "cover" the story about Mary Baker Eddy which was then occupying some space in the newspapers, and which is mentioned at length in the last part of Chapter XXI of Miss Wilbur's "Life of Mary Baker Eddy."

He told me that they were sent to Pleasant View at that time to dig up the truth about Mrs. Eddy. Their orders from the city desk were positive. They were to use what methods were necessary, but they were to find out the facts. If Mrs. Eddy was dead and someone was impersonating her, if she was mentally incompetent and physically in ill health, they were to bring back the story, sparing no one.

He also told me that naturally, being reporters, they hoped this would be the case—that something of a sensational nature would be uncovered. If Mrs. Eddy was merely living in saintly retirement, working and praying for mankind, it was not news. But if any of the other rumors about her were true, it would be a great story. All upon the old reportorial adage that if a dog bites a man it isn't news, but if a man bites a dog it is.

He said that they were a hard-boiled, belligerent bunch of old-timers who went down there. That they hoped and expected to "dig up" a lot of scandal. That they were news hounds baying on the trail.

As he told it to me, they were in Concord for some rather long period of time, investigating the story and as I remember it, covering the happenings surrounding the suit brought by George Glover, Dr. Foster Eddy and George W. Baker.

They took rooms at some hotel in Concord.

He said that while they were there a member of the Christian Science Church and someone close to Mrs. Eddy was appointed as a sort of news representative for Mrs. Eddy. This man was to give them the information from Mrs. Eddy's side of the case and to handle their requests and deal with them in all matters pertaining to the press.

The man appointed, so he said, was Mr. Irving Tomlinson.

He said that they were all greatly amazed at the kind and loving treatment accorded them. I remember his exact words, "If ever anyone had a right to hate anyone else, surely those Christian Scientists had a right to hate us. We were there to vilify their Leader if we could. We had no reverence and no decency, as I knew. We didn't believe anything but the worst about anybody. And we wanted if possible to hold Mrs. Eddy up to scorn and ridicule, to expose and denounce her if we could."

They were therefore much surprised to receive kindly treatment.

One member of their group—Mr. Weadock did not give me his name and I am not just now able to get in touch with him, but I will later and will send it to you—was a reporter from a big New York newspaper, a hard drinker, and altogether the type of old newspaper man.

He had been afflicted for some years with a very severe throat condition. Mr. Weadock did not know whether this was a cancer or not, but the boys thought maybe it was. Anyway, it was extremely painful, and at times overwhelmed this man completely.

One evening they were all sitting in his room at the hotel, drinking and smoking, bored with their stay in this small New England town. The reporter I have mentioned was at this time suffering tortures with his throat. He had lost his voice entirely and was not able to speak a word.

The telephone rang and it was yourself, calling and asking for this reporter. He had asked for some information and you were calling to give it to him.

Mr. Weadock answered the phone and said he would take the message as the reporter in question was too ill to come to the phone and couldn't speak anyway. But Mr. Tomlinson insisted upon speaking with him, saying that whether he could speak or not he could hear the message.

So the reporter went to the phone, showing decided anger. He listened a few moments, and those in the room of course could not hear what was being said. But when the reporter turned away from the phone, he could not only speak perfectly, but he was completely healed.

Mr. Weadock said the healing scared them all. They sat around, looking at each other, not able to comprehend this thing, and more startled by it than anything else.

They were closely enough in touch with Christian Science at that time to understand the claim of Christian Scientists to heal the sick, and they knew that their comrade had been healed. They could not understand the method, but he said they did understand one thing, and all voiced it. If Christian Scientists were loving enough to want to heal those reporters who had come for the purpose they had, they were certainly loving their enemies and were showing a Christ spirit far beyond anything they had ever before encountered.

They were just enough to give full credit for the great Love shown in the gentleness and the healing, even though they could not understand what had happened.

Mr. Weadock said that this circumstance completely changed their outlook on Christian Science, and swung them very decidedly over to a fair viewpoint in the proceedings, and animated them with a real desire to be fair in dealing with Mrs. Eddy and in fact made them hope that she would be thoroughly vindicated—which of course she was.

The reporters scattered after this, and Mr. Weadock does not know what became of this man, but he said he saw him several times afterwards and the healing was perfect and was still puzzling him greatly—so we know that we can leave him in God's hands, confident that his very wonder will one day lead him to the Truth.

Mr. Weadock himself has in the past two years turned to Christian Science for help. The claim of drunkenness had him pretty well down and out at that time, and the demonstration is not yet complete, but he asks for treatment, goes to church, and does his lessons, and believes entirely that Christian Science is the finest and most wonderful religion on earth today.

He has often stated to me that his contact with Christian Scientists in those early days, and his one interview with

Mrs. Eddy, did so much to convince him of this, so that in his hour of greatest woe he turned back to it. And it has made me see more and more clearly that much of our "duty to our Leader" [*Church Manual,* page 42] is to live Christian Science in just this way, so that we will bring others to the Truth just by our daily living.

This experience as told to me has been a great help to me many times, and I have also given it as a testimony—without any names, of course—in several Wednesday evening meetings, and it has brought much help to others.

It is a great happiness to me to relate it to you.

(Adela Rogers St. Johns's letter of October 25th, 1926: Tomlinson reminiscences)

∼

A healing which I recall with much interest occurred in the year 1907, at the time of the "Next Friends" suit, when many newspapers were sending their reporters to Concord in the hope of securing interviews with Mrs. Eddy. Since it would have taken nearly all her time if she had seen all these representatives of the press, she appointed me as a receiver and giver of messages. At this time there were three or four reporters particularly determined to see Mrs. Eddy. . . .

The chief man among this group, representing a big New York newspaper, was known as a particularly hard-boiled reporter and a steady drinker. He had been afflicted for some years with an extremely painful growth on his throat, which may have been cancerous and which at times completely overwhelmed him. . . .

Mrs. Eddy had asked me to call these men by telephone and inform them that it was impossible for her to see them. But she cautioned me at the same time, "Be sure to ask for the leading man and speak directly to him."

The telephone rang and one of the younger reporters answered the call. According to instructions, I asked to speak to the head man, whose name he mentioned, but was told that this man was too ill to come, could not come, and could not speak if he did come to the telephone, and could not speak any way. Remembering Mrs. Eddy's instruction I said, "Tell him to come to the telephone; he can hear what I say even if he can't talk."

Accordingly, the suffering newspaper man came to the telephone, showing decided anger (as I was later informed). He listened for a few moments. Those in the room, of course, could not hear what was being said, but when this man turned away from the telephone, he not only could speak perfectly, but was healed. . . .

Some years later a relative of this man called at my office in Boston, and gave me the following message: "My uncle requested me to see you and to tell you in his last days he turned to Christian Science, and he knew that he owed a debt of gratitude to Mrs. Eddy for his healing in Concord." (Irving Tomlinson, *Twelve Years with Mary Baker Eddy*, pages 69–71)

Storm dispelled (1907)

On several occasions I saw Mrs. Eddy dispel a storm; the first time was on August 3, 1907, in the late afternoon. The sky was overcast and it was very dark. Mrs. Eddy sat in her chair in the tower corner of her study, watching the clouds with a smile and a rapt expression on her face. She seemed to be seeing beyond the storm, and her present surroundings, and I do not think that she was conscious of my presence. In a few moments the clouds broke and flecked, and the storm was dissolved into its native nothingness. About half an hour later I took her supper tray to her, and she said to me, "Ada, did you see the sky?" I replied, "Yes, Mrs. Eddy." Then she said, "It (meaning the cloud) never was; God's face was never clouded." This agrees with what another student has recorded as having been said by Mrs. Eddy, namely, "When I wanted to dispel a storm, I did not say, 'there is no thunder, and no lightning,' but I said, 'God's face is there, and I do see it.' " (Adelaide Still reminiscences)

Lame arm healed (1908–1910)

Sunday afternoon, April 12, 1931, the writer [Irving Tomlinson] with Mrs. Tomlinson took for a drive Mrs. Martha McGaw. . . . While passing the Reservoir on Beacon Street, at the entrance to the Reservoir, Mrs. McGaw said: "Here a friend of mine had a wonderful case of healing. He had been troubled for a long time with a disabled arm. It was in such a bad condition that he could not lift his hand to his head. He hoped that he might see Mrs. Eddy, and while he was standing at the entrance to the Reservoir park, Mrs. Eddy came toward him in her carriage. He lifted his hand to his head to tip his hat to her, forgetting all about himself, forgetting that he had a lame arm, but he did it naturally and without inconvenience to himself. From that moment, he found himself completely healed and has been free from any inconvenience in that arm ever since. (Irving Tomlinson reminiscences)

Laura Sargent healed of exhaustion (1910)

One night in April, 1910, error seemed to strike at Mrs. Sargent quite severely. Miss Eveleth and I stayed with her until midnight when she seemed somewhat better, but when morning came she said she was not equal to her work and it seemed best for her to take a little time off to recuperate. Mrs. Eddy missed her very much and kept asking when she was coming back. She asked me what was the trouble with Laura, and I told her that she was just tired out and needed a rest. Mrs. Eddy immediately took a pad and wrote the article, "A Pæan of Praise," [*The First Church of Christ, Scientist, and Miscellany,* page 355] and gave instructions for it to be printed in the next issue of the *Sentinel.* She also wrote a note to Laura, and when she received an answer stating she would return in a few days, she was very happy. Laura came back a day earlier than she had promised, and surprised Mrs. Eddy. (Adelaide Still reminiscences)

[Mrs. Eddy's note follows:]

Apl 17, 1910

Give my love to Laura and tell her I have taken her up and it helped her and she can come back to me. Tell me when she will come. Tell Laura I healed her. (Document L10875)

A PÆAN OF PRAISE

"Behind a frowning providence
He hides a shining face."

The Christian Scientists at Mrs. Eddy's home are the happiest group on earth. Their faces shine with the reflection of light and love; their footsteps are not weary; their thoughts are upward; their way is onward, and their light shines. The world is better for this happy group of Christian Scientists; Mrs. Eddy is happier because of them; God is glorified in His reflection of peace, love, joy.

When will mankind awake to know their present ownership of all good, and praise and love the spot where God dwells most conspicuously in His reflection of love and leadership? When will the world waken to the privilege of knowing God, the liberty and glory of His presence,— where

"He plants His footsteps in the sea
And rides upon the storm."

MARY BAKER EDDY

APPENDIX

Biographical
Glossary

Biographical Glossary

*T*HE FOLLOWING ARE SKETCHES of individuals mentioned in this book or whose reminiscences have provided source material for the accounts of Mary Baker Eddy's healing works. For many, their association with Mrs. Eddy came about from the need for healing. Some were healed by her directly, others by reading her book *Science and Health with Key to the Scriptures,* and others were healed by her students.

A number of the people discussed in this glossary are said to have had Christian Science class instruction—Primary or Normal. A Christian Science teacher, one who has earned a certificate from the Board of Education of The First Church of Christ, Scientist, is qualified to teach Primary classes. Each teacher may hold one Primary class a year of not more than 30 pupils. A student who takes a Primary class is preparing to be a Christian Science practitioner—a Christian healer. Attending a Normal class—taught every third year—prepares an experienced Christian healer to be a Christian Science teacher.

Joseph Armstrong *(1848–1907)* A lumberman and banker in Kansas, Joseph Armstrong took up the study of Christian Science after his wife's healing of invalidism in 1886. He took three classes taught by Mrs. Eddy. Early in 1893 she asked him to serve as publisher of *The Christian Science Journal* and soon after placed him on The

Christian Science Board of Directors, the administrative board of The Mother Church. Mrs. Eddy asked Mr. Armstrong to be the Publisher of her own writings after she dismissed her adopted son from that position in 1896. Armstrong's duties as Publisher of the *Journal* were assumed by the Trustees of the newly reorganized Christian Science Publishing Society in 1898. At that time Mrs. Eddy made him Manager of the Publishing Society. He served in all three capacities—Director, Manager, and Publisher of Mrs. Eddy's writings—until his passing.

Addie Towns Arnold *(1858–1937)* Born in Tilton, New Hampshire, Addie Towns was acquainted with members of Mrs. Eddy's family there. Mrs. Eddy's niece, Ellen Pilsbury, was her school teacher. Addie was a child when she first saw Mrs. Eddy (then Mrs. Patterson) in 1862. Mrs. Patterson's husband Daniel was a prisoner of war in the South, and she was staying with her sister Abigail Tilton. Mrs. Arnold became interested in Christian Science in 1885 when she was healed of invalidism caused by rheumatic fever. It wasn't until after her healing, when she read of Ellen Pilsbury's healing in the Twentieth edition of *Science and Health,* that she realized that Mrs. Eddy and the Mrs. Patterson she had known as a child were the same person. During the winter of 1886–1887 Addie was taught Christian Science by Susie M. Lang, a student of Mrs. Eddy's. She devoted the rest of her life to the public practice of Christian healing.

Sarah Bagley *(1824–1905)* After being displaced from Captain Nathaniel Webster's house in Amesbury, Massachusetts, Mrs. Eddy (then Mrs. Glover) went to live in Miss Bagley's home for two months during the summer of 1868. She spent another six weeks there in the spring of 1870. Originally a spiritualist, Miss Bagley gave up that belief when she became Mrs. Eddy's fourth student. Although remaining a friend, Sarah never gave up head rubbing as part of her practice after Mrs. Eddy told her students in 1872 that they must discontinue this method as part of their healing treatment. Miss Bagley never joined her teacher's students' association or the church and never claimed to be a Christian Scientist. The two lost contact with each other after the mid 1870s.

Joshua F. Bailey *(1831–1907)* A Boston school teacher in the late 1850s, Joshua Bailey became a Special Agent of the United States Treasury Department in 1861. Working for Thomas Edison's Telephone and Light Company, he lived in South America from 1870 to 1874 and then in Europe until 1887. He took three classes from Mrs. Eddy: two Primary classes in 1888 and 1889, and a Normal class in 1889. She appointed him Editor of *The Christian Science Journal* in February 1889. Under her instructions he wrote the *Journal* article, "Christian Science and its Revelator," which is quoted on page 6. Mr. Bailey began teaching Christian Science in 1891 and continued in this work in New York City, along with his healing practice, until his passing.

Abigail Ambrose Baker *(1784–1849)* Mrs. Eddy's mother was a Puritan and very loving by nature. Her family was second in her affections only to God, and she felt closest of all to Mary, her youngest. Likewise no one was dearer to Mrs. Eddy than her mother. After Mary was born, Abigail Baker told her close friend, Sarah Gault, "I don't know what is to become of this child. While I bore her I had such sinful thoughts . . . a voice seemed to say to me, 'that which shall be born of thee shall bring about a great revolution.' " In addition, a conviction had come over her that the child she was carrying was some holy and consecrated thing. A voice would at times tell her, "That which shall be born of you will be born of God." And another recurring voice insisted throughout the nine months, "You can heal the sick." In describing her experience in the attic (see page 4), Abigail told Sarah, "My work and all around me and my own body disappeared before me. The world all seemed to combine in me and I seemed to take the place of God."[1]

Abigail Barnard Baker (Tilton) *(1816–1886)* Mrs. Eddy's elder sister. In her later years, Abigail declared, "I loved Mary best of all my brothers and sisters,"[2] but this love could not endure Mary's devotion to Christian Science (see page 39). In 1837, she married Alexander Tilton who owned a number of large textile mills. The town of Sanbornton Bridge was eventually renamed Tilton for his family. At the time of her passing, the newspapers reported, "Mrs. Tilton was the wealthiest lady in town and undoubtedly the most charitable, giving money liberally and in such a quiet manner that it was not generally known. She subscribed liberally toward the improvement of the village."[3]

Albert Baker *(1810–1841)* Mrs. Eddy's second eldest brother, whom she was closest to after her mother. One time when young Mary was sick in bed, Albert read to her Psalm 103 and she was healed (see pages 52–54). He served as her tutor between terms at Dartmouth College. He graduated with honors in 1834, and then accepted an offer from the former governor of New Hampshire, General Benjamin Pierce, to live with him and study law with his son, Franklin, a future President of the United States. In 1837 Albert was admitted to the bar of Suffolk County, establishing his practice in Hillsborough as successor to Franklin Pierce, who was then in Washington. Albert Baker served in the state legislature from 1839 to 1841. At the time of his passing, he had been nominated for the United States Congress in a district where such nomination by the political party practically guaranteed election.

Anna B. White Baker *(c1860–c1928)* Raised as a Quaker, she was married to Dr. Alfred E. Baker, a homeopathic physician from Philadelphia, Pennsylvania. They had Primary class instruction in 1896 with Flavia Knapp, whose husband Ira was a Director of The Mother Church. She went through Normal class with Mrs. Eddy in her last class in 1898. The following year Mrs. Eddy called Alfred Baker to serve as a Christian Science practitioner in

Concord, New Hampshire. Anna Baker was called to serve in Mrs. Eddy's household from time to time until they left Concord in 1902. In Mrs. Baker's reminiscences she recounts: "Mrs. Eddy had told us of Miss E[aton], a young child of 12 yrs. whom she had healed of cataracts in her early work in Science—She was visiting the parents, and seeing the child in a very ugly attack of temper, sternly rebuked her saying, 'when you can see to do right you will see with your eyes'—then naming the expression, 'you have no eyes.' The child instantly became still and her sight was restored."[4] Mrs. Eddy wrote the Bakers afterwards, "I write to say I forgot my close to that sentence to the blind Miss Eaton. It was this, 'You have no eyes'—meaning 'having eyes ye see not' then the cataract moved off."[5]

Elizabeth P. Baker Mrs. Eddy's stepmother, who married Mark Baker on December 5, 1850. Elizabeth Baker was Daniel Patterson's aunt, and it was through her that Mary met her second husband. Stepmother and daughter were on affectionate terms throughout their lives. Mrs. Baker's letter testifying to Ellen Pilsbury's healing of enteritis appeared in *Science and Health* from the Third edition through the 225th edition (see pages 223–224). A glimpse into their relationship can be seen in a card Elizabeth wrote to Mary on April 6, 1875: "My own Dear Daughter. It is a long time sinse I have heard one word from you, hope you are well and injoying the light of God's countanance and surrounded with kind friends, a good Minister, and good society. . . ."[6]

George Sullivan Baker *(1812–1867)* Mrs. Eddy's youngest brother, whom the family often called Sullivan. When a boy, he was healed of a severe ax wound to his leg when his father put little Mary's hand on the gash. When George left home in 1835, he found employment teaching weaving at the Connecticut State Prison. Three years later he returned to Sanbornton Bridge, joining his sister Abigail's husband, Alexander Tilton, as a partner in the mills which would become famous for the tweeds produced there. In 1849 he married Martha Rand and moved to Baltimore, Maryland, to establish himself in millwork. Toward the end of his life he became blind and returned to New Hampshire to spend his remaining years close to his family. He turned down his sister Mary's offer to pray for him.

Mark Baker *(1785–1865)* Mrs. Eddy's father was a Calvinist and an orthodox Congregationalist who, according to his youngest daughter, "kept the family in the tightest harness I have ever known."[7] "My father was very particular about the books his children read. He even objected to my reading the books that my brother brought from College such as Locke & Bacon, & forbade my reading under his roof Voltaire or Hume."[8] Mark Baker was well respected in Bow, sometimes acting as a lawyer for neighbors and even for the town itself. Although a farmer by occupation, he was civically active. He served as clerk for his church, chaplain for the town's militia, county coroner, and for ten years as a trustee of Sanbornton Academy. Mark, along with his eldest daughter Abigail, was responsible for removing Mary's son, George, from her care when he was a young child.

Martha Rand Baker Married to George Sullivan Baker in 1849, she was Mrs. Eddy's sister-in-law. Martha and Mary had become good friends while George was courting her, but their lives went separate ways after Martha and George moved to Baltimore, Maryland. Martha was present when Mary healed their niece, Ellen Pilsbury, in July 1867. In the 1880s when Mrs. Eddy invited Martha Rand Baker to attend one of her classes on Christian Science, she declined. Mrs. Eddy learned later that Martha had influenced Mrs. Eddy's father and her sister Abigail against her after she discovered Christian Science.

Martha Smith Baker (Pilsbury) *(1819–1884)* Mrs. Eddy's second elder sister was a school teacher before she married Luther C. Pilsbury at the end of 1842. Martha was Mary's nurse for a period in 1851 and 1852 to the extent that she had to give over the care of her two young daughters to relatives. She also loaned Mary and husband Daniel Patterson money for their home in North Groton. After Mrs. Eddy discovered Christian Science, Martha called on her sister when her twenty-two-year-old daughter, Ellen, was dying of enteritis (see pages 223–225). A number of years later, after Ellen had married, Martha again called on Mary for help when she had received news that Ellen was not expected to live through childbirth. Mrs. Eddy told her sister, "Go and when you reach there you will find her well." And so it was when Martha arrived at her daughter's home.[9]

Maryann Baker *(1746–1835)* Mrs. Eddy's grandmother, who shared the homestead with Mark and Abigail Baker and their family at the time Mary was born. With the Bible as a lesson book, she taught Mary to read.

Nancy Baker *(1802–1881)* Mrs. Eddy's cousin, daughter of Mark Baker's brother, James. Before Mark moved his family to Sanbornton Bridge, New Hampshire, Mary healed Nancy of a severe headache. Mrs. Eddy (then Mrs. Glover) and her student Miranda Rice visited Miss Baker in Bow, New Hampshire, in the late 1870s.

Samuel Dow Baker *(1808–1868)* Mrs. Eddy's eldest brother was responsible for introducing her to her future husband, George Washington Glover. Samuel married Glover's sister Eliza in 1832. After Eliza passed away, he married Mary Ann Cook in 1858. In 1862 Samuel and his wife escorted Mrs. Eddy (then Mrs. Patterson) to Portland, Maine, to be treated by Phineas Quimby. From 1895 to 1902, Mrs. Eddy oversaw and paid for her sister-in-law's care, providing her with a home and a nurse in her last years.

Samuel Putnam Bancroft *(1846–c1925)* One of Mrs. Eddy's earliest students, Samuel Bancroft went through her second class, which she taught in November and December of 1870. He was a charter member of the Christian Scientist

Association, organized in 1876, and he helped Mrs. Eddy to establish the Massachusetts Metaphysical College in 1881. He privately published his reminiscences in 1923 under the title, *Mrs. Eddy As I Knew Her in 1870*. In this work he writes: "She had the gift of the true orator, the ability to make her listeners forget the speaker in what she was saying. I had the privilege of being present and listening to her discourse with the deep thinkers of the past generation, Emerson, Bronson Alcott, and others. I have heard her at the public forum, where questions were propounded, and have never known her to fail to interest or at loss for an answer."[10]

Julia S. Bartlett *(1842–1926)*   At age sixteen, Julia Bartlett was left parentless and had to care for and raise five brothers and sisters, the youngest being three years old. She came to Christian Science in 1880 for the cure of physical ailments that had made her bedridden for periods at a time. Mrs. Eddy's husband, Asa Gilbert Eddy, treated and healed her. She was taught by Mrs. Eddy four times. Julia taught her own first class in Christian Science in 1884 and served in a number of prominent positions in the Church of Christ (Scientist) in Boston during the 1880s. She was one of twelve chosen Charter Members of The First Church of Christ, Scientist, when Mrs. Eddy reorganized her Church in 1892. She lived for a time at the Massachusetts Metaphysical College in Boston in the early to middle 1880s when Mrs. Eddy was working and teaching there. William Bradford Turner came to know Miss Bartlett when they were both members of the Church's Bible Lesson

Committee, and from time to time she would tell him of different experiences she had had with her teacher. After being taught by Mrs. Eddy, Miss Bartlett devoted the remainder of her life to Christian healing and teaching Christian Science.

Elsie Bergquist A Christian Scientist, she gave a reminiscence to The Mother Church in 1951 in which she related her father's encounter with Mrs. Eddy in 1909 and the healing that resulted therefrom (see page 218). She also wrote that her father "spoke so much about it [to the members of his church] that the minister of the church asked him not to relate the experience anymore there."

Harriet L. Betts *(1846–1937)* A Christian Science practitioner and teacher, Harriet Betts had Primary class with Mrs. Eddy in 1888 and Normal class in 1898. She worked in Mrs. Eddy's household for six weeks during December 1902 and January 1903. Mrs. Betts wrote of the time after she first arrived at Pleasant View: "Those first days were very happy ones. Whenever I was called to [Mrs. Eddy's] room she had many things to tell me. . . . When she wished to impress on my mind some instruction she would turn to her Bible, open it at random apparently, then read aloud a passage and say to me, 'There don't you see?' Once, on such an occasion [Mrs. Eddy] said: 'I could hear God's voice as distinctly as I could hear my son's voice.' " At another time Mrs. Eddy told her that "she wished she had taken certificates of her healing but people now would deny it. Healed every form of disease known. A dead body was nothing to her. A little corpse was handed to her, and he was alive. A mother sent for her saying 'You are too late, he is dead, but I wanted you to see him.' She told the mother to go away for an hour. The mother went and never dreamed the child would be restored. Three times she told the child to arise, then he sat up and rubbed his eyes. Then she told him to get down from the bed then she called him to her and took him in her lap. Mentally she commanded 'Come out of him.' The boy said 'I *is* tick, I *is* tick,' and doubled his fists to fight her. She had all she could do to keep him from pommeling her face. Then she made a plaything of two spools and he threw it on the floor. He was a wicked little boy of an awful temper. His face was purple for awhile from brain fever. In an hour's time he went to the door and met his mother."[11]

Mary B. G. Billings See Mary Baker Glover.

Clara Sweet Brady The daughter of Ella Peck Sweet, who was a member of Mrs. Eddy's household from June to November 1904. Mrs. Brady was a Christian Science practitioner from 1927 to 1935. In her reminiscences she recounted two of Mrs. Eddy's demonstrations of Christian Science that her mother witnessed: dissolving a gathering storm, and healing Mrs. Sweet of injuries received from an accident (see pages 277–278). Regarding the storm Mrs. Brady wrote, "During the period of [my mother's] stay at Pleasant View frequent severe storms of weather occurred. Mrs. Eddy perceived in them certain threatening phases of evil to be overcome. She would often call all the workers together and instruct them to handle these weather conditions. On one particular occasion the evidences of gathering storm being unusually ominous, Mrs. Eddy directed them all to work. They assembled in a room, as I understood, downstairs where were long french windows or doors. They had stood for a time in a group near one of these windows working without much effect, when very quietly Mrs. Eddy was heard descending the stair and approaching. She presently stood in their midst, pushing them gently aside, and said, 'It is very evident you are not making the demonstration, you are all mesmerized by the appearances.' As she stood and worked a few moments, the clouds broke and the black ominous appearing faded away."[12]

James Brierly *(1852–1926)* Brought up in the Congregational church, James Brierly began attending the Methodist Episcopal church after he married. "It was in the year 1884 that I first heard of Christian Science and became interested in it. It came about through the healing of my wife, who from a child 'had suffered many things of many physicians' who had failed to heal her of neuralgia, womb, stomach, and kidney troubles."[13] Mrs. Eddy taught Mr. Brierly in a Primary class in 1885, and a Normal class in 1887.

Arthur Brisbane *(1864–1936)* A nationally known journalist, he began at the age of nineteen working for the *New York Sun.* Later he was managing editor of the *New York World* for seven years, and after that, in 1897, became editor of the *New York Evening Journal.* At one point he was the publisher of the *New York Daily Mirror.* He finished his career as an editorial writer for the Hearst Syndicate and as America's highest paid newspaper writer, earning $260,000 per year. Mr. Brisbane was one of three newspapermen whom Mrs. Eddy granted an interview in her home at Pleasant View just prior to the "Next Friends" suit in 1907. At this meeting, Mrs. Eddy healed him of fatigue. He told Helena Hoftyzer and her husband about his healing of fatigue at the time of the interview, and she recounted it in a letter to The Mother Church in 1942.

Ezra M. Buswell *(1844–1906)* A veteran of the Civil War, Mr. Buswell became interested in Christian Science in 1884. He was healed by reading *Science and Health* of a disease his doctors had told him was incurable. He had four classes with Mrs. Eddy, including her last class in 1898. Mr. Buswell was arrested, tried, and acquitted for practicing medicine without a license in Nebraska in 1893. Mrs. Eddy called him to Concord, New Hampshire, in 1895 to practice Christian healing in her city. He also served, at Mrs. Eddy's request, as First Reader of the Concord church from 1897 to 1899. He returned to Nebraska in 1899 and devoted his remaining years to Christian healing and teaching Christian Science.

Stephen Chase *(1839–1912)* Originally a Quaker, Stephen Chase became interested in Christian Science as a result of being healed of blood poisoning. He was taught by Mrs.

Eddy in a Primary class in 1887. She appointed him as one of the original Directors of The Mother Church, a position he held from 1892 to 1912. He was also Treasurer of the Church from 1896 to 1912.

***Clara E. Choate** (1850–1916)* Mrs. Choate went through a Primary class taught jointly by Mr. and Mrs. Eddy in 1878 and took another Primary class with Mrs. Eddy in 1882. Mrs. Eddy healed her young son, Warren, in the early 1880s when he was sick (see pages 111–112) and healed Clara of severe diphtheria in 1881 (see pages 241–242). Mrs. Choate served as one of the directors of the Church of Christ (Scientist) in Boston for a period of time. She was dismissed from the Church and Mrs. Eddy's students' association in 1884 for working against the interests of the Cause. In 1904, after expressing regret for past actions, Mrs. Choate, at Mrs. Eddy's suggestion, joined The Mother Church.

In her reminiscences Mrs. Choate writes of one of her first visits with Mrs. Eddy: "One of my most precious memories of Mrs. Eddy is an interview I had with her in 1877—She had invited me to call to confer about class instruction with her. I had been wonderfully healed and this fact kept our attention fixed upon the healing—She emphasized this work of Christian healing as laying the foundation for her future work in *Science & Health*, as we then termed the Cause, more often than its present term of Christian Science, as near as I can quote her from memory she said this, 'Healing is what the world needs—Christ

taught this healing—our religious advancement or right-
eous living, one and the same, can be better gained by *good
healing* than in any other way.' 'To be a good healer, or a
true follower of Christ, you must demonstrate the law of
God, for His law does overcome disease. In overcoming
this you overcome sin.' I replied, why this will be glorious,
and she remarked in her sweet winsom and persuasive
manner, 'Your enthusiasm is just what I need to carry
forward this work of healing to the hearts of the people, for
healing is what *they* desire and what you and I and dear
Gilbert and other of my students must give them. I must
turn my attention from now on, to other departments of
the work of *Science and Health* which I am trying to
systematize. We must have a system. This great Cause
cannot progress in a desultory fashion. Everything must be
done decently and in order.' She then explained how the
students might be led, or swayed into thinking of *less*
important ways of the work, but healing is *the* work needed
first and last. She wished us all to follow her plans of
healing the sick for in so doing she could bring the Cause
and *Science and Health* into the acceptance of the *whole*
world and this could *not* be done in any other way. She
praised my voice, so earnest and honest and said my work
of healing the sick would be a great help to her in many
ways, and of useful service to the world. The healing was
the need of the hour she strongly urged—just the faithful,
patient healing work, by a life devoted and willing. This
was what *she* prayed for, so *she* might write, and form, and
plan, for the *wider* spread of the cause and the *real* uplifting

of man. I could not resist this appeal, who could? My healing had inspired *me*, and I longed to heal others, and by this wonderful truth as taught in Mrs. Eddy's *Science and Health*.

As she sat so unconsciously stately, in her modest rocking chair of black hair cloth, with the curls of brown ringlets tossing unnoticed upon her shoulders, her plain gown unornamented except by a long gold chain with which she toyed, and with eloquent upturned face, beaming with the glorious hopes of a soul inspired, I felt she was pleading for the sick world; the *whole sick world,* and is still pleading for the students to do this work, tho[ugh] now from an impersonal standpoint she still speaks. I was then a very young mother and oh this did touch my heart most deeply. She continued, 'all the emoluments in the world, all the admiration that can ever be excited is not, nor can be *surpassed* by the gratitude of a sick person healed, or, by the dejected painful, suffering one relieved and restored'— Mrs. Eddy never belittled this part of the work—She always impressed upon me that soul healing would inevitably come with the demonstration of *bodily healing.* 'I join the work of Christ when *I* heal the sick.' As she said this she rose and laying her hand gently upon my shoulder, with tears in her deep glorious eyes, 'Then are we the true soldiers of the Christ and His followers. What a help such work will be and how hopefully I am inspired to go on with my part and my writings.' She pointed to the groups of manuscript that lay in little piles about the floor around her chair, the black rocker in which she had been seated. Here let me say, 'Key to the Scriptures' and the chapter on 'Recapitulation' was not then in *Science and Health*, and she was considering including them so she told me. In concluding this all too short interview with Mrs. Eddy I resolved to join the class as she proposed, and remember the joy of my decision and the 'God bless you, my dear girl' which she so tenderly and impressively uttered as she accompanied me to the door of her home 8 Broad St. Lynn, Mass. All the way home I marvelled at her *faith* in God, at her divine healing and still feel to this day Mrs. Eddy really walked and talked with God. The effect upon me was to read *Science and Health*, and that very night a clearer consciousness came to me of what her mission was, and of the purpose of her book *Science and Health*."[14]

Lottie Clark Miss Clark was Julia Bartlett's nurse at the Christian Science Benevolent Association in 1924. Eight years later she gave to The Mother Church her reminiscences of what Miss Bartlett had told her about Mrs. Eddy. In 1939 Miss Clark wrote to The Mother Church about Mrs. Eddy's healing of a partially paralyzed woman in 1903 when she had welcomed Christian Scientists to Pleasant View (see pages 192–193). From 1948 to 1955 Miss Clark advertised in the *Journal* as a Christian Science practitioner in Boston.

Joseph I. C. Clarke *(1846–1924)* A journalist, dramatist, and poet. Between 1870 and 1906, Mr. Clarke worked for the *New York Herald*, the *New York Journal*, and *The Criterion*. His interview with Mrs. Eddy (see pages 183–184) was published in the *New York Herald* on May 1, 1901, and served as the basis for a chapter in his 1925 memoir, *My Life and Memories.* Excerpts from this interview appear in *The First Church of Christ, Scientist, and Miscellany*, pages 341–346.

Rev. Joseph Cook *(1838–1901)* A well-known lecturer who spoke throughout the United States, as well as in Great Britain and the Far East. He was also the founder and editor-in-chief of the periodical *Our Day.* His "Boston Monday Lectures" in Tremont Temple were famous in their time. It was in response to one of these lectures that Mrs. Eddy delivered a defense of Christian Science at the Temple in 1885.

Hiram Crafts A shoemaker by trade, Hiram Crafts was Mrs. Eddy's first student. She taught him in 1867 using her exegesis of Matthew 14 to 17. She lived in the Craftses' home in East Stoughton (now Avon), Massachusetts, for five or six months during the winter of 1866–67. In April 1867 the Craftses moved to Taunton and Mrs. Glover moved with them, staying three to four more months. Hiram set up his healing practice under his teacher's guidance, but after she left, he returned to shoemaking. In 1901 when various charges were being made in the press about the early days after Mrs. Eddy's discovery of divine Science, Mr. Crafts came to his teacher's defense.

Sarah Crosby She and Mrs. Eddy (then Mrs. Patterson) met while both were patients of Phineas Quimby. In the latter half of the summer of 1864, Mrs. Patterson stayed with Sarah Crosby in Albion, Maine. While there she healed Mrs. Crosby of injuries from vitriolic acid spilled on her face (see pages 32–33). Mrs. Patterson taught her Christian Science in 1870. Her spiritualistic leanings eventually caused her to put aside Mrs. Eddy's teachings.

George B. Day An ordained minister, George Day was taught twice by Mrs. Eddy in 1886, first in a spring Primary class and then in an autumn Normal class. He became pastor of the Chicago Christian Science church that same year. As chairman of the National Christian Scientist Association's convention in June 1888, he introduced her at the public meeting in Chicago's Central Music Hall. Even though she had previously stipulated that she would not be speaking, George Day told her, right as they were about to go on the platform, that the printed programs stated she would be delivering an address. "Science and the Senses" (*Miscellaneous Writings*, pages 98–106), was the title she subsequently gave to her talk, which she based on the ninety-first Psalm (see pages 129–130). The Reverend Mr. Day left the church in 1890 because of a resurfacing of traditional Protestant beliefs that caused theological turmoil within his thought.

Walter Scott Day In 1935 Mr. Day sent to The Mother Church his reminiscences of his encounters with Mrs. Eddy (see page 272). He was taught by Pamelia J. Leonard, a student of Mrs. Eddy's, who also served in her household several times between 1900 and 1907. Mr. Day was listed in *The Christian Science Journal* as a Christian Science practitioner in Chatham, Ontario, Canada, from 1903 to 1948.

Adam Dickey *(1864–1925)* Formerly a Methodist, Adam Dickey became interested in Christian Science as a result of his wife's healing in 1893. He received Primary class instruction in Christian Science from Henrietta Graybill in 1896 and entered the full-time healing practice in 1899. He received his teaching certificate in 1901 after attending The Mother Church's Board of Education Normal class taught by Edward Kimball, a student of Mrs. Eddy's. Mr. Dickey joined Mrs. Eddy's household as a secretary in 1908. While still a member of Mrs. Eddy's staff, he was elected to The Christian Science Board of Directors at her suggestion in 1910 and he served until his passing in 1925. He also served as Treasurer of the Church from 1912 to 1917.

In his memoirs Mr. Dickey writes of his three years as a member of Mrs. Eddy's household when she lived in Chestnut Hill, Massachusetts. At one point, in reference to *Science and Health,* she told him, "when I turn to this book, I am like a mechanic who turns to his tools and picks up the one he wants." At another time she called all of her household together and asked them, "can a Christian Scientist control the weather?" After each one had responded affirmatively, she told them, "They can't and they don't." Then she said, "They can't, but God can and does. Now, I want you to see the point I am making. A Christian Scientist has no business attempting to control or govern the weather any more than he has a right to attempt to control or govern sickness, but he does know, and must know, that God governs the weather and no other influence can be brought to bear upon it. When we destroy mortal mind's belief that it is a creator, and that it produces all sorts of weather, good as well as bad, we shall then realize God's perfect weather and be the recipients of His bounty in that respect. God's weather is always right. A certain amount of rain and sunshine is natural and normal, and we have no right to interfere with the stately operations of divine Wisdom in regulating meteorological conditions. Now I called you back because I felt you did not get my former instructions correctly and I want you to remember that the weather belongs to God, and when we destroy the operations of mortal mind and leave the question of regulating the weather to God, we shall have weather conditions as they should be."

Mary E. Dunbar Mrs. Dunbar's mother was a Baptist, her father was a Universalist who served as a justice of the peace and a Vermont state senator. Mary Dunbar was chronically ill as a child, and her health grew worse as an adult: "I never had health until the healing power of Truth and Love in Christian Science gave me my divine inheritance of health. All that human parents, doctors, money and care could do was done for me."[15] She went to a Christian Science practitioner for treatment in May 1886 and was healed in three days. The following Sunday Mrs. Dunbar heard Mrs. Eddy preach a sermon in Boston, and that night her little daughter Ethel was healed of lameness (see pages 127–128). Mrs. Eddy taught Mary Dunbar in an 1887 Primary class and an

1889 Normal class. She was called on occasion to serve in Mrs. Eddy's home for a day or two at a time. Mrs. Dunbar advertised in the *Journal* as a Christian Science practitioner in Boston from 1887 to 1929.

John Randall Dunn Mr. Dunn was taught Christian Science in 1906 by one of Mrs. Eddy's students, Sue Ella Bradshaw. His Normal class instruction was conducted by another of her students, Ella W. Hoag, who served in Mrs. Eddy's home several times from 1908 to 1910. Mr. Dunn entered the public healing practice in 1907. He served on the Board of Lectureship from 1916 to 1920 and 1923 to 1943. He was First Reader of The Mother Church from 1920 to 1923 and was appointed Editor of the Christian Science periodicals in 1943, a position he held until his passing in 1948. Two of his poems appear in the *Christian Science Hymnal.* Nemi Robertson told John Randall Dunn about her conversation with Mrs. Eddy related on page 80.

Joseph S. Eastaman *(1836–1910)* Joseph Eastaman was a sea captain for twenty-one years, having begun his career at sea as a cabin boy when he was just ten. When he returned from his last voyage, Captain Eastaman found his wife very ill. He turned to Mrs. Eddy to heal her, but she told him that he could learn how to heal her himself, so he went through Mrs. Eddy's Primary class in 1884. During this instruction he did heal his wife, and she accompanied him to the last lesson. For about a year Captain Eastaman was a member of the first Christian Science Board of Directors.

Mrs. Eddy created this Board through her 1892 Deed of Trust, which conveyed the land on which The Mother Church edifice was to be built. Considered by Mrs. Eddy to be quite a good healer, he devoted himself to its public practice. Six months before his passing, in 1910, Captain Eastaman wrote Mrs. Eddy a letter of gratitude in which he said: "You told me more than twenty-five years ago to take an office and to go to work on Christian Science healing. I did as you told me, and took *this room* on lease. It is just twenty-five years to-day since I began the most holy work (to my sense), and Oh, beloved Teacher, how many are the people that I have been the instrument to heal and help in that time, and how many are the people that are living in comparative health to-day who were given up by the medical profession and through my efforts in Christian Science to save them are to-day well and praising God for Christian Science."[16]

David Augustus Easton *(1843–1894)*   A Congregational minister, the Reverend Mr. Easton became interested in Christian Science through the healing of his wife of an incurable illness. He had previously attended Antioch College and Andover Seminary and was a member of the Alpha Delta Phi Society along with James Russell Lowell and Phillips Brooks. Mrs. Eddy healed him of consumption in 1891. With her recommendation, he was appointed as associate pastor of The Mother Church from 1893 to 1894. The Reverend Mr. Easton had previously been a guest preacher at the Church of Christ (Scientist) in Boston.

Asa Gilbert Eddy *(c1832–1882)*   Mrs. Eddy's third husband. They were married on January 1, 1877. A native Vermonter, Gilbert Eddy was a sewing machine salesman at the time he and Mrs. Glover were introduced by a mutual friend, who knew he was suffering from a heart condition. He was so improved by his future wife's treatment that he asked her to teach him Christian Science. In the spring of 1876, four weeks after completing his instruction, he established himself in the Christian healing practice and became the first of her students to announce himself publicly as a Christian Scientist. He also organized the first Christian Science Sunday School in 1881. Throughout their marriage, Gilbert devoted all his effort to supporting his wife in her mission to establish Christian Science.

Ruth Ewing *(1846–1923)* Mrs. Ewing became interested in Christian Science through her husband's healing of incurable respiratory problems: "I love to recall my earliest experiences as an investigator of its merits. By its means my husband was raised from what physicians pronounced immediately impending death. When, after having been restored to health and activity, he manifested a tendency to relapse, I went to see the practitioner in Chicago—a young student from under Mrs. Eddy's personal tuition—to whom my husband had been referred by the one in the East who had so wonderfully helped him. Betraying my anxiety, as I told my story of hope uplifted and then again depressed, she said to me with great earnestness, 'Why don't you study Christian Science and learn how to take care of your own family?' I was astonished and said to her, 'Can anybody take it up?' Her answer was, 'It is for every man, woman and child; it is simple Christianity.'"17 Mrs. Ewing took the advice and attended three of Mrs. Eddy's classes in the Massachusetts Metaphysical College. She lived in Chicago and devoted the rest of her life to the practice of Christian healing and to teaching Christian Science. Her husband, Judge William G. Ewing, was a well-known Christian Science lecturer from 1899 to 1910.

Alfred Farlow *(1857–1919)*   Raised as a Methodist in Illinois, Alfred Farlow became interested in Christian Science when he first encountered *Science and Health* in 1885. A neighbor who had been healed of invalidism, had loaned the book to his mother. After he was taught Christian Science by Janet Coleman, one of Mrs. Eddy's students, he applied to Mrs. Eddy herself for instruction. He attended her class in May 1887. Mrs. Eddy taught him two more times: in the Normal class in the autumn of 1887, and another Primary class in 1889. After his first class with Mrs. Eddy, Mr. Farlow left his manufacturing business to enter the full-time public healing practice. Mrs. Eddy called him to Boston at the beginning of 1899 to serve on the Church's three-member Committee on Publication, which was the organization's contact point with the news and publishing media. A year later she reduced the size of the Committee to one, with Mr. Farlow serving as that one with the title of Manager. He served in this position until 1914, when he retired to California to resume his work as healer and teacher.

Julia Field-King A student of Mrs. Eddy's, Mrs. Field-King was originally a homeopathic physician, having graduated from Oberlin College in Ohio and from Hahnemann Medical College in Philadelphia, Pennsylvania. Mrs. Eddy taught her in an 1888 Primary class and again in an 1889 Normal class. She appointed her as Editor of *The Christian Science Journal* in November 1891. Mrs. Field-King served in that position until September 1892, when she resigned. Four years later, Mrs. Eddy sent her to establish Christian Science in England. Her efforts proved successful and resulted in the formation of First Church of Christ, Scientist, London, and the dedication of the church's edifice in 1897. In June 1902 Mrs. Field-King was placed on probation as a member of The Mother Church due to her working against the interests of the Church because of theological misconceptions of Christian Science. Three months later she was dismissed at her own request. She reunited with the Church as a probationary member in 1917, remaining as such until her passing in 1919.

Lida W. Fitzpatrick A Methodist investigating Christian Science in 1887 for her diabetic husband, Mrs. Fitzpatrick took Primary classes from two of Mrs. Eddy's students: George Day and Hannah Larminie. This resulted in her healing her spouse. In 1888 Mrs. Eddy taught her in a Normal class, and afterward Mrs. Fitzpatrick established a public healing practice and taught Christian Science in Cleveland, Ohio. She was instrumental in organizing both First and Second Churches of Christ, Scientist, in that city.

Mrs. Fitzpatrick served in Mrs. Eddy's household three times: from May 1903 to February 1904, and from February to June and August to September in 1907. Mrs. Eddy would often share metaphysical ideas with her and the other members of the household. On one occasion Mrs. Eddy said, "If you have a patient who does not respond, would you say, I have done the best I could, and give up? No; it is the opportunity to rise higher and meet the demand." After Lida Fitzpatrick returned to Cleveland she devoted herself to healing and teaching until her passing in 1933.

Addie P. Forbes Miss Forbes became interested in Christian Science after her father, a Civil War veteran, was healed by reading *Science and Health.* She went on to enter the full-time healing practice as a Christian Science practitioner. She wrote to The Mother Church in 1959 about her meeting Mrs. Eddy while living in Concord, New Hampshire (see page 271).

Marie Chalmers Ford She wrote to Mrs. Eddy in 1906 about the healing she had experienced at the time they briefly encountered each other in Concord, New Hampshire, several years earlier (see pages 178–179). In describing this incident, Mrs. Ford wrote, "My eyes were flooded with tears of joy and my heart was overflowing with gratitude to you for this wonderful healing which had come to me through the Christ-love radiating from your consciousness."[18] Five months after sending this letter, Mrs.

Ford advertised in *The Christian Science Journal* as a full-time Christian healer in Toledo, Ohio.

Minnie Ford See Minnie Ford Mortlock.

Ebenezer J. Foster Eddy *(1847–1930)* A homeopathic physician from Vermont, Dr. Foster had graduated from the Hahnemann Medical College in Philadelphia, Pennsylvania, in 1869. After seeing a friend healed by reading *Science and Health,* he entered one of Mrs. Eddy's Primary classes in 1887, and was again taught by her in a Normal class in 1888. In November of that year, she adopted him as a son for his devotion to her and the support he had shown capable of giving to her life's work. Dr. Foster Eddy served as Mrs. Eddy's publisher from 1893 to 1896. His high opinion of himself and continual disobedience of her instructions caused Mrs. Eddy to send him to Philadelphia to establish himself as a Christian healer in that city and to shepherd the church there. Unable to work in harmony with his fellow Scientists, he was expelled from the church and went to visit his brother in Wisconsin for an extended stay. He resurfaced in 1907, at the time of the "Next Friends" suit, when he joined with Mrs. Eddy's birth son, George, as a plaintiff against Calvin Frye and Church officers. After the suit was dismissed, Mrs. Eddy wrote "Benny," as she called him, inviting him to come for a visit: "If you would like to call on me now, I have a little leisure, and would be pleased to see your dear face once more for a chat with you after the old way."[19] He did not accept the invitation and the two never saw each other again. Her final wish to him was a gift of $45,000 from her estate.

Alice Cluff French She was born and raised in Lynn, Massachusetts. Mrs. French's grandmother, Deborah J. Cluff, a Methodist, was a friend of Mrs. Eddy (then Mrs. Glover) at the time the latter was living in Lynn. Mrs. Glover, in fact, "asked Deborah if she might use the large front 'spare' bedroom on the second floor to write in,— that she was writing Science & Health and did not have much opportunity to get entirely away from others in her own home. Deborah graciously granted the request at once. Then when Mrs. [Glover] had finished writing the book she asked Deborah how much she owed her for the use of this spare room, but Deborah would not think of accepting money for it. Then Mrs. [Glover] said she knew what she would do—she would give Deborah a First edition of the book—Science and Health—which she did do, writing an inscription in it to Deborah from her."[20] Mrs. French sent her reminiscences of her father's healing by Mrs. Glover (see pages 234–235) to The Mother Church in 1937.

Calvin A. Frye *(1845–1917)* His father attended Harvard University and was in the same graduating class as Ralph Waldo Emerson. Originally a member of the Congregational church, Calvin became interested in Christian Science after his mother was restored to sanity by one of

Mrs. Eddy's students, Clara Choate. Mrs. Eddy first taught him in 1881 in Lynn, Massachusetts. He subsequently went through two other classes with her. As Mrs. Eddy's private secretary, Mr. Frye served from 1882 until her passing at the end of 1910 without ever taking a vacation. His duties as Mrs. Eddy's assistant changed and overlapped in accord with her activities. Apart from his secretarial responsibilities, he was, at times, her bookkeeper, coachman, aide, steward, spokesman, confidant, and metaphysical physician. Mrs. Eddy highly valued Calvin Frye's unwavering devotion to her and her lifework. After Mrs. Eddy's passing, Mr. Frye served as First Reader in First Church of Christ, Scientist, Concord, New Hampshire, and then in 1916 he was elected to a term as President of The Mother Church.

Mary G. Gale The wife of a physician in Manchester, New Hampshire. Mrs. Gale's healing of pneumonia, consumption, and morphine addiction in 1868 was the first catalyst that eventually caused Mrs. Eddy (then Mrs. Glover) to write *Science and Health*. In appreciation for her healing, Mrs. Gale gave Mrs. Glover a copy of William Smith's *Dictionary of the Bible*. This was particularly valuable to Mrs. Glover at this period, as she was devoting her full time to studying the Bible.

Sarah (Sally) Knox Gault (1784–1870) Her farm abutted the Bakers' in Bow, New Hampshire. Sarah, a Methodist, was one of the closest friends of Mrs. Eddy's mother. Her children were about the same age as the Baker children and all were playmates. Sarah and Abigail often discussed Scriptural passages and prayed together about challenges that came up in their daily lives. Mrs. Eddy sent a copy of *Science and Health* to Mrs. Gault's son, Matthew, when it was first published.

Caroline Getty *(1864–1955)* A dressmaker from Great Britain, Mrs. Getty began studying Christian Science when her elder sister sent her a copy of *Science and Health* in 1903. Not long after, she received Primary class instruction from Lady Victoria Murray, and in 1908 entered the full-time healing practice. In 1912 she moved permanently to Paris, and the following year was taught by Mrs. Eddy's student Laura Sargent in a Normal class. This resulted in her being the first Christian Science teacher in France. From 1914 to 1917, Mrs. Getty served on the three-member translation committee responsible for translating *Science and Health* into French. Later, she also worked on translating three other works of Mrs. Eddy's: the *Manual of The Mother Church, Rudimental Divine Science,* and *No and Yes.* In 1931 Mrs. Getty sent to The Mother Church her account of Mrs. Eddy healing an actor of smoking (see pages 275–276).

William I. Gill Originally from England, William I. Gill was a Methodist minister with Unitarian ideas. At the time he became interested in Christian Science he was pastor of a congregation in Lawrence, Massachusetts. Mrs. Eddy taught him in a March 1886 Primary class. In May of that year he was invited to serve on a trial basis as assistant pastor for the Church of Christ (Scientist) in Boston. In September he became Editor of *The Christian Science Journal,* but held the position for only four months. His firmly held orthodox beliefs about the reality of evil so interfered with his understanding of Christian Science that his separation from the Church was inevitable, and he resigned as assistant pastor in January 1887. Over the next few years he aligned himself with the "mind-curists" in Boston and Chicago.

James F. Gilman *(1850–1929)* Primarily a landscape artist, James Gilman spent the first twenty years of his adulthood drawing and painting mostly Vermont farm scenes. He became interested in Christian Science in 1884 via friends in Barre. At the end of 1892 he moved from Montpelier, Vermont, to Concord, New Hampshire, and met Mrs. Eddy for the first time on December 20. In March 1893 she asked Mr. Gilman to work with her on illustrating a new poem she had written, "Christ and Christmas." They worked together throughout the spring and summer to get the pictures just as she wanted them. The book was published at the end of November with both Mrs. Eddy and Mr. Gilman listed as "Artists." The following year Mr. Gilman moved to Gardner, Massachusetts, and then in 1899 to Athol, where he was instrumental in organizing a Christian Science Society. From 1895 to 1905 he advertised in local newspapers as a "Christian Science Healer." After this he decided to devote himself to his artwork again and did so until his passing.

George Washington Glover *(1811–1844)* Mrs. Eddy's first husband. They met in 1832 at her brother Samuel's wedding to Eliza Glover, George's sister. He jokingly told Mary at that time he would come back and marry her when she had grown up. Eleven years later, on December 10, 1843, they married and moved first to Charleston, South Carolina, and then to Wilmington, North Carolina. Six months later he passed on from yellow fever. A construction contractor, he was preparing to go to a job in Haiti with Mary at the time of his passing.

George Washington Glover II *(1844–1915)* Mrs. Eddy's son, George was born at the Baker's home in Sanbornton Bridge, New Hampshire, three months after his father's passing. After his grandfather, Mark Baker, remarried, he was sent to live with a family friend. Mrs. Eddy told one of her secretaries about this in 1906: "When my father married the second time, he refused to have George in the house any longer. After praying over him the whole night, I sent George to the old nurse, who had been called to the family for years in every case of sickness. Her name was Mary [Mahala] Sanborn, and she was married to a man by the name of Cheney. My agreement with them was that George should go to school and receive a liberal education. I married the second time, Dr. Patterson, for the express purpose of having the boy with me, but my husband thought that I cared more for George than I did for him, and again I had to send my son away. The last time I saw George [as a child], he was about ten years old. The Cheneys then moved to the far West [Minnesota]."[21]

After a number of years George ran away and joined the Union Army to fight in the Civil War. He was shot in the neck during a battle and expected to die, when his mother healed him (see pages 26–27). Mother and son did not meet again until his visit to Lynn, Massachusetts, in November 1879. At this time he was a gold prospector with a wife, Nellie, and two children, Edward and Mary. He had just moved from a farm in Fargo, North Dakota, to the Black Hills of Deadwood, South Dakota. Mrs. Eddy tried to teach him Christian Science, but he would not continue after the first lesson. In the winter of 1887–88 George brought his family (with another daughter, seven-year-old Evelyn) east for a six-month visit to his mother in Boston. In 1893 he brought his son, four-year-old George, for a brief visit to Pleasant View in Concord, New Hampshire. He visited his mother again in 1902, this time bringing his daughter Mary with him. In 1907 he and the same daughter were plaintiffs, along with other relatives, in the "Next Friends" suit against Calvin Frye and Church officers, claiming his mother to be mentally incompetent. After the suit was dismissed, he agreed to a $245,000 settlement from her estate with the condition that he not contest her will after her passing. He did not keep his promise.

Mary Baker Glover *(1877–1968)* Mrs. Eddy's grand-daughter was born in Fargo, North Dakota. She was healed by her grandmother of crossed eyes at the time her father was visiting his mother in 1879. Mary met her grand-mother for the first time in November 1887. In 1907 she was one of the plaintiffs in the "Next Friends" suit, along with her father and a few other relatives. The estrangement was not a continuing one, despite the family's actions contesting Mrs. Eddy's will. Mary and her two sons, Harry and Marion Billings, enjoyed a warm relationship with Christian Scientists and Mrs. Eddy's church. All three joined The Mother Church as members in 1936.

Mary Crane Gray After doctors advised Mrs. Gray to commit her husband to a sanitarium because of insanity, which she refused to do, a neighbor gave her *Science and Health:* "I was drawn to the statement on page 10 of the Preface . . . 'The divine Principle of healing is proved in the personal experience of any sincere seeker of Truth.' " She then went to the Rector of the Episcopal church of which she was a member and asked him to heal her husband. "His reply was: 'My dear child. If I should start doing that work, I wouldn't have any time for the regular church work. Take your physicians' advice, and place him where he can have proper care.' As I left the Rectory, I thought what is the regular church work, if it isn't healing the sick? It is one of our Lord's commandments. Then the 'still small voice' said, 'why don't you try Christian Science?' It is our God-given right to think and act rightly for ourselves, was my answer, and I wrote at once to Mrs. Eddy, asking her to heal my husband, explaining that I had confidence in her because of what I had just been reading of her writings."[22] Mrs. Eddy healed her husband in 1905. Mrs. Gray wrote all of this in a letter to The Mother Church in 1935.

Charles E. L. Green Mrs. Eddy (then Mrs. Glover) healed Charles Green's four-year-old daughter, Josephine, of brain fever in 1873 (see pages 233–234). Around 1907 Mr. Green gave Alfred Farlow a statement about this incident. In that statement he said, "Nobody took any stock in it [Josephine's healing], and the event was forgotten." Mr. Green included at the end of his statement a testimony of his own recent healing. "Two years ago when I turned to Christian Science I was a wreck from rheumatism, nervous prostration, and was in hell from fear of the insane asylum. The Doctors could do me no good. I went to a C. S. practitioner for two weeks, with no perceptible benefit; then I went to work for myself with the aid of the book [*Science and Health*]. I was healed of the rheumatism, nervous troubles and eczema of 16 years standing. When my son came home and I showed him my arm that had been so disagreeable before and which was so completely healed, he would not credit it as the work of Christian Science. Rheumatism so completely gone that I can now run like a boy, at the age of 63 years, where before I had to slide down stairs because my knees refused to bear my weight, and when I moved them they squeaked like a rusty hinge. This summer I took a walk of 11 miles in one stretch."[23]

Helen M. Grenier Mrs. Eddy healed her around 1880 when Helen was a little girl in Lynn, Massachusetts. Her statement of this healing was given to The Mother Church in 1917. At the end of her statement, Mrs. Grenier writes, "Though I have passed through many trials and afflictions which might have been averted had I known and understood her [Mrs. Eddy's] teachings then, I am convinced that the benediction of that hour has at last brought me to the Truth. I have had many demonstrations of Divine Love in my own body. One—an instantaneous healing after being deformed for four years and pronounced incurable by physicians. The deformity was caused by a shock to the nerves of the spine. Another—the healing of a crushed finger which was caught in a cog wheel; the healing was marvelous, to sense, but under treatment I suffered no pain or loss of finger, although loss of arm—blood poison—etc. was predicted. The bone grew in and the flesh filled in where it had been torn away, healing rapidly."[24]

Septimus J. Hanna *(1844–1921)* Judge Hanna is best known as the Editor of the Christian Science periodicals from November 1892 to June 1902. His wife, Camilla, served as assistant editor. They were both in Mrs. Eddy's last class, which she conducted in November 1898. In December 1886 he had gone through a Primary class taught by Rev. J. S. Norvell, a student of Mrs. Eddy's, who had previously been a Baptist minister.

Septimus Hanna was admitted to the Illinois bar in 1867 and then moved to Council Bluffs, Iowa, where he held the office of judge of the county court. In 1871 he moved to Chicago, Illinois, to practice law, remaining there until 1879, when he moved to Leadville, Colorado, for his health. Judge Hanna became interested in Christian

Science in 1886 because of the healing Camilla experienced from reading *Science and Health*.

A year and a half after Mrs. Eddy first met Judge Hanna in 1891 she asked him to become the Editor of *The Christian Science Journal*. In March 1894 she appointed him to the pastorate of The Mother Church. When she ordained the Bible and *Science and Health* as the Pastor of her Church at the end of 1894, Judge Hanna became the First Reader in the Church. He served on The Christian Science Board of Directors in October 1895, but had to withdraw from this after a month because his other official responsibilities, such as Editor and First Reader, were all that he could effectively handle. He was elected President of the Church in October 1896 and served for two years. In 1902 he retired from his positions of Editor and Reader and was appointed to the Church's Board of Lectureship. He served as a Christian Science lecturer until 1914. In 1898 Judge Hanna was elected vice-president of the Church's Board of Education, and taught the Normal course in 1907. Upon Mrs. Eddy's passing, he succeeded her as president of that Board, serving in this office until his own passing in 1921.

Margaret E. Harding Mrs. Harding's account of the healing of George Norton's club feet by Mrs. Eddy (then Mrs. Patterson) was sent to The Mother Church in 1929. The incident was told to Mrs. Harding by George's mother, "Mrs. James Norton, the wife of a well-known musician of the old school, some time before 1900—while all three members of the Norton family were alive."[25] Mrs. Harding's daughter, Elizabeth, became interested in Christian Science as a result of being told about this healing.

Frances Thompson Hill (1886–1979) Her parents were pupils of Augusta Stetson, a student of Mrs. Eddy's. When she was twenty, Frances came to Boston to study music. Three years earlier she had been among the ten thousand Christian Scientists who were attending the annual meeting of The Mother Church and were invited to visit Pleasant View. She heard Mrs. Eddy speak from the second-floor balcony. Later Frances also had a private visit with Mrs. Eddy and at that time played for her the hymn "'Feed My Sheep'" which begins with the words "Shepherd, show me how to go." In 1911 Frances married Calvin C. Hill, who had worked for Mrs. Eddy for a number of years while she lived in Concord. His reminiscences appear in the biography *We Knew Mary Baker Eddy*. Mrs. Hill became active in gathering the reminiscences of others who had contact with Mrs. Eddy and gave these to The Mother Church in 1946. She served on the *Christian Science Hymnal* revision committee that produced the Church's current hymnal. She also wrote the text of the "Easter Hymn," no. 413. In 1944 Mrs. Hill advertised in *The Christian Science Journal* as a Christian healer, devoting the rest of her life to the full-time healing practice.

Emma C. Hopkins *(1849–1925)* Formerly a member of the Congregational church, Emma Hopkins was taught by Mrs. Eddy in an 1883 Primary class and the following year was appointed Editor of *The Christian Science Journal.* She lasted only seven months in this position before Mrs. Eddy had to remove her because of the influence over her of another student (Mary Plunkett). Mrs. Plunkett led her into the "mind-cure" school of healing. Mrs. Hopkins then became editor of the *Mind Cure Journal* (later renamed the *Mental Science Journal*). In 1886 she and Mrs. Plunkett went into partnership, forming "Christian Science institutes" in Chicago, Detroit, St. Paul, and other cities in the midwestern United States. Mrs. Hopkins served as teacher and Mrs. Plunkett, as business manager. Emma Hopkins was especially interested in mysticism and theosophy. In the 1890s she became a leader in the New Thought movement. She taught Ernest Holmes, the founder of the Church of Religious Science. Two other prominent students were Charles and Myrtle Fillmore, founders of the Unity School of Christianity.

Charles Carroll Howe Curiosity rather than interest in Christian Science motivated Charles Howe to attend the first service held in the Original Edifice of The Mother Church on Sunday, December 30, 1894. He saw Mrs. Eddy on a number of public occasions between 1895 and 1900. Mr. Howe actually met her when she was entering the Church on January 5, 1896, to deliver a Communion address. It was at this time that he was healed of disabilities caused by typhoid fever. While he read *Science and Health* and other Christian Science literature, he never joined the Church. He sent his reminiscences to the Church in 1932.

Emilie B. Hulin Originally a member of the Congregational church, Mrs. Hulin attended Mrs. Eddy's Primary class in November 1888. The previous year she had been taught Christian Science by Pamelia J. Leonard, a student of Mrs. Eddy's. Emilie served in Mrs. Eddy's household a number of times, first in the spring of 1895, then from the following winter for almost a year, and after that as the need arose. In her reminiscences she wrote, "I saw [Mrs. Eddy] in her own home life and in various conditions of belief calling for demonstration, and I never saw her fail, but she adhered to what she taught and lived. Many were the lessons I learned at this time and which I have been most grateful for throughout the subsequent years, and never have I lost faith in Christian Science or its Discoverer, because I have seen her many wonderful demonstrations over the claims of the deceitful senses. At one time the 'First Members' were called to Concord to receive a lesson from her. It was a hot season in July. Twenty-five responded to her call. I was seated in the bay window of her home when I noticed the appearance of a storm gathering and it was very violent and cyclonic in its appearance. Mrs. Eddy's attention was drawn to it by the flapping of the window curtains. She ceased talking for a few minutes and was perfectly silent. The clouds came to a sudden stop and then disappeared and the sun was shining again. The Concord paper the next day spoke of it as a wonderful phenomenon."[26] Mrs. Hulin advertised as a practitioner and teacher in *The Christian Science Journal* from 1890 to 1931. She lived in Brooklyn, New York, until 1924, and then moved to Brookline, Massachusetts. From 1923 to 1926 she was vice-president of The Mother Church's Board of Education, teaching the Normal class in 1925.

***William B. Johnson** (1839–1911)* Born in England, William Johnson came to the United States with his parents when he was a child. During the Civil War, he served three years in General Joseph Hooker's brigade. He became interested in Christian Science in 1882 after being healed of disabilities caused by injuries received in the war. Taught by Mrs. Eddy in one of her 1884 Primary classes, he then joined the Church of Christ (Scientist) in Boston. Mr. Johnson became Clerk of the Church in 1887 and held that position continuously until 1909. Mrs. Eddy appointed him to The Christian Science Board of Directors when she created that Board in her September 1, 1892, Deed of Trust, which served to reorganize the Boston congregation into The Mother Church, The First Church of Christ, Scientist. He remained on the Board through May 1909. In a letter of gratitude to Mrs. Eddy he wrote that he was devoting all his time to study and practice.

Julia Michael Johnston Her mother, Annie R. Michael, was a student of Mrs. Eddy's, having taken a Normal class in 1887. Julia received her Primary class instruction in

Christian Science from her mother. She first advertised as a full-time Christian healer in *The Christian Science Journal* in 1913. She became a teacher of Christian Science after attending The Mother Church's Normal class taught by Clifford P. Smith in 1916. Mrs. Johnston herself taught the Normal class in 1940. After this she wrote the biography, *Mary Baker Eddy: Her Mission and Triumph,* which was published in 1946. Over the years, from the 1930s through the 1950s, she wrote a series of articles about two children growing up in Christian Science at the turn of the century. These were gathered together and published in 1959 as a booklet entitled *Elizabeth and Andy.*

Elizabeth Earl Jones *(1881–1963)* Though they never personally met, Miss Jones saw Mrs. Eddy three times when she was visiting Concord, New Hampshire, in 1902 and 1903. The two did briefly correspond in the years following. Miss Jones became interested in Christian Science when she was healed by it in 1898 of chronic headaches, dyspepsia, and neuralgia, which she had suffered from since childhood. She was taught Christian Science by one of Mrs. Eddy's students, Sue Harper Mims. After that she decided to devote her full time to Christian healing. In 1940 she became a Christian Science teacher when she went through the Church's Normal class taught by Julia M. Johnston.

Richard Kennedy *(1849–1921)* Born in Barnet, Vermont, Richard Kennedy first met Mrs. Eddy (then Mrs. Glover) in Amesbury, Massachusetts, in 1868, when he was nineteen years old and boarding at the Websters' home. He became Mrs. Glover's second student that same year. This was during the period when she was devoting most of her time to Bible study. In February 1870 the two moved to Lynn and formed a legal partnership, wherein she was to guide his healing practice and he would pay her a portion of his earnings. During the latter half of 1871 Mrs. Eddy discovered Richard Kennedy's immorality with one or more patients, and their partnership was dissolved in May 1872. After this Mr. Kennedy did whatever he could to turn Mrs. Eddy's students away from her. He did this through mental and verbal manipulation. Richard Kennedy was committed to an insane asylum in Vermont in 1918. He passed away three years later from an unsuccessful operation for intestinal trouble.

Edward A. Kimball *(1845–1909)* With only an eighth-grade education, Edward Kimball became a successful Chicago businessman, working twenty years in lumber and manufacturing before becoming interested in Christian Science in 1887. He learned of Christian Science from his sister after he had spent more than twelve months in a sanatorium, barely able to digest the simplest of foods. Healed, he attended two of Mrs. Eddy's Primary classes in 1888 and 1889. He was also a member of her last class in 1898. In 1893, at Mrs. Eddy's request, Mr. Kimball coordinated the Christian Science activities at the Chicago World's Fair and World Parliament of Religions. Mrs. Eddy appointed Edward Kimball to the original Christian Science Board of Lectureship in 1898. Considered one of the ablest lecturers of Mrs. Eddy's day, he served as chairman of the Board of Lectureship and went on to deliver more than eighteen hundred lectures during the next twelve years. In 1898 Mrs. Eddy also asked him to serve as teacher in the Church's new Board of Education. He taught four Normal classes to prepare new teachers of Christian Science. In January 1901 Mrs. Eddy asked him to oversee her defense in the libel suit that had been brought by Josephine Woodbury in 1899. Six months later the suit was decided in Mrs. Eddy's favor. In September 1901 she chose Mr. Kimball, along with William McKenzie, to act as editorial assistants to her when she was working on her final major revision of *Science and Health with Key to the Scriptures,* which was published at the beginning of 1902 in its 226th edition.

George Kinter After years of struggling with ill health, George Kinter became interested in Christian Science when his mother-in-law was healed and she loaned him *Science and Health.* He regained his health in 1888 while reading this book. Later that same year he was taught Christian Science by Annie V. C. Leavitt, a student of Mrs. Eddy's. In 1890 he decided to devote his full time to Christian healing and advertised as a practitioner in *The Christian Science Journal.* Mr. Kinter became a teacher of Christian Science upon completion of the Normal class taught by Edward Kimball in The Mother Church's Board of Education in

1901. Mrs. Eddy called Mr. Kinter to serve in her household as a secretary and metaphysical worker in December 1903. This first time in Mrs. Eddy's household Mr. Kinter remained for one year. After that she asked him to work in her home for shorter periods during 1905, 1907, 1909, and 1910. After Mrs. Eddy's passing he devoted the rest of his life to teaching and practicing Christian Science in Chicago, Illinois.

Ira O. Knapp *(1839–1910)* A school teacher, farmer, and local politician, who held virtually every office in the town of Lyman, New Hampshire, Ira Knapp felt most comfortable with Universalism as a faith before he became interested in Christian Science through his sister-in-law. Both he and his wife, Flavia, were healed by it in 1884, and that same year they attended one of Mrs. Eddy's Primary classes. They also went through another of her Primary classes the following year. In 1887 and 1888 Ira Knapp again had classes with Mrs. Eddy, the last, a Normal class. Mr. Knapp was one of the original Directors of The Mother Church appointed by Mrs. Eddy in 1892. He served as chairman of The Christian Science Board of Directors from the time he was appointed until 1903, and he remained on the Board up to the time of his passing.

Annie M. Knott *(1850–1941)* Born in Scotland and raised a strict Presbyterian, Annie Macmillan came to North America with her parents when she was twelve. Due to her family's connections (her cousins founded the Macmillan publishing company), she had the opportunity while still a girl to meet Bronson Alcott, Susan B. Anthony, and Elizabeth Cady Stanton. After her marriage, Annie Knott lived in London, England, from 1877 to 1882. She first heard of Christian Science when she moved to Chicago, Illinois, and was told about healings that had been accomplished through this new faith. But she didn't consider turning to it until after her young son, not expected to live after swallowing much of a bottle of carbolic acid, was quickly healed in Christian Science. After witnessing the healing, Mrs. Knott studied Christian Science with Bradford Sherman, one of Mrs. Eddy's students in Chicago. She moved to Detroit, Michigan, in 1885 and began a public practice of Christian healing. In 1887 she was taught by Mrs. Eddy in a February Normal class, and the following year attended another class with her. In 1898 Mrs. Eddy appointed her to The Mother Church's Board of Lectureship, where she served until 1903 when she became an Associate Editor of the Christian Science periodicals. Mrs. Knott was the first woman to be elected to the Church's Board of Directors. She served from 1919 to 1934, when she retired to devote her full time to Christian healing and the teaching of Christian Science.

John Lathrop *(1871–1941)* Raised in the Presbyterian church, John Lathrop became devoted to Christian Science after his mother, Laura, was healed by it in 1884 of a chronic illness that had left her an invalid. Several years after Mrs. Lathrop was taught by Mrs. Eddy, he went through one of his mother's Primary classes. In 1898 he was taught by Mrs. Eddy in her last class. At her request, he came to Boston from September to December 1899 to help with her defense during Josephine Woodbury's libel suit. He was also called to serve as a member of Mrs. Eddy's household from May to November 1903 and from September 1907 to February 1908. When Mr. Lathrop was about to return to his home in New York City this last time, Mrs. Eddy told him to devote himself to becoming the best Christian healer he could be (see page 209). In 1911 Mr. Lathrop was elected to serve as First Reader in The Mother Church and then as President of the Church from 1914–1915. He was appointed to the Church's Board of Lectureship in 1918, and served as a lecturer for seven years. After that he devoted his full time to Christian healing and the teaching of Christian Science.

Laura Lathrop *(1843–1922)*   The daughter of a Methodist minister, Laura Lathrop had become an invalid at seventeen from several physical problems that doctors would eventually pronounce incurable. After her husband's passing in 1884, and at the urging of friends, she traveled to Chicago, Illinois, in January 1885 to have Christian Science treatment, though she was highly skeptical of it. After nine weeks of treatment by Caroline Noyes, a student of Mrs. Eddy's, Mrs. Lathrop was so improved that she decided to attend Mrs. Noyes' Primary class in April. Four months later she was a pupil in one of Mrs. Eddy's Primary classes in the Massachusetts Metaphysical College. After the class Mrs. Eddy asked her to go to New York City to help establish a Christian Science church there. In 1886 and 1887 Mrs. Lathrop again had class with Mrs. Eddy. In 1891, again at her teacher's request, she organized Second Church of Christ, Scientist, New York City. Mrs. Eddy healed Mrs. Lathrop of heart disease when the latter was invited to visit her teacher in the winter of 1886–87 (see pagess 266–267). Mrs. Lathrop devoted her life to Christian healing and the teaching of Christian Science.

Ellen Brown Linscott Ellen Brown was a young woman when she was first taught Christian Science by Mrs. Eddy in 1883, and she was one of four students who lived at the Massachusetts Metaphysical College for several months during that year. In 1885 and in 1887 she attended class with Mrs. Eddy. Ellen Brown married John Linscott in 1887, and together they worked to establish Christian Science in Chicago, Denver, Washington, D.C., and other cities. Ellen Linscott devoted her entire adult life to the full-time public practice of Christian healing and to teaching Christian Science.

John Freeman Linscott *(1837–1931)* At the age of fourteen John Linscott went to work on a whaling ship. After four years at sea he worked for a time in a law office until the Civil War broke out and he joined the Massachusetts cavalry, serving throughout the conflict. In the years following the war he entered the United States Secret Service where he worked to uncover and apprehend counterfeiters. He also learned quite a bit about liquor and drugs from his work, which led to a very successful career in lecturing for the temperance movement. It was during this period of his life that he first heard about Christian Science. In 1887 Captain Linscott was taught by Mrs. Eddy in both a Primary and a Normal class. After this he devoted himself to Christian healing and the teaching of Christian Science. He also worked with his wife, Ellen, to establish Christian Science churches in a number of cities around the country. He was appointed to The Mother Church's Board of Lectureship in 1900 and served in this capacity until 1904. Three years later the Church placed Captain Linscott on probation as a Christian Science teacher and Church member. He remained on probation for the rest of his life.

Delia S. Manley *(1850–1919)*   Raised in the Baptist church, Delia Manley was in poor health until she turned to Christian Science in the early 1880s. When she was thirteen she had had typhoid fever which left her with consumption. As an adult she was diagnosed and treated by numerous physicians, but all of them said her case was hopeless. When one of the doctors advised Mrs. Manley to try Christian Science, her husband contacted Mrs. Eddy's student, Clara Choate, to treat her. After her healing, she was taught by Mrs. Eddy in an 1882 Primary class. When Gilbert Eddy passed away, Mrs. Manley stayed several days with her teacher. Mrs. Manley went through class again with Mrs. Eddy in 1884 and in 1887. She lived in Fall River, Massachusetts, and devoted the rest of her life to the public healing practice and to teaching Christian Science to others.

Arthur A. Maxfield "In the spring of 1891 my father, a civil war veteran, came under treatment by Captain J. S. Eastaman, C.S.D. of Boston, Massachusetts. He, the Captain, visited my father twice a week. I used to meet him at the depot with a horse and carriage, take him to see my father, then back to the depot in time for him to take the train back to Boston. On one of these trips he told me of a healing by Mrs. Eddy which he had witnessed that happened a day or two previously."[27] This healing appears on page 147. Mr. Maxfield joined The Mother Church in 1895 and sent his reminiscences to the Church in 1934.

William P. McKenzie *(1861–1942)* The son of a Presbyterian minister, William McKenzie himself became one, graduating in 1889 from Knox Theological College, Toronto, Ontario, Canada. After attending the Auburn Theological Seminary in Ohio, he was ordained by the Presbytery of Rochester, New York, in 1890 and served as pastor to a small church for four years. During this period he also taught English literature and rhetoric at the University of Rochester. He first heard of Christian Science in 1891 at the home of a friend who had invited Daisette Stocking, a Christian Scientist from Cleveland, Ohio, to explain her new faith to afternoon guests. He immediately bought a copy of *Science and Health* and began to study it. He also began a correspondence with Miss Stocking asking her many questions. He was taught Christian Science by Daisette's teacher, Pamelia Leonard, one of Mrs. Eddy's students. Mr. McKenzie was also a member of Mrs. Eddy's last class in 1898. The two had first met when she invited him to visit her on Christmas Day, 1894, and by the following September he advertised in *The Christian Science Journal* as a practitioner, devoting his full time to the practice of Christian healing. In 1896 Mrs. Eddy appointed him to The Mother Church's Bible Lesson Committee, which prepared the weekly Lesson Sermons used in all Christian Science church services on Sunday. He remained on this committee for twenty-one years. On January 25, 1898, Mrs. Eddy reorganized The Christian Science Publishing Society and appointed Mr. McKenzie to the three-man Board of Trustees. He served as a Trustee until 1917, when he was elected Editor of the Christian Science periodicals. In 1922, he was again made a Trustee and held the position until elected to The Christian Science Board of Directors ten years later. He served as a Church Director for the rest of his life. Mr. McKenzie married Daisette Stocking in 1901.

Archibald McLellan *(1857–1917)* A successful businessman who had also earned a degree from Kent College of Law in Chicago, Illinois, Mr. McLellan became interested in Christian Science after seeing the benefit it brought to the health of his wife. He was so impressed by what he heard when Mrs. Eddy spoke in Chicago in 1888[28] that he began to study Christian Science in earnest and received Primary class instruction, along with his wife, from Ruth B. Ewing, a student of Mrs. Eddy's. He became very involved with Christian Science church work in Chicago, and was appointed Committee on Publication for the state of Illinois in 1900. He was never a Christian Science practitioner or teacher, but he did attend a Board of Education Primary class taught by Edward Kimball in 1903. Mrs. Eddy appointed Mr. McLellan as Editor of the Christian Science periodicals in 1902. A year later she put him on The Christian Science Board of Directors, where he served as its chairman. He continued in both positions up to the time of his passing. He was a frequent visitor both in Pleasant View and Chestnut Hill. "He is one of Nature's noblemen,"[29] Mrs. Eddy said of him. In 1913 he wrote to a friend, "It is for me to fulfill the trust reposed in me by our Leader as I see it, and leave the results with divine Love."[30]

Adelaide Morrison Mooney   Her father, Henry H. Morrison, was the Western Union Manager in Concord, New Hampshire: "I was employed as a Western Union operator in my father's office at this time. While Mrs. Eddy lived at Pleasant View it was her custom to take daily drives to the city. At one time no one was permitted to stop her carriage except our Western Union Messengers. They always spoke of her genial smile and generosity to them. Many times my father would go out to her carriage, when she would stop at the office for telegrams and sometimes would ask his advice."[31] In her reminiscences, which she sent to The Mother Church in 1943, Mrs. Mooney recounts her father's healing by Mrs. Eddy: "At the time of the 'Next Friends' suit, father and I worked from ten to fifteen hours daily sending newspaper copy. This was done without any sense of fatigue. . . . Mrs. Eddy presented autographed copies of *Science and Health* and *Miscellaneous Writings* to my father."[32]

***Dr. Alpheus Morrill** (1808–1874)* Dr. Morrill was related to Mrs. Eddy through his marriage to Hannah Baker, a first cousin. He graduated from Dartmouth Medical College, afterward settling in Columbus, Ohio, where he became one of the leading physicians in the state. By 1847, when he returned to New Hampshire and opened his office in Concord, he had become a homeopathist. The first president of the New Hampshire Homeopathic Medical Society, Dr. Morrill introduced Mrs. Eddy (then Mrs. Glover) to the practice around 1848. She wrote that, "homœopathy came like blessed relief to me."[33] After she had studied homeopathy in order to treat not only herself, but others, too, he counseled her in her practice. They maintained a warm relationship throughout his lifetime.

Henry Morrison See Adelaide Morrison Mooney

Minnie Ford Mortlock As a teenager, Minnie Ford came to know Mrs. Eddy after her family emigrated from England in 1893, settling on a small farm near Pleasant View: "One day as Mrs. Eddy was driving by our house our guinea hens made such a noise that they scared her horses, and that evening she sent word over to ask my Father if he would loan her two of them to put into her stable so that her horses could get used to them, which he did. That is how she came to hear about us. She became quite interested in us and especially in me. I was then about 16 years old [in 1896]. Miss Shannon, Mrs. Eddy's maid, would occasionally take me for a drive, and that is really how I came to go into Mrs. Eddy's home. Her household consisted of Mr. Calvin Frye, secretary, Miss Shannon, maid, and Miss Morgan, cook. "I became quite useful to both Miss Shannon and Miss Morgan."[34] Of her healing of tuberculosis after a visit with Mrs. Eddy, she wrote: "The healing must have taken place immediately as I don't recall of any illness after that. And today I am in perfect health. Thanks to dear Mrs. Eddy and Christian Science."[35] Though never a member, Mrs. Mortlock gave her reminiscences to The Mother Church in 1937.

***Lady Victoria Murray** (1877–1926)* A godchild of Queen Victoria and the daughter of the Earl and Countess of Dunmore, she became a student of Christian Science after her mother's healing in 1892 of spinal problems that doctors had diagnosed as incurable. Lady Victoria was taught the Primary class of Christian Science by a student of Mrs. Eddy's, Julia Field-King. After that she entered the full-time public practice of Christian healing, advertising in the *Journal* in 1900. The following year, at Mrs. Eddy's invitation, she and her sister and parents attended the Normal class of The Mother Church's Board of Education taught by Edward Kimball. Immediately after that class Mrs. Eddy called them to Pleasant View where she gave them "a beautiful and inspiring talk on the application of Christian

Science, being informed at the same time that we were now teachers. Seeing that none of us had anticipated for a moment such a calling, we probably seemed hesitant, but Mrs. Eddy was firm and gave us additional counsel, expressing the while much satisfaction with the healing we had already done. It was evident to us that everyone was expected to be at work and that, whatever our seeming lack, Mrs. Eddy knew we could reflect the one [divine] Mind,— the only Teacher and Healer."[36] After returning to England, Lady Victoria decided to live in Manchester. Her work to establish Christian Science in that city was instrumental in a branch of The Mother Church being dedicated there in 1908. Her remaining years were devoted to Christian healing and the teaching of Christian Science.

James Neal (1866–1930) James Neal was introduced to Christian Science while working as a cashier in Joseph Armstrong's bank in Irving, Kansas. He was first taught this Science in December 1887 by Mr. Armstrong, who had just returned from one of Mrs. Eddy's Primary classes. Immediately after this, Mr. Neal left his bank job and began working full time as a Christian healer. In May 1888 he went through another Christian Science class, this time taught by another student of Mrs. Eddy's, Janet Coleman. Nine months later he took Mrs. Eddy's Primary class. In 1898 he attended Mrs. Eddy's last class, and thereby became a Christian Science teacher. Mr. Neal had come to Boston, Massachusetts, at the end of 1892 to work as a Christian healer. At Mrs. Eddy's request he also worked in

The Mother Church's publishing activities. In January 1897 he wrote to her of his desire to devote his full time to the healing practice. She gladly agreed, writing him an eloquent letter on the vital significance of healing to the Cause of Christian Science (see pages 170–171). One year later she appointed him to the three-man Board of Trustees of the newly reorganized Christian Science Publishing Society. Ten months after that Mrs. Eddy wrote Joseph Armstrong, the Manager of the Publishing Society, who was also a Director of the Church:

"I feel and discern the *need* of Mr. Neal giving his whole attention to healing the sick. No man can serve in C.S. two masters and do his duty to both. Mr. Neal consents to this change and he thinks it will not interfere with Mr. Joseph Clark's work for the Pub. So. to have him take his (Neal's) place on the Board of Trustees. Have you any objection?

"I have named Mr. Clark to the Board and called for Mr. Neal's discharge on the grounds that he is needed to devote himself to healing. It is not right that he should lose aught of his spiritual power by so much material thought. Hence my duty and his in the case."[37]

In 1911 Mr. Neal was again made a Publishing Society Trustee. He served a little more than a year. In June of the following year he was elected President of the Church, but resigned a month later when he was elected to The Christian Science Board of Directors. He remained a Director for seventeen years before retiring "to have more time for my practice and teaching work."[38]

Carol Norton *(1869–1904)* A cousin of Henry Wadsworth Longfellow, he was born on Christmas Day in Maine and reared as a Unitarian. Carol Norton lost his parents while still a boy and was raised in New York City by an aunt and uncle. He became interested in Christian Science when he turned to it because of a physical ailment that had plagued him for some time and which his doctors had been unable to cure. The healing so impressed him that he decided to devote his life to this new faith, leaving a promising business career behind. Augusta Stetson, a student of Mrs. Eddy's, taught him in one of her Primary classes, and it was not long before he became her assistant at the New York City Christian Science Institute. Through Mrs. Stetson, Mr. Norton came to know Mrs. Eddy personally, as they were both invited to Pleasant View a few times, and a regular correspondence grew between him and Mrs. Eddy. In 1893 Mrs. Eddy revised a poem he had written, "The New World," and asked the Christian Science Publishing Society to publish it as a booklet, which she wanted to have available at the Christian Science exhibit at the Chicago World's Fair. At her invitation, Carol Norton attended Mrs. Eddy's last class in 1898, the same year she appointed him to The Mother Church's Board of Lectureship. He devoted himself to this work in his remaining years. Mrs. Eddy considered Carol Norton one of her most promising students, and especially appreciated his understanding of true womanhood. In one of his lectures he said, "The present age witnesses woman's ascension to her rightful place as man's equal. . . . Woman's spiritual leadership will not supersede that of man, because man will rise to the possession of a spirituality and love that is ideal. Then there will be fulfilled the vision of genuine sex co-operation."[39]

Elizabeth Norton She and Carol Norton were married in April 1901. Elizabeth had previously received Primary class instruction in Christian Science from Augusta Stetson, a student of Mrs. Eddy's. Upon reading a letter to her husband from Mrs. Eddy, she was healed of a severe ankle injury (see pages 273–275). Not long after her husband's sudden passing, Mrs. Eddy invited her for a visit: "I shall never forget the first time I talked with [Mrs. Eddy]. She had sent for me to call upon her. On entering the room she extended her hand and asked me to be seated. I walked across the room and sat down in a chair. Mrs. Eddy very deliberately arranged her dress and sat down on a sofa. She looked at me so tenderly and, patting the sofa beside herself, she said, 'You are too far away from Mother, darling.' I immediately went to her. She took me in her arms and kissed me. She was not afraid to express her love humanly, and I did not mistake it, for I learned then and there, that divine Love must be expressed humanly in order to heal the broken hearted."[40] Mrs. Norton attended the Normal class of The Mother Church's Board of Education in 1910, taught by Bicknell Young, a student of Edward Kimball. She lived in Boston, devoting the rest of her life to Christian healing and the teaching of Christian Science.

Edward E. Norwood *(1868–1940)* Raised in the Methodist church, Edward Norwood early on desired to become a minister, but chronic ill-health interfered with his college training. In the spring of 1893, at the suggestion of a friend, he contacted a Christian Science practitioner to treat his mother, who had been diagnosed as having an incurable disease, and he also began reading *Science and Health* to her. What he read so amazed him, he couldn't put the book down. After three weeks he was completely healed of his ailments and his mother was much improved. He wrote to Mrs. Eddy in great gratitude for what had happened. In her reply she asked him, "Are you thinking of making Christian Science a study and practice? The spirit of love you manifest inclines me to ask this."[41] Two years later his advertisement as a full-time Christian healer appeared in *The Christian Science Journal.* Edward was taught Christian Science in an 1895 Primary class by Carol Norton. In 1898 he attended Mrs. Eddy's last class at her invitation. In 1902 Mrs. Eddy wrote Mr. Norwood a letter of deep gratitude for his search and discovery of evidence that her first husband, George W. Glover, had been a member of the St. Andrew's Masonic Lodge in Charleston, South Carolina. He had taken on this investigation in order to counteract a newspaper article that had attacked Mrs. Eddy's character and that of Colonel Glover's. In the latter half of 1906, Mrs. Eddy requested him to oversee in Washington, D.C., the production of new printing plates for *Science and Health.* Mr. Norwood devoted his adult life to Christian healing and teaching Christian Science in

Washington, D.C. His testimony of being healed when first reading *Science and Health* appears in that book's last chapter, "Fruitage," on pages 694–695.

Harriet O'Brien "In August, 1910, it was my inspiring privilege to see Mary Baker Eddy on her daily drive just as she was leaving her Chestnut Hill home. . . . As her carriage came out the gate her love drew me right over to the carriage wheels. Mrs. Eddy, who was occupying the seat on the farther side of the carriage, turned her small, black parasol aside, leaned forward in her seat, turned toward me, and looked straight into my eyes, while her face was illumined with a wondrous smile. Although she did not speak to me audibly, these words from Scripture came distinctly to me three times, every word clearly, 'Man shall not live by bread alone, but by every word that proceedeth out of the mouth of God.' It seemed to me the carriage stopped, but that evidently was due to my losing, for a moment, the thought of time and being wholly absorbed in spiritual unfoldment and a new born love for her whose teachings had raised me from a death bed and healed me from wheel-chair invalidism; a condition due to the teaching of old theology and a major surgical operation in which the ligaments controlling the limbs had been severed by mistake.

"'Transparency' is the word that best expresses my impression of Mrs. Eddy from this experience. Instinctively I felt her great love, and I was conscious that no one I had ever seen loved me as much as she did. My entire thought was filled with a spiritual illumination and there was a glory in the sunshine and landscape, as though a breath of heaven had swept earth and enveloped me, while tears of gratitude rained down my cheeks unheeded. I had caught a glimpse of the great difference between a mortal and spiritual man in God's image and likeness.

"My trip to Boston was for the purpose of determining whether the time had come for me to open a practitioner's office. After seeing Mrs. Eddy all my questions were fully answered and I returned to Kansas City and opened my office at once, healing desperate illnesses and sometimes raising the dying in one or two visits. . . .

"This experience helped me see how inseparable and how much alike Mrs. Eddy and her writings are."[42]

Less than a year later, in 1911, Miss O'Brien's advertisement as a Christian healer appeared in *The Christian Science Journal* and remained there until March 1964. Mrs. Mary E. Dunbar personally told Miss O'Brien about the healing of her little daughter Ethel, which Miss O'Brien recounted for The Mother Church's archives in 1935 (see pages 127–128).

***Mary Godfrey Parker** (1868–1945)* Mrs. Eddy (then Mrs. Glover) healed Mary Godfrey of membranous croup when she was a little girl in Lynn, Massachusetts. Before that she had healed Mary's mother of a badly infected finger, which the doctors had said would need to be amputated.[43] Her mother was responsible for introducing Asa Gilbert Eddy to Mrs. Glover. Mary Godfrey Parker was raised in the Universalist church and was teaching in a Universalist Sunday School at the time she became interested in Christian Science. Her interest stemmed from two events: in 1898 her husband was healed of the aftereffects of pneumonia, and at the same time Joseph Armstrong, the Manager of The Christian Science Publishing Society, called her to help in putting out the new *Christian Science Weekly* (later renamed the *Christian Science Sentinel*). She joined The Mother Church three years later and continued her work in the Publishing Society. In 1902 Mrs. Parker wrote Mrs. Eddy, "For the many, many blessings that have come to me through Science, I feel that I must express my gratitude to you. My childhood recollections of you in the Lynn house, when I was there with my cousin, Mr. Nash, and my mother, Mrs. Christiana Godfrey, are so full of love for you, that since becoming interested in Christian Science within the last few years, I have felt that I must tell you. When I look at the First edition of Science & Health, which you gave mamma so many years ago, I feel that I wish you knew how I appreciate it, and the great blessings that have come to me through it."[44]

Daniel Patterson *(1818–1896)* Daniel Patterson, an itinerant dentist with an interest in homeopathy, was a nephew of Mrs. Eddy's stepmother, Elizabeth. Mrs. Eddy married him in June 1853, not only out of love, but also in the hope that she could regain custody of her son George Glover II. Daniel did not keep his promise to reunite her with her son, partly out of fear that the young boy's rambunctious behavior would adversely affect her health. On a commission from the governor of New Hampshire to deliver funds to Southerners loyal to the Union during the Civil War, Daniel was captured by Southern forces and placed in a prisoner of war camp. He escaped and rejoined his wife in Portland, Maine, where she was being treated by Phineas Quimby. In the fall of 1865 they moved to Lynn, Massachusetts, where he reestablished his dental practice. Mary would often help his patients when they were in pain. The following spring Daniel ran off with one of his female patients, but her husband tracked them down and retrieved his wife. Mrs. Eddy (then Mrs. Patterson) forgave Daniel, but he deserted her again a few months later and when he returned a second time, she would not take him back. For a time he sent money to support her, but the payments eventually stopped, and he disappeared forever from her life. She was granted a divorce in November 1873. Unbeknownst to her, Daniel passed away impoverished in Maine in 1896.

Dorr Phillips Mrs. Eddy (then Mrs. Patterson) healed Dorr Phillips of a badly infected finger when he was a boy in Lynn. This was one of the first healings she accomplished after she discovered Christian Science. Mrs. Eddy stayed with his family twice for brief periods in 1866. At one point a little later on, Mrs. Patterson wrote up an agreement to teach Dorr the "art" of healing,[45] but for reasons unknown this never came about.

Ellen Pilsbury *(1844–c1905)* Mrs. Eddy's niece, the daughter of her sister Martha. In 1867 Mrs. Eddy (then Mrs. Patterson) healed Ellen, who was dying from enteritis (see pages 223–225) and again several years later when she was not expected to live through childbirth. After her first healing Ellen accompanied her aunt back to the her home with the Craftses in Taunton, Massachusetts. The austerity of their house and her aunt's work regimen proved too severe for Ellen's sensibilities and she returned to New Hampshire in a short time. In 1899 Henry M. Goddard, a psychologist from Clark University, Worcester, Massachusetts, wrote to Ellen Pilsbury Philbrook in preparation for a book he was thinking of writing. She responded, "In reply to your letter asking for information in regard to Mrs. Eddy I would say I have none to give you along the desired lines. In my childhood I was taught to regard my 'Aunt Mary' as a suffering saint. I removed west before Christian Science became the *Science* it is."[46]

Lyman P. Powell *(1866–1946)* The author of *Mary Baker Eddy: A Life Size Portrait.* Raised in the Methodist church, Lyman Powell graduated from Johns Hopkins University in 1890. From 1892 to 1895 he was a Fellow at the Wharton School of Finance of the University of Pennsylvania. Then his life took a very different direction when he entered the Episcopal Divinity School in Philadelphia. He graduated in 1897 and was ordained to the ministry. After serving as pastor to two congregations in Pennsylvania, he became

Rector of St. John's Church in Northampton, Massachusetts, in 1904. His interest in Christian Science around this time appears to have come from its effect on his own congregation and his involvement with the Emmanuel Movement, which also promoted spiritual healing. In 1907 he wrote a highly critical book, *Christian Science, the Faith and its Founder.* Of this, his biographer, Charles Macfarland, wrote, "I read the book which, it was clear, had been written in a spirit of extreme irritation. I remember my own observation that it was neither judicial nor judicious."[47]

Over the next twenty years, Dr. Powell's opinion of the religion and its founder would radically change. Beginning in 1918, and for the next seven years, he went on the lecture circuit, speaking primarily about education and the United States as a world influence. One of his lectures, "America's Greatest Woman," was about Mrs. Eddy. Dr. Powell returned to the ministry in 1926, becoming Rector of St. Margaret's Church in the Bronx, New York. He served for ten years before retiring as one of the more well-known clergymen, lecturers, and authors in America. Over his lifetime he wrote more than twenty books and booklets. In 1930 Dr. Powell published his biography of Mrs. Eddy. In contrast with his previous book on the subject, his deep appreciation of her and his kind consideration of her Church are evident throughout. He followed the publication with a series of lectures on the subject, "Mary Baker Eddy, Educator," where he especially shone light on her humility and tolerance.

Julia E. Prescott *(1849–1924)* Raised in the Free-Will Baptist church, Julia Prescott first heard of Christian Science in 1885 from a relative. She was healed of curvature of the spine while reading *Science and Health* and receiving treatment from a Christian Science healer. Not long after this she healed her own young son who was suffering greatly from a severe attack of the croup. Julia Prescott was taught by Mrs. Eddy in a Primary class in 1886. Soon after her instruction, she started the Christian Science church in Reading, Massachusetts, with the help of another Christian Scientist. She first advertised as a healer in *The Christian Science Journal* in 1895, and four years later began teaching. One of her students had known Phineas Quimby at the time Mrs. Eddy (then Mrs. Patterson) was consulting with him. Mrs. Prescott asked this student, "Was Dr. Quimby's treatment anything like Christian Science?" Her pupil replied, "Oh no, it seemed like clairvoyance."[48] Mrs. Prescott served in Mrs. Eddy's home from August 1905 to February 1906, and again for a number of weeks throughout 1907. In her reminiscences she wrote that one day while at Pleasant View Mrs. Eddy called her into her study "and the sense of God was so great that tears came into my eyes. [Mrs. Eddy] noticed that I was affected and she asked: 'Why those tears, dear? Are you homesick?' 'Oh no,' I responded, 'But I feel that you are an angel.' She asked: 'You don't mean my personality?' 'Oh no,' I answered. 'I mean that you give us messages from God.' She concluded: 'You mean that I am the window. We are right under the focus of divine Love.' I went to my room, feeling that all the world was filled with God, good."[49] When Mrs. Eddy moved to Chestnut Hill, Massachusetts, in 1908, she asked Julia to come with her as a regular member of the household, but Mr. Prescott wrote "that it seemed more of a sacrifice than he could make."[50] Mrs. Prescott lived in Reading, Massachusetts, and devoted her remaining years to Christian healing and the teaching of Christian Science.

Lewis Prescott After reading Lyman Powell's biography of Mrs. Eddy in 1931, Mr. Prescott wrote to thank him and also told him about his own contact with Mrs. Eddy: "In 1882 I was healed in Christian Science of consumption after eight years of invalidism. Preceding my full healing I met Mrs. Eddy and heard her lecture [in Lawrence, Massachusetts, in the autumn of 1882]. After this healing I went to Boston to hear Mrs. Eddy preach, whenever she addressed her church. In those early days of C. S. Mrs. Eddy preached on Sunday afternoons. Sunday mornings I went to Trinity Church and listened to Bishop [Phillips] Brooks. He was a gifted preacher, a fine man. A very whole man! . . . One Easter I heard Bishop Brooks preach on the "Resurrection." A splendid discourse. After luncheon I listened to Mrs. Eddy preach on the *same subject* in Chickering Hall, Tremont St. . . . I would like to tell you one impression Mrs. Eddy's sermon made upon me. As I listened, her words seemed to cause me to actually see Jesus stepping forth from the tomb, a victor over the 'last enemy,' and his body so glorified that he could pass through closed doors into his disciples' presence, proving, as Christian Science teaches, that matter is not substance. No longer was the resurrection a beautiful Bible-story to be believed in blind faith. It was an actual fact. What power gave Mrs. Eddy ability to show forth the living Christ? It was something more than a beautiful word-picture. And the spirit of that sermon healed. The power was divine. And it set forth not only Mrs. Eddy's great spiritual discovery—Christian Science, but also showed what Mrs. Eddy had suffered and experienced."[51] Mr. Prescott was taught Christian Science by Susie M. Lang, a student of Mrs. Eddy's. He first advertised as a healer in *The Christian Science Journal* in 1895. He lived in Lawrence, Massachusetts, devoting the rest of his life to this work till his passing in 1944.

Phineas P. Quimby *(1802–1866)* A clockmaker by profession, Phineas Quimby first became interested in mesmerism in 1838 when he heard a professional mesmerist lecture and demonstrate his skill. Literature and lecturers on mesmerism were not uncommon at this period in New England. It was from these sources that Mr. Quimby gained an understanding of its methods, and through his investigation found he had a special talent for "magnetizing" others, putting them into a mesmeric sleep. For a period of time he toured Maine and New Brunswick, Canada, giving exhibitions, placing an assistant in a somnambulistic state and, through him, diagnosing illnesses and prescribing cures. Eventually he saw he did not need a middleman, and in the 1840s he returned to his home in Maine, beginning a regular therapeutic practice as a "magnetic doctor," first in Belfast, then Bangor, and finally in Portland. He encountered Mrs. Eddy (then Mrs. Patterson) in Portland in 1862. Dr. Quimby's mesmeric treatment was based primarily on clairvoyance. He would first talk with his patients, discuss their problems, tell them what he perceived to be the source of their trouble, and then vigorously rub their heads or stomachs depending on where he saw the illness to be centered. The theory behind his practice was that man has two identities: one, the fleshly mind, which receives information through the material senses; the other, the clairvoyant mind, which is completely mental in nature, untouched by the senses. He believed that he could mentally influence or manipulate the clairvoyant mind in a patient, which would affect the fleshly, or "natural" mind, which would in turn affect the physical body for good or ill.

It wasn't until Mrs. Eddy suggested to him that there was a "science" behind his practice, that Dr. Quimby first started referring to it with that term. After a while he received so many insights from their many discussions about his work and her "views of mental therapeutics" that he began to praise her to others. As to his "manuscripts," which created quite a stir a number of years after Mrs. Eddy discovered Christian Science, it is highly unlikely that the bulk of these writings could be his own. Phineas Quimby was barely literate and found it difficult to write an articulate sentence. While he wrote simple notes to himself about specific cases he treated, it is not conceivable that he could have been the author of what has been published as *The Quimby Manuscripts*. While his concepts are woven throughout, it is obvious that others have rewritten and added much to his notes in an attempt to make his ideas comprehensible to readers and to insinuate that they are the source of Christian Science.[52] The vast majority of the original notes in Dr. Quimby's hand were destroyed by his son George, who refused to let anyone inspect them after Mrs. Eddy had become well-known in Boston. When quotations from some of the doctor's alleged writings were published in 1887, Mrs. Eddy responded, "Some words in these quotations certainly read like words that I said to him, and which I, at his request, had added to his copy when I corrected it."[53] Considering all the evidence, one is left to conclude that Mrs. Patterson's influence on Dr. Quimby was far greater than any lasting effect he might possibly have had on her. (See Emma A. Thompson entry, pages 382–383).

William R. Rathvon *(1854–1939)* As a boy of nine, William heard Abraham Lincoln deliver his Gettysburg Address: "I was within a few feet of the President as he stood upon the rough board platform over which Old Glory was draped, and as I looked into his face he seemed even to my boyish imagination to be a prophet and seer as he uttered the closing words of his address."[54] Raised in the Lutheran church, Mr. Rathvon became interested in Christian Science in 1893: "I became very successful in business, but my wealth, mostly in silver mines, was wiped away in the panic of '93, and we were left practically penniless. While sojourning temporarily in Chicago, through association with friends of former years we learned of Christian Science and without resistance it entered our lives, ever to remain. Before leaving Chicago we were taught by Mrs. Mary W. Adams, an early student of Mrs. Eddy's and the following year (1894) left for Colorado, to begin pioneer work in Christian Science in the little town of Florence, the center of the oil district."[55] In 1902 he and his wife, Ella, moved to Boulder, Colorado, where he divided his time between a job at an oil refinery and the public Christian healing practice. The following year he was taught by Edward Kimball in a Primary class in The Mother Church's Board of Education. Then in 1907 he attended that Board's Normal class instruction taught by Septimus J. Hanna.

Mr. Rathvon was called to serve in Mrs. Eddy's household in 1908. Not long after joining her household, Mr. Rathvon asked Mrs. Eddy: "Mother, would you object if I were to impart to my dear wife at times some of the good and helpful things you are constantly giving us? She is working bravely in Colorado to overcome the claim of separation and is making it much easier for me here than if her work was not so well done. I know some things I could tell her would help us both." Mrs. Eddy replied, "By all means, tell her such things and give her my love this night. And you must both know that what you are doing and giving is not a *sacrifice,* but an *offering.*"[56] Ella Rathvon was called to serve in Mrs. Eddy's home nine months later. A few months after Mr. Rathvon arrived, Mrs. Eddy asked her staff, "What is the highest attainment one can cherish?" Several answers were offered, but then she said, "Healing the sick. That requires the abandonment of everything. Away go automobiles and all else material. I gave up everything and I healed the sick. I saw a man crippled so that when he moved he was almost doubled up and had his hands on the ground to assist locomotion. I saw him seated on the curb with his head between his knees, on my way to a patient. As I passed I placed my hand on his head and said, 'Do you know that God loves you?' At once he straightened up, erect as he ever had been."[57]

In 1911 Mr. Rathvon was elected to The Mother Church's Board of Lectureship and over the next seven years gave lectures in Europe, Asia, and Australia. He retired from this work when he was appointed Treasurer of The Mother Church in June 1918. Four months later he was elected to The Christian Science Board of Directors and remained on that Board until his passing.

Bertha S. Reinke *(1859–1939)* Else Buchenberger wrote The Mother Church that Bertha Reinke "was born in Camionken, Kreis Loetzen, East Prussia, on 4 February 1859, where her father owned an estate. Her parents were Lutherans. . . . As a young girl, when she was to be confirmed, she rebelled against the strict doctrines of her church and refused to accept them; her pastor—so she often told us—allowed her then to write her own confession of faith and accepted her in his congregation. Her governess had punished her severely for her apparent stubbornness, but bread and water and a locked room did not compel her to yield and give vows, which even as a child she knew she could not obey. In 1888 an insatiable thirst for learning led her to Paris, where as lady companion to Countess Kessler and governess of their daughter, she had opportunity to study French and literature. In Paris she met two German teachers, who were then living in U.S.A. and accompanied them to America in the hope of studying there psychology, theology, and especially medicine, which was not open to women in Germany."[58] It was during this visit that she heard Mrs. Eddy preach in Boston. Miss Reinke was taught Christian Science in the mid1890s by Laura Lathrop, a student of Mrs. Eddy's. Else Buchenberger's account continues: "In 1902 [Bertha] received word from her mother that she was seriously ill, given up by the physicians, and filled with longing to see her daughter once more. Miss Reinke took the first steamer, declared the Truth as best she then understood it, and when she arrived in Berlin, where her mother lived, she had the joy of finding her well. . . . Miss Reinke began the practice of C.S. in Berlin . . . and has been a practitioner in Germany since 1902. In May 1913 at the call of a group of Scientists in Hamburg, she moved to that city, to help them organize as First Church of Christ, Scientist, Hamburg, Deutschland." From the time of her return to Germany, Miss Reinke devoted her life to Christian healing.

Else Buchenberger sent her account of Bertha Reinke's encounter with Mrs. Eddy to The Mother Church in 1939. In her reminiscence she wrote, "It has been my privilege to know Miss Reinke 22 years—as practitioner and truest friend in the highest sense of the word."

Miranda Rice When she became interested in Christian Science, Miranda Rice was a homemaker and a Methodist. Even though she was unable to pay, she was taught by Mrs. Eddy (then Mrs. Glover) in her fourth class in 1872. Her sister, Dorcas Rawson, had been taught two years earlier. In the beginning, Mrs. Rice could not do enough for Mrs. Glover, due in part, perhaps, to Mrs. Glover's metaphysical assistance at the birth of a child (see pages 235–236). Mrs. Glover herself was helped by her student at a time of physical distress: In 1874 Samuel Bancroft notes in his diary that he had received a letter from George Barry about "a strange experience my teacher passed through." He goes on to relate that when Mr. Barry and a friend entered Mrs. Glover's rooms, "she arose to meet them, but fell back, lost consciousness, and, to their belief, was gathering herself on the other side. George went after Mrs. R[ice], who came, and immediately a change took place. George had called on her mentally to come back, but Mrs. R[ice] called loudly, as for someone afar off, and the answer came, faintly at first, but stronger and stronger, till she was able to sit up and have the Bible and manuscripts read to her, and, finally, recovered."[59] It came as a great shock to Mrs. Eddy when Mrs. Rice, along with seven other students, deserted her at the end of October 1881, signing a letter that accused their teacher of unchristian behavior. As Mrs. Eddy understood it, these students were victims of mesmerism and the mental malpractice of Richard Kennedy and Daniel Spofford. By 1884 Miranda Rice had moved to San Francisco and was teaching classes in Christian Science, taking these occasions as opportunities to denounce Mrs. Eddy. Three years later Mrs. Rice studied with Emma Hopkins, and not long after this became mentally unbalanced. Upon her release from an asylum, she returned to Massachusetts. In 1906 Mrs. Rice became a source for the *New York World's* muckraking attacks on Mrs. Eddy.

Nemi Robertson First taught by Mrs. Eddy in 1889, Nemi Robertson entered the full-time healing practice in Orange, New Jersey, in 1896. She also attended Mrs. Eddy's last class, held two years later. She devoted her life to Christian healing and the teaching of Christian Science until her passing in 1926.

Henry Robinson After beginning his law practice in Concord, New Hampshire, in 1875, Henry Robinson became interested in politics and served as a New Hampshire state senator from 1883 to 1885. He was elected mayor of Concord in 1895 for a two-year term. He also served as postmaster of the city from 1890 to 1894, and from 1898 to 1903. Mr. Robinson had the opportunity to be intimately involved in the evolution of the city during its transition from the nineteenth to the twentieth century, with the introduction of all the innovations and new technologies that attended that period. Though never a student of Christian Science, Mr. Robinson did develop a friendly relationship with its Founder due to her prominence. In 1894 he wrote to her of his desire to prepare a biographical sketch of her for the local press. He interviewed her for this purpose in 1895, but due to his other duties was unable to complete his work on it at that time. In 1903 he did finish the sketch, and Mrs. Eddy was very pleased with what he produced. The article was published by a local newspaper as a booklet entitled, "A Biographical Sketch of Rev. Mary Baker G. Eddy."

Adela Rogers St. Johns *(1894–1988)* A journalist who covered major stories for the William Randolph Hearst newspapers for more than sixty years, she became a well known American personality. In the movie *His Girl Friday,* the character of Hildy Johnson was based in part on Adela St. Johns. Mrs. St. Johns studied Christian Science on her own. She wrote to Irving Tomlinson in 1926 the account of the newspaper reporter's healing, which appears on pages 278–279.

John Salchow *(c1865–1945)* John Salchow grew up on a farm in Kansas, his parents having emigrated from Germany. "I remember my folks had always felt very bitter towards religion as a boy. . . . We were, therefore, never allowed to go to church. As a young man I instinctively felt that there must be a God and I remember asking others about their religion, hoping that they would be able to tell me the right way. But they always turned me off and never seemed to be able to offer anything that satisfied. Finally, I think sometime in 1883 or 1884, my sister Bertha secured a few copies of the first Christian Science Journals and passed them on to me to read. My curiosity was aroused and just when I was wondering how I could find out more about this new religion, Mr. Joseph Mann came from the East to visit his brothers Christian and Frederick at Junction City. I knew both brothers well. . . . While Joseph was staying with his brothers I went down to see them all and then learned of his wonderful healing from an almost fatal bullet wound."[60] At once John ordered by mail a copy of *Science and Health*. The book arrived while he was working in the fields: "I was so anxious to see what it was all about that I immediately read a page or two. I had been suffering from an acute attack of stomach trouble that day, a condition which had been chronic for years, and after I read those few pages it entirely disappeared. In fact, I forgot the condition so completely that it was not until almost six months afterwards that I realized I had been free all that time."[61] As a result of his interest, and their own reading of the textbook, John Salchow's entire family embraced the new faith. He, his father, mother, and one of his sisters were taught Christian Science by Joseph Mann, a student of Mrs. Eddy's. In January 1901, on the recommendation of Mr. Mann, John Salchow was called to serve in Mrs. Eddy's household. Mr. Salchow was with Mrs. Eddy up to the time of her passing. After that he went to work for The Christian Science Publishing Society.

Laura E. Sargent *(1857–1915)* The daughter of a sea captain who had become a ship builder, Laura Sargent learned of Christian Science in 1882 from a friend who was then receiving treatment from a practitioner. She was also in need of help, having spent much on physicians, but finding no permanent cure. After she was healed by a Christian Science practitioner she began to study *Science and Health.* Laura was taught Christian Science in the class Mrs. Eddy conducted in Chicago in May 1884. She also attended another of Mrs. Eddy's Primary classes in December of the same year. In 1886 and 1887 she went through other classes with Mrs. Eddy.

Mrs. Eddy asked Laura Sargent to join her household staff in 1890. She would serve her teacher in this capacity for the next twenty years, off and on, for months or years at a time, depending on the need. From 1895 to 1899 Mrs. Eddy appointed her as custodian of the Mother's Room in The Mother Church. From 1903 to the time of Mrs. Eddy's passing, Mrs. Sargent lived continually in Mrs. Eddy's homes at Pleasant View and then Chestnut Hill. Laura Sargent was one of several workers in the home that were especially depended on for prayerful support during challenging times. Often Mrs. Eddy would call her staff together and give them instructions or lessons about a particular point in Christian Science. Mrs. Sargent would afterward write down some of these lessons. One time she wrote, "[Mrs. Eddy] said to ask ourself each day 'How do I know that I am a C[hristian] S[cientist]?' The only answer must be by what we demonstrate of the healing power of Love and Truth." At another time she wrote, "Mother called us and told us the secret of C. S. healing was in these words, 'All things are possible with God.' " And after Mrs. Eddy spoke of herself, Laura wrote, "Mother said that she was simply the window that admitted the Light and that we must not mistake the window for the wall or spatter the window and thus dim the light to ourselves."[62] In 1913 Mrs. Sargent taught The Mother Church's Board of Education Normal class.

Victoria H. Sargent *(1848–1930)* Victoria Sargent was Laura Sargent's sister. (The two had married brothers, thus the same last name.) Like her sister, Victoria Sargent was also healed in Christian Science. This occurred in the summer of 1884 from reading *Science and Health*. Victoria attended Mrs. Eddy's Primary class in December of the same year. In October 1886 she went through Mrs. Eddy's Normal class. After this she began to devote time to her Christian healing practice and in 1895 taught her first class. From that point on she gave her full time to healing and teaching. In 1907 Mrs. Eddy called Victoria Sargent to Concord, New Hampshire, to help in prayer about the "Next Friends" lawsuit. She was there for several weeks and visited Pleasant View a few times. In 1915 The Mother Church appointed Mrs. Sargent custodian of the Chestnut Hill home. Apart from this responsibility she devoted her time to Christian healing and the teaching of Christian Science.

Amos Scribner Mrs. Eddy (then Mrs. Glover) boarded at Amos Scribner's home at 7 Broad Street, Lynn, Massachusetts, for a short time in 1874 and for the first three months of 1875. While living there she bought the house across the street, number 8 (now 12 Broad Street). Even though Mrs. Glover had healed Mrs. Scribner and her child of physical ailments and she witnessed what it did for her husband (see pages 82–83), Mrs. Scribner remained quite hostile toward Christian Science as a practical explanation of God and man. So it's not surprising that after Mrs. Glover moved, the Scribners disappear from the pages of her life story.

Clara Shannon *(1858–1930)* Born in England, Clara Shannon emigrated with her family to Montreal, Ontario, Canada, in 1873. Upon reaching adulthood she began a professional singing career, and was soloist at St. George's Anglican Church. She became interested in Christian Science after being healed by it in 1887 of a severe physical ailment. The following year she attended one of Mrs. Eddy's Primary classes, and afterward she began a public healing practice in Montreal. In 1889 she took the Normal class at the Massachusetts Metaphysical College and began teaching Christian Science to others. She also established the Montreal Institute of Christian Science and helped to organize what became First Church of Christ, Scientist, Montreal.

In 1894 Mrs. Eddy asked Miss Shannon to join her at Pleasant View. She remained a member of the household until 1903, when she went to live in London, England. There she devoted her full time to the Christian healing practice. In 1907 she served again at Pleasant View for three weeks and upon her return to England began teaching Christian Science at Mrs. Eddy's request. She wrote that on one occasion, "Mrs. Eddy showed us how it is *God* who heals and not the student and that we must have faith in God, in the allness of God, in the omnipotence of Truth, and know that God is *all,* and then we will see the healing."[63] Miss Shannon was preparing to return to her teacher's home at the beginning of December 1910, but Mrs. Eddy passed on before she left London. She remained there, healing and teaching for the rest of her life.

Emma C. Shipman *(1871–1958)* Reared in the Congregational church, Emma was healed of a physical problem by reading *Science and Health* when she was fourteen. For a time she lived in Lisbon, New Hampshire, with three aunts who were Christian Scientists, two of whom had been taught by Mrs. Eddy. When she was seventeen Emma took the Primary class in Christian Science from Annie Louise Robertson. She went on to attend Boston University and after graduation became a school teacher in Brookline, Massachusetts. During her summer vacations, she helped to organize the White Mountain church in Fabyans, New Hampshire. Miss Shipman was present when Mrs. Eddy delivered her first address in The Mother Church on May 26, 1895, and was present again when she gave the Communion sermon in January 1896.

Mrs. Eddy taught Emma Shipman in her last class in November 1898. The following year she began devoting her full time to the public practice of Christian healing. In 1900 Miss Shipman took a Christian Science Primary class taught by Alfred Baker in the Church's Board of Education, and the following year, at Mrs. Eddy's request, she attended the Normal class taught by Edward Kimball. Miss Shipman conducted her own first Primary class in 1905. The year before she had been invited for a week's visit to Pleasant View. Mrs. Eddy told her that she wanted to get to know some of her newer students better, and the two had daily conversations about Christian Science. From 1915 to 1922 Miss Shipman served on the Church's Bible Lesson Committee; in 1949 she was elected to a term as President of The Mother Church; and in 1952 she taught the Board of Education's Normal class. When not involved with church duties, Miss Shipman devoted her time to Christian healing and teaching Christian Science.

In the early years of the century Emma Shipman had been a member of the Church's Literature Distribution Committee. At one time the committee received a large number of periodicals from Mrs. Eddy's home at Chestnut Hill. In the *Christian Science Sentinel* for January 6, 1906, was a quotation from Phillips Brooks, the Episcopal pastor of Trinity Church in Boston, "God has not given us vast learning to solve all the problems, or unfailing wisdom to direct all the wanderings of our brothers' lives; but He has given to every one of us the power to be spiritual, and by our spirituality to lift and enlarge and enlighten the lives we touch." Under this quotation Mrs. Eddy had written in pencil, "The secret of my life is in the above."[64]

Alice M. Sibley *(1864–1939)* Lucretia Brown, one of Mrs. Eddy's students, first brought fifteen-year-old Alice to hear Mrs. Eddy deliver her Sunday sermons in 1879. It was not long before they were introduced and became quite fond of one another. Mrs. Eddy especially appreciated Alice's loving nature, her innocence, and liveliness of thought. She gave Alice a copy of her newly published Third edition of *Science and Health* as a birthday present. In July 1882, after Asa Gilbert Eddy's passing, Alice accompanied Mrs. Eddy during her month-long stay in Barton, Vermont. When they returned to Boston in August, she went through Mrs. Eddy's Primary class. But after 1883 the two lost contact with each other. Alice Sibley went on to become a school teacher in Boston, where she taught many years. She did not pursue her interest in Christian Science.

Hanover P. Smith Not long after Mrs. Eddy healed him of deafness and dumbness when he was nineteen. Hanover Smith went through one of her Primary classes in 1880. He was one of a small group of students that lived for a time at the Massachusetts Metaphysical College in Boston when Mrs. Eddy taught there in the 1880s. In 1887 he attended another one of her classes. That same year he published, with Mrs. Eddy's assistance, a fifty-two page pamphlet entitled, "Writings and Genius of the Founder of Christian Science." Mr. Smith advertised in *The Christian Science Journal* as a Christian healer from 1887 to 1893.

Daniel Spofford *(1842–1924)* A shoemaker in Lynn, Massachusetts, Daniel Spofford became interested in the teachings of Mrs. Eddy (then Mrs. Glover) at the time his wife, Addie, was studying with her in November 1870. After studying copies of Mrs. Glover's teaching manuscripts which his wife had, he began to practice healing a little. He himself studied with Mrs. Glover in April 1875 at her invitation. In April 1876, at Mrs. Glover's request, he took on the task of running the Christian Scientist Publishing Company, previously a two-man operation. It meant he was in charge of promoting and selling her new book *Science and Health.* Unfortunately, he was not successful in this position, and Mrs. Glover became very dissatisfied with his ineffectiveness. After she married Asa Gilbert Eddy at the beginning of 1877, Mr. Spofford's relationship with his teacher fell apart. He came to feel that she was unworthy to carry on the mission of Christian Science and launched out on his own to practice healing.

In May 1878, Edward Arens, a student of Mrs. Eddy's, persuaded her to bring a lawsuit against Mr. Spofford for unpaid tuition. The case was dismissed the following month because of defects in the writ and insufficient service. Four months after that, at the end of October, Mr. Arens and Mr. Eddy were arrested for conspiracy to murder Mr. Spofford, who had gone into hiding as part of an elaborate hoax. By the time the case came to trial in January 1879, the deception had been exposed and it was dismissed. Much of the evidence points to Richard Kennedy as the instigator of this strange episode.

Mr. Spofford fades from the scene at this point until he reappears in 1904 as one of Georgine Milmine's sources for her muckraking articles about Mrs. Eddy, which appeared in 1907 in *McClure's Magazine*. An appreciation for his old mentor, however, shines through his misconceptions of her as can be seen in a September 18, 1904, letter he wrote to Miss Milmine in which he said: "I have always considered her as my spiritual mother and the only teacher of Moral Science" and "You ask 'what was the power she evidently possessed by which she attracted and held her followers?' To me it was that she had come with the Truth for which the christian world had been looking for lo these eighteen centuries. . . ."[65]

Augusta Stetson *(1841–1928)* In her book of reminiscences and writings, Augusta Stetson writes: "During the spring of 1884, I heard of several cases of Christian Science healing in Boston and was invited to attend a lecture which was to be given by Mrs. Eddy, in a handsome home on Monument Hill, Charlestown, Massachusetts. I went to the lecture weighted with care and nearly prostrated from the effects of watching for one year in the room of an invalid husband. During this lecture I lost all sense of grief, physical weakness, and prostration."[66] In November of that year Mrs. Stetson reluctantly attended Mrs. Eddy's Primary class in the Massachusetts Metaphysical College at the latter's suggestion. After the class Mrs. Stetson encountered a number of opportunities to test her new learning through healing and soon found herself with a public practice that took all her time. In 1885 Augusta Stetson would substitute when needed for Mrs. Eddy in the pulpit, conducting the Sunday services in the Church of Christ (Scientist) in Boston. The following year, in February, she attended Mrs. Eddy's Normal class and then went to New York in November at Mrs. Eddy's request to help Laura Lathrop and Pamelia Leonard establish Christian Science there through healing and teaching. She was a charter member of First Church of Christ, Scientist, New York City, which was organized in 1887. Augusta Stetson regularly preached for this church and was appointed its pastor in 1888. In 1889 she took the Primary class again with Mrs. Eddy. And the following year she formed the New York City Christian Science Institute.

Mrs. Eddy was more patient and long-suffering with Mrs. Stetson than any other of her students. She saw such potential in her that time and again she strove to help her overcome worldliness, ambition, and ego. Unfortunately, this effort was in vain. Mrs. Stetson let these malignant qualities erode her Christianity to such a degree that she actively tried to ruin anyone in New York City whom she considered a rival. In 1909 The Christian Science Board of Directors revoked her status as a practitioner and teacher, and removed her from membership in The Mother Church. Her remaining years were spent in explaining herself and her actions and attempting to continue teaching. In one of Mrs. Eddy's many Bibles she noted that Romans 8:5–8 pertained to "Augusta": "For if men are controlled by their earthly natures, they give their minds to earthly things; if they are controlled by their spiritual natures, they give their minds to spiritual things. Because for the mind to be given up to earthly things means death; but for it to be given up to spiritual things means Life and peace. Abandonment to earthly things is a state of enmity to God. Such a mind does not submit to God's Law, and indeed cannot do so. And they whose hearts are absorbed in earthly things cannot please God."[67]

M. Adelaide Still (1873–1964)   In her reminiscences Adelaide Still writes, "I started the earthly dream in Banwell, a village of Somersetshire, England. My parents belonged to the working class. They were good, honest persons, Nonconformists; my father being of the Puritan type and very strict." When Adelaide was fifteen, she joined the Congregational church. "In 1900 Christian Science was introduced by a teacher of a Bible Class which my sister and I attended in this church. I was very much interested and in November of that year bought the textbook [*Science and Health*]."[68] She took the Primary class in Christian Science in 1901 from E. Blanche Ward, a Christian Science teacher.

Miss Still came to the United States in 1906, and the following year was invited to join Mrs. Eddy's Pleasant View household. She began as a housekeeper but after a few months Mrs. Eddy asked Adelaide to become her personal maid, a position she held up to the time of Mrs. Eddy's passing. She wrote that, "As soon as Mrs. Eddy was dressed she went to her chair in the study, and opened, first her

Bible, and then her *Science and Health*, and read whatever verse or paragraph her eyes first rested upon. She usually read these aloud to whomever was in the room with her, sometimes calling the [metaphysical] workers and giving them a lesson from them. . . . After reading the selections and explaining them, she sat in her chair, thinking and praying until nine-thirty, when she went downstairs. . . . She was usually in bed by nine-thirty. Always her *Science and Health*, and a pad and pencil were placed on the small marble topped table at the head of her bed, and occasionally she would call us all in after she had retired, and give instructions as to handling certain phases of error or some special problem which needed solving."[69]

For several years after Mrs. Eddy's passing, Miss Still remained in the Chestnut Hill home as a caretaker and companion to Laura Sargent. After that she worked for a period in the Treasurer's office of The Mother Church.

Marguerite F. Sym Originally a Presbyterian, Marguerite Sym was taught Christian Science in Mrs. Eddy's Primary class in 1889, and the following year began to devote her full time to the public practice of Christian healing. She had met Mrs. Eddy prior to the class: "While on a visit to Boston in the autumn of 1888 I was taken by a student of Mrs. Eddy's to call upon her and we spent the evening at her house. . . . On taking leave of me that evening she took my hand in hers and said, 'put your hand in God's hand, let Him lead you.'"[70]

Abigail Dyer Thompson *(c1878–1957)* Christian Science was introduced into Abigail Thompson's home in 1884, when she was a little girl. At that time her mother, Emma, was healed of neuralgia by studying *Science and Health*. Abigail met Mrs. Eddy two years later: "My first impression of Mary Baker Eddy was gained in early childhood, in August 1886, at the time my mother received her Primary class of instruction in the Massachusetts Metaphysical College."[71] A few months after their first meeting, upon a return visit to Boston, Mrs. Eddy instantly healed Abigail of an inherited "lung trouble" that doctors had diagnosed as terminal: "One morning as I stood looking over the mail Mrs. Eddy passed through the hall on her way to hold a few moments consultation with a student. . . . Almost instantly after our Leader began her conference with him the sound of my prolonged rasping cough attracted their attention, and finally when I leaned on the banister for support, Mrs. Eddy held up her hand to stop the conversation and listened for a moment, then she said, 'I do not like the sound of that child's cough.' Closing her eyes for a short time she worked earnestly. The coughing ceased at once, and not only did the distressing phase of the condition yield, but the whole mortal law which lay back of the trouble was broken down, and through the many years that have followed I have rejoiced in complete freedom from any return of this so-called family inheritance."[72] A year or so after this Mrs. Eddy again healed her, this time of a severe hip ailment.

When Abigail Thompson was about twenty she entered the full-time public practice of Christian healing. A year later, in 1898, she and her mother were students in Mrs. Eddy's last class. Miss Thompson devoted the rest of her life to healing and teaching Christian Science to others. In her reminiscences she wrote, "Mrs. Eddy made very little of a diagnosis of disease. She often said, 'Let the patients talk freely at first, it is the way they lay their burdens down; mentally you must walk a short distance with them, but never permit people to indulge in daily descriptions of their feelings.' "[73]

Emma A. Thompson *(1842–1913)* Growing up near Portland, Maine, Emma Thompson, although an energetic child and a brilliant student, was afflicted with severe attacks of pain in the head that physicians pronounced an extremely acute form of neuralgia. No method of medical treatment brought relief. In a notarized affidavit Emma Thompson, related what happened when she was twenty: "I became acquainted with Dr. P. P. Quimby for the first time late in the year 1862. As I recall it, his home was then in Belfast, Me. He traveled about the country giving a form of treatment similar to magnetic healing. At this time I was at the home of my father, Pitman Morgan, near Portland, Me. I had been very ill with severe neuralgic pains in the head and Dr. Quimby was called to give me treatments." She continued, "I then tried other courses of treatments and remedies, without success, until 1884, when I was finally and permanently healed through the reading of 'Science and Health with Key to the Scriptures,' by Mary Baker G. Eddy.

"Upon my first visit to Dr. Quimby I saw Mrs. Eddy in his office in Portland, as a patient. He had cited my case to her, and she remained in the room during my treatment. There was nothing in Dr. Quimby's method of treating disease which bears any resemblance to the teachings or methods of Christian Science. He never spoke of God to me, or referred to any other power or person but himself. (As far as I know he had no manuscripts or books relating to his subject.) He gave me nothing to read and no explanation of his treatment. In fact he had no explanation. I distinctly recall that before he left our home [the morning of my first treatment], my father offered him a check for one thousand dollars if he would impart to him or any member of his family his method of treating disease, to which the doctor replied, 'I cannot. I don't understand it myself.'

"I have been through three classes under Mrs. Eddy's teaching; have been in active practice of Christian Science for over twenty years, and can testify that the instruction and methods of healing disease are in no way similar to those employed by Dr. Quimby,—but on the contrary are diametrically opposed thereto."[74] Emma Thompson began her public Christian healing practice soon after her own healing had occurred from reading the Christian Science textbook. She devoted the rest of her life to this healing work.

Irving C. Tomlinson (c1860–1944) The son of a minister, Irving Tomlinson became one himself. After graduating from Akron University in Ohio with a Bachelor's degree from the Classical Department in 1880 and a Master's in

1884, he attended the Theological Department of Tufts College in Medford, Massachusetts, and graduated as a Bachelor of Divinity in 1888. He immediately entered the ministry and became pastor of the First Universalist Church of Arlington, Massachusetts. In investigating the role of healing in the Christian church, Reverend Tomlinson attended a Sunday service of The Mother Church in Boston in 1884. After going to a number of weekly testimony meetings he became convinced "that there was at least one church carrying out the Master's injunction to heal the sick."[75]

He attended class with Flavia S. Knapp, one of Mrs. Eddy's students. Soon after this he resigned from the Universalist church, and in 1897 entered the public practice of Christian healing. In 1898 Irving Tomlinson was one of the five members appointed to the newly created Board of Lectureship. Mrs. Eddy also placed him on the Bible Lesson Committee, where he served for over twenty years. And in November 1898 she invited him to her last class. The following year, 1899, Mrs. Eddy called him to Concord, New Hampshire, to be First Reader of the Christian Science Church in that city. He held this position until 1906. While living in Concord, especially after 1900, Mr. Tomlinson was in almost daily contact with Mrs. Eddy, carrying out the assignments she gave him. When she moved to Chestnut Hill, he joined her household and became one of her secretaries. Irving Tomlinson is perhaps best known for his biography, *Twelve Years with Mary Baker Eddy*, which he began in the early 1930s as an effort to write out his reminiscences and ended with the posthumous publication of the book in 1945. In writing his reminiscences, Tomlinson used notes he had made in calendar notebooks while working with Mrs. Eddy. He wrote: "In the years the writer knew Mrs. Eddy there was not a single moment given to idleness—the welfare of mankind and their highest good was always her constant care."[76]

William Bradford Turner *(c1870–1937)* "My earliest recollections of Christian Science carry me back to the city of Minneapolis, Minnesota, as a lad of fourteen. From infancy I had never known what it was to be well, never known what it meant to feel strong. Nervous disorders racked me physically, and frightened me mentally. A wonderfully sweet mother and a devoted father did all they could to put me in the way of health. Relief would come, temporarily; but I heard it whispered that probably I would not live long. Organic difficulties of a serious nature developed, from which, also, I obtained, now and again, relief, but only temporarily."[77] Around 1884 William Turner's father introduced him to Emma Thompson, who had been healed that year by reading *Science and Health.* "I received help through Mrs. Thompson's Christian Science treatment, but it was not until eleven years later that I was impelled to an earnest study of the subject." In the latter part of the 1890s he was taught the Primary class in Christian Science by Flavia Knapp, a student of Mrs. Eddy's. "Mrs. Eddy herself I never came personally in contact with, though it was my rare privilege to hear her speak a number of times, twice in the original edifice of The Mother Church, once in Tremont Temple, Boston, and each time, besides, that she spoke to the Annual Meeting visitors invited to her home at Pleasant View, in Concord, New Hampshire."[78] Mr. Turner served on the Bible Lesson Committee at the same time as Julia Bartlett. He first advertised as a full-time Christian healer in *The Christian Science Journal* in 1903. He devoted himself to this practice for the rest of his life.

Ludie M. Waldron Formerly a Baptist, Ludie Waldron wrote The Mother Church in 1946, "I should like to mention, before closing, that Mr. Waldron as a young student of preparatory school for Yale University, enjoyed a most unique and beneficial acquaintance with our Leader, Mary Baker Eddy. It was in Concord, [New Hampshire], and he was working his way through this school. It happened that Mrs. Eddy needed some one to translate her foreign letters. As my husband speaks several languages, he was fortunate in getting this work to help him with his expenses of schooling. My husband is not a student of Christian Science, but he cherishes many beautiful memories of our Leader, and it is a privilege to listen to his reminiscences of those times. Such as the loving gifts she gave him; the various events connected with those of her household. He often had the privilege of occupying a room at Pleasant View; and was well acquainted with the coachman, the cook, etc., and loved Mrs. Eddy with his boyish enthusiasm. He recalls the healing of a young lineman, who was working in front of her home, and was hit in the eye by a wire; someone ran into the house to ask the owner to send for a doctor; the young man was brought into the house, and our Leader talked with him; also had him put to rest in a quiet room. The next day Mr. Waldron saw the same young lineman; and he was healed."[79]

Mary Webster A spiritualist, "Mother" Webster was the wife of Nathaniel Webster, a retired sea captain, who was superintendent of cotton mills in Manchester, New Hampshire. A young neighbor wrote in later years, "The Websters were loved by all, and she did many loving acts of kindness, no one called on her in vain, she was always ready to go."[80] A "healing medium," Mother Webster would prescribe various remedies for boarders and friends in need. Mrs. Eddy (then Mrs. Glover) stayed in the Websters' Amesbury, Massachusetts, home for ten months beginning in the autumn of 1867. She devoted most of her time there continuing to write out her notes on the first book of the Bible, Genesis. The young neighbor in Amesbury wrote: "I saw Mrs. Glover when she first came to 'Grandma' Webster, and I have always remembered her eyes, just so full of love and tenderness. I often saw her and Mrs. Webster when they went to walk the first of the evening, they went across a little bridge over the Powow (a branch of the Merrimac) and stood on the bank of the Merrimac. The view was beautiful at sunset."[81]

Janette E. Weller *(1840–1925)* As a young woman, Mrs. Weller was a school teacher in Littleton, New Hampshire. In her reminiscences she wrote of her introduction to Christian Science: "In March 1884, I first heard of Christian Science and its healing work. I immediately purchased a copy of the Seventh edition of *Science and Health with Key to the Scriptures* by Mary B. G. Eddy, and read it through carefully, giving most of my time for three weeks to its study. I had not heard that the reading of the book healed the sick but, before those three weeks had passed, I awoke to find that all the claims of disease and pain from which I had suffered for more than twenty years had vanished and that I was free as a bird." That same year Mrs. Weller attended one of Mrs. Eddy's Primary classes in the Massachusetts Metaphysical College. Five years later, in 1889, she was in the last Normal class Mrs. Eddy taught in Boston.

Five months after the Primary class, Mrs. Eddy wrote to Mrs. Weller, "Do you find any difficulty in healing? If so, strike for the higher sense of the *nothingness* of *matter.* Do not care to search into causation there, for there is no cause and no effect in matter; *all is Mind,* perfect and eternal. When ever you treat a patient, include in your under-standing of the case that no ignorant or malicious mind can affect the case and there *is no relapse.* Science tells us this— is all it manifests. *Progress* is the law of the Infinite, and finite views are but supposition and belief. Now *realize* this. And be a law to every case, when you commence treating it, that there is but *one Mind* and this one governs your patient, that there are not minds to interfere, error is not

Mind, has *no power* over *you* or the patient. These are the rules for you to work out every hour of your life."[82] According to her reminiscences Mrs. Weller devoted the ten years after her Primary class to Christian healing work in Littleton, New Hampshire; Binghamton, New York; Philadelphia, Pennsylvania; and Spokane, Washington, before settling in Boston, Massachusetts. She worked for a few months in Mrs. Eddy's home at the end of 1896 and the beginning of 1897. After this Mrs. Weller devoted the rest of her life to Christian healing.

Sally Wentworth (1818–1883) In September 1868 Mrs. Eddy (then Mrs. Patterson) came to live in the Went-worths' home on a farm in East Stoughton, Massachusetts. A Universalist at the time, Sally Wentworth became Mrs. Eddy's third student. On August 11, 1869, she wrote out the following contract: "For value received in instruction which enables me to heal the sick and to teach others the science whereby I have learned to heal I hereby agree to give Mrs. M. M. Patterson board free from expense so long as, and whenever she requires it; and when she is absent from my home to pay her the sum of two dollars per week. This sum to be paid her on condition that I am practicing or teaching this science."[83] Mrs. Eddy lived with the Wentworths for a year and a half.

Parsons Whidden (1801–1869) Parsons Whidden took his degree of M.D. at Dartmouth Medical College in 1836. Over his lifetime he practiced in the New Hampshire towns of Danbury, Alexandria, Pembroke, Warner, and Northfield. He married Mary P. Tilton of Sanbornton Bridge in 1832, and in this way became distantly related to Mrs. Eddy through her sister Abigail Baker Tilton. In the summer of 1849 Mrs. Glover went to Warner for two months to be treated by Dr. Whidden for what had been diagnosed by her regular physician as dyspepsia caused by a disease of the spinal nerves.[84] She took advantage of her time in Warner to study allopathy with Dr. Whidden because she needed this knowledge to study homeopathy, which was her prime interest at that time.[85] (Allopathy employs medicines to produce effects different from those resulting from the disease being treated.) In later years she wrote of this pursuit: "I returned [from the South] to my Father's at Tilton, New Hampshire. Read Allopathy and qualified myself for a Homeopathic student and afterwards in Homeopathy for a physician. Studied Grahams system of dietetics and qualified myself for an Homeopathic physician only to abandon that practice for Metaphysics."[86]

Lilian Whiting *(1847–1942)*   American journalist, essayist, and poet. Two of her articles on Margaret Fuller were published in the *Cincinnati Commercial,* which led to her being employed by that paper. That experience enabled Lilian Whiting to become a reporter for the *Boston Traveller.* She later became the paper's literary editor, holding that position until 1890. She wrote a weekly feature called "Boston Letters" for western newspapers, and became editor in chief of the *Boston Budget.* Miss Whiting interviewed Mrs. Eddy in 1885 and at one point asked about entering her September Primary class that year. Due to an overly full schedule she did not go through with this.

In the interview that was published in the *Ohio Leader,* Miss Whiting wrote, "Mrs. Eddy impressed me as a woman who is—in the language of our Methodist friends—'filled with the spirit.' It seems to be a merely natural gift with her. She is, by nature, a harmonizer. My own personal experience in that call was so singular that I will venture to relate it. I went, as I have already said, in a journalistic spirit. I had no belief, or disbelief, and the idea of getting any personal benefit from the call, save matter for press use, never occurred to me. But I remembered afterward how extremely tired I was as I walked rather wearily and languidly up the steps to Mrs. Eddy's door. I came away, as a little child friend of mine expressively says, 'skipping.' I was at least a mile from the Vendome, and I walked home feeling as if I were treading on air. My sleep that night was the rest of elysium. If I had been caught up into paradise it could hardly have been a more wonderful renewal. All the next day this exalted state continued. I can hardly describe it; it was simply the most marvelous elasticity of mind and body."[87] (See also pages 263–264.)

Rev. James Henry Wiggin *(1836–1900)* After graduating from the Meadville Theological Seminary in 1861, James Wiggin became a Unitarian clergyman. He retired from the active ministry in 1875 to devote himself to writing and editing. A friend of John Wilson, the owner of the

University Press (printers of *Science and Health* from the Third edition until 1930), James Wiggin became engaged in proofreading, revising, and editing manuscripts. In an article in the December 1906 issue of *The Christian Science Journal,* Mrs. Eddy wrote of her past relationship with her editorial assistant, which had begun in 1885: "I engaged Mr. Wiggin so as to avail myself of his criticisms of my statement of Christian Science, which criticisms would enable me to explain more clearly the points that might seem ambiguous to the reader. . . . My diction, as used in explaining Christian Science, has been called original. The liberty that I have taken with capitalization, in order to express the 'new tongue,' has well-nigh constituted a new style of language. In almost every case where Mr. Wiggin added words, I have erased them in my revisions."[88]

Mrs. Eddy asked James Wiggin to become editor of the *Journal* in 1886. He served in this capacity from January to August, and again from January 1887 to January 1889. While he never became a student of Christian Science, the Reverend Mr. Wiggin did accept Mrs. Eddy's offer to sit through one of her Primary classes in 1886. The Sixteenth edition of *Science and Health,* published that year, included an index for the first time. It had been prepared by James Wiggin. At one time when he was not feeling well, Mrs. Eddy wrote him the following letter: "My dear Mr. Wiggin: Mr. Frye told me yesterday you were not as well as usual. I have taken the liberty to send a team to your door with your drive prepaid to take you out in the cool of the day. Now step right into it and leave all cares behind and tell the driver to take you into pleasant places as long as you care to drive. Most truly, M. B. G. Eddy. P.S. Remember the City lieth four square and every side is *safe, harmonious.* This City is the kingdom of Heaven already within your grasp. Open your spiritual gaze to see this and you are well in a moment."[89] In his last years James Wiggin unfortunately became publicly critical of his former employer and benefactor, and her discovery.

Sibyl Wilbur (1871–1946) An American journalist and an organizer of the Woman's Suffrage Party in New York City, Sybil Wilbur wrote a series of articles about Mrs. Eddy for the magazine *Human Life* in 1906–7. She used these as the basis for her 1908 biography, *The Life of Mary Baker Eddy.* What is especially significant about this biography is that Miss Wilbur was able to personally interview people in Mrs. Eddy's past, who had known the religious leader before she became famous. Irving Tomlinson read Miss Wilbur's book to Mrs. Eddy in 1909, and he wrote to The Christian Science Board of Directors about this in 1929. In his letter he stated, "When the account of the cures recorded on pages [140] to [144] was read to Mrs. Eddy she remarked, 'The account of cures told is told just as they occurred.'"[90]

Sibyl Wilbur began her journalistic career as a society reporter for the *Minneapolis Journal,* which three years later sent her to report from Europe. As a national reporter for the *Minneapolis Times,* she toured the West and also reported on Southern interests. In 1896 she wrote a series of articles exposing governmental fraud and graft for the *Washington Times*. In order to write a series for the *New York World* on the conditions of working women in America, Miss Wilbur took jobs as a waitress, hospital nurse, office stenographer, and a telephone operator. As labor editor for the *Chicago Journal,* she scooped all other reporters with her account of the Virdin riot in Illinois.

In 1904 Sybil Wilbur became a reporter for the *Boston Herald.* Miss Wilbur first interviewed Mrs. Eddy in May 1906; her story about the interview sold 60,000 extra copies of the *Herald.* What she was learning of Christian Science prompted her the following year to take Primary class instruction with Alfred Farlow, but she never became a member of The Mother Church. After finishing her biography of Mrs. Eddy, she became deeply involved with the women's suffrage movement.

Cordelia Willey A Presbyterian, Cordelia Willey had been an invalid for ten years when her doctors told her family to prepare for her passing. One of Mrs. Eddy's students, Ellen Brown [Linscott], healed her in April 1887 after being contacted by the family. Miss Willey first met Mrs. Eddy in June 1888 at the reception held after the latter had given her address "Science and the Senses" in the Central Music Hall in Chicago. Three months later she was taught by Mrs. Eddy in a Primary class. During one of the lessons, Mrs. Eddy healed her of an overwhelming fear (see pages 267–268). After this Miss Willey devoted her life to the

Christian healing practice, advertising in *The Christian Science Journal* from 1891 until her passing in 1943.

Abigail Winslow Well-to-do Quakers, Abigail and her husband, Charles, were close friends of Mrs. Eddy's (then Mrs. Patterson) in Lynn, Massachusetts, in 1866. Mrs. Eddy had met them previously while living with the Thomas Phillipses. (Abigail Winslow was Mr. Phillips's sister.) Mrs. Eddy stayed with the Winslows briefly in the autumn of 1866 and kept in touch with them over the next few years. Even though she healed Abigail of hip disease during a visit in 1868 (see pages 226–227), the Winslows tried to dissuade Mrs. Eddy from continuing her efforts to promote divine Science because they felt the world would say she was mad if she continued to preach divine healing.

Josephine Curtis Woodbury *(c1850–1930)* In a booklet she published, Josephine Woodbury wrote that her parents "were numbered among progressive Unitarians and prominent Abolitionists."[91] She grew up in Milford, Massachusetts, and first became interested in Christian Science when she was about thirty; in 1880 her son was healed of membranous croup and she was restored to health with the help of a Christian Science healer. In 1884 Mrs. Woodbury took Mrs. Eddy's Primary class, and followed this by going through two other classes in 1886 and 1888. In the latter half of the 1880s she was quite involved in church work in Boston, assisting for a time in editing *The Christian Science Journal,* and in 1886 establishing, as an "institute" for teaching, the Academy of Christian Science.

At the beginning of December 1889, Mrs. Woodbury withdrew her membership from the Boston Church of Christ (Scientist), explaining she was simply following Mrs. Eddy's lead in disassociating herself from organizations. More likely her withdrawal was prompted by the embarrassing condition she found herself in. In June 1890, she bore a child and declared she had been unaware of the pregnancy. Having told her students that she had abstained from marital relations with her husband for some years prior to this event, she explained that the baby was the result of an immaculate conception. In actuality she had been having an affair with a man in Montreal, Ontario, Canada. After Josephine Woodbury visited Pleasant View in 1894, Mrs. Eddy wrote her, "you seemed deeply penitent and I pitied you sincerely. . . . I forgave you then and there and told you I would try to have you admitted to our church if you so desired. . . . I have asked the Church to reconsider and restore you not at all because you deserved this at my hand but because it is doing as I would be done by and gives you one more chance for repentance and reformation under the teachings of the Bible and my book."[92] Notwithstanding Mrs. Eddy's attempts to save her, Josephine Woodbury began an all-out attack of her teacher in 1899, first through an article in the *Arena* magazine and then in a libel suit seeking $150,000 in damages. The suit was dismissed in 1901. By 1909 Mrs. Woodbury had moved to England and devoted the rest of her life to vilifying Mrs. Eddy through private lectures and teaching.

Alice Swasey Wool While living in Beverly, Massachusetts, Alice Swasey Wool went to be treated by Mrs. Eddy sometime during the summer of 1876 or '77. She healed her of an abdominal pain that doctors had been unable to relieve (see pages 239–240). This experience did not cause her to become interested in Christian Science at that time, but about fifty years later she began its study and then joined The Mother Church in 1928. Mrs. Wool sent her reminiscences to the Church in 1932. Not long after, a friend of hers wrote that Mrs. Wool remembered "that in appearance Mrs. Eddy was slender, had dark hair parted in the middle and waved on the side & that she wore a dark dress. She was principally impressed with Mrs. Eddy's eyes—which she said looked right through her: and that it would be impossible to lie to those eyes. Mrs. Wool never saw her again. She felt that this healing influenced her life, though she did not come into Christian Science until many years later."[93]

Wallace W. Wright The son of a Universalist minister in Amesbury, Massachusetts, Wallace Wright was twenty-five years old when he wrote to Mrs. Eddy (then Mrs. Glover) on March 10, 1871, asking nine questions about Moral Science, her teaching of it, and the results therefrom. He was considering taking her class at the time. Mrs. Glover's answers prompted him to join her April class. Not long after this he moved to Knoxville, Tennessee, and began a successful healing practice. This success, however, was short-lived as he was unable to maintain the discipline of living in the "strait" and "narrow way" that Jesus requires of his followers.[94] By August of that year Mr. Wright was demanding back the money he had paid for tuition plus two hundred dollars. Mrs. Eddy refused, and Mr. Wright then wasted the next few years of his life trying to ruin her by alleging publicly that Moral Science was mesmerism. To Mrs. Eddy that was no different than claiming that white was black, and she responded to this effect in the *Lynn Transcript* during the first months of 1872. This conflict served to focus Mrs. Eddy's thought on the importance of presenting to the public a clear statement of the divine Science she had discovered and was then teaching. God's direction for her was exceedingly clear when one day in February 1872 she opened her Bible to Isaiah 30:8, "Now go, write it before them in a table, and note it in a book, that it may be for the time to come for ever and ever."[95] That month she began writing the manuscript for *Science and Health*.

NOTES

Church History documents either written or dictated by Mary Baker Eddy are usually identified by a number preceded by a letter. Document numbers preceded by the letter "L" refer to correspondence from Mrs. Eddy. "A" documents refer to non-correspondence material, such as notes, sermons, and articles. "V" documents refer to facsimile copies of documents for which the originals are no longer extant. "F" and "H" documents refer to copies of documents where the originals reside in an organization outside of The First Church of Christ, Scientist, but the copyright of the documents is owned by the Church. Other documents in the Church History department that are identified by a combination of numbers and internal letters are correspondence written to Mrs. Eddy.

TITLE PAGE

1. Emma Shipman reminiscences. See Biographical Glossary, p. 374.

PREFACE

1. Mary Baker Eddy, *The First Church of Christ, Scientist, and Miscellany,* p. 111.
2. John 8:58.
3. *Science and Health,* p. 150. See also *Rudimental Divine Science* by Mrs Eddy, 2:23.
4. Church History document A10234b.

PART ONE
CHAPTER 1

1. The authors use Mary Baker Eddy's unique capitalization of certain

words that she considered synonymous with God: Principle, Mind, Soul, Spirit, Life, Truth, and Love.

2. Clara Shannon reminiscences. Mrs. Eddy related this to Miss Shannon.

3. Abigail Baker was thirty-seven. Adam Dickey recounted in his *Memoirs* that Mrs. Eddy told her household that she felt the circumstances of her birth were similar to Isaac's birth in the Bible, referring them to Hebrews 11:11.

4. Irving C. Tomlinson notes, Church History. These notes, jotted down at the time or soon after the words were spoken, were the basis for his book, *Twelve Years with Mary Baker Eddy.*

5. *The Christian Science Journal,* April 1889, p. 4. The *Journal* is the official organ of The First Church of Christ, Scientist. This article was written by Joshua F. Bailey. See p. 293.

6. Quoted in a pamphlet by Septimus J. Hanna, *Christian Science History,* 1899.

7. Tomlinson notes.

8. *Ibid.*

9. Harriet Betts reminiscences, Church History.

10. Tomlinson notes. Mrs. Eddy actually moved from Bow when she was fourteen and a half.

11. Alfred Farlow notes.

12. Tomlinson, *Twelve Years with Mary Baker Eddy: Amplified Edition* (Boston: The Christian Science Publishing Society, 1996), p. 5.

13. Tomlinson notes. And, in Sibyl Wilbur's *The Life of Mary Baker Eddy* (Boston: The Christian Science Publishing Society, 1907, 1976), pp. 33–34; she recounts how this man appeared during a Sunday church service and stood beside Mary during hymn singing. Afterward he allowed himself to be taken away without any resistance.

14. *Retrospection and Introspection,* pp. 8–9. See also I Samuel, chapter 3. In an interview she gave to the *New York World,* published April 17, 1898, Mrs. Eddy recounted this experience: "Even when I was a child my life was different. There were strange things in it; strange things happened to my mother before my birth. Once a minister, a good old soul, held me to his side and told my mother she ought to consecrate me to God.

"When I was very little I used to hear voices. They called me. They spoke my name, 'Mary! Mary!' I used to go to my mother and say: 'Mother, did you call me? What do you want?' And she would say: 'No, child, I didn't call you.' Then I'd go away to play, but the voices would call again distinctly.

"There was a day when my cousin [23-year-old Mehitable Huntoon], whom I dearly loved, was playing with me when she too heard the voices. She said: 'Your mother's calling you, Mary,' and when I didn't go I could hear them again. But I knew it wasn't mother. My cousin didn't know what to make of my behavior, because I was always an obedient child. 'Why, Mary,' she repeated, 'what do you mean by not going?'

"When she heard it again we went to my mother and my cousin said: 'Didn't you call Mary?' My mother asked if I had heard voices and I said I did. Then she asked my cousin if she had heard them, and when she said 'yes' my mother cried. She talked to me that night, and told me when I heard them again—no matter where I was—to say: 'What wouldst Thou, Lord? Here am I.' That is what Samuel said, you know, when the Lord called him. She told me not to be afraid, but surely answer.

"The next day I heard voices again, but I was too frightened to speak. I felt badly. Mother noticed it and asked me if I had heard the call again. When I said I was too frightened to say what she had told me to, she talked with me and told me that the next time I must surely answer and not fear.

"When the voice came again I was in bed. I answered as quickly as I could, as she had told me to do, and when I had spoken a curious lightness came over me. I remember so well. It seemed to me I was being lifted off my little bed, and I put out my hands and caught its sides. From that time I never heard the voices. They ceased."

In later years, after talking to one of her household workers, Janette Weller, about this incident, Mrs. Eddy said, "I have no *words* to describe *what* I saw, but I saw Heaven" (Weller reminiscences, Church History).

It is possible Mrs. Eddy was also thinking of this experience when she wrote, "The effects of Christian Science are not so much seen as felt. It is the 'still, small voice' of Truth uttering itself. We are either turning away from this utterance, or we are listening to it and going up higher. Willingness to become as a little child and to leave the old for the new, renders thought receptive of the advanced idea" (*Science and Health,* pp. 323–324).

15. See *Science and Health with Key to the Scriptures,* p. 40.

16. Church History document A10134.

17. *Ret.,* pp. 13–14.

18. *Ibid.*

Chapter 2

1. Church History document L02682.

2. *Christian History,* vol. VII, no. 4, p. 35. This is an excerpt from Finney's *Lectures on Systematic Theology,* 1846–1847. His ideas of "Christian Perfection" came to him in the late 1830s.

3. Church History document A11134. This document is an early version of *Retrospection and Introspection.*

4. *Ret.,* p. 21.

5. Irving C. Tomlinson notes, Church History.

6. Mary Baker Glover, *Science and Health,* First edition (Boston: The Christian Scientist Publishing Company, 1875), p. 315.

7. Church History document A11031.

8. *Ret.,* p. 20.

9. *Ibid.* The details of the "plot" are given in the May 1983 *Journal,* "An important historical discovery" by Jewel Spangler Smaus.

10. *The First Church of Christ, Scientist, and Miscellany,* p. 345; see Norman Beasley, *Mary Baker Eddy* (New York: Duell, Sloan and Pearce, 1963), p. 346.

11. To prepare herself for instruction in homeopathy, Mrs. Patterson first studied allopathy with Dr. Parsons Whidden for two months in the summer of 1849. See Parsons Whidden entry, pp. 389–390.

12. *Science and Health,* p. 156.

13. Beasley, p. 347.

14. Tomlinson diary: September 9, 1907, Church History.

15. *Miscellaneous Writings,* p. 355.

16. Church History document L101006.

17. Church History document A10402.

18. I John 4:19.

19. *Ret.,* p. 24.

20. Published in *The Covenant,* October 1846. This periodical was published by the Odd Fellows, a fraternal organization.

21. F. B. Eastman affidavit, Church History.

22. *Science and Health,* p. viii.

23. *Ibid.*

CHAPTER 3

1. II Corinthians 10:4.
2. Church History document A10222.
3. Tomlinson notes, Church History.
4. *Ibid.,* and Alfred Farlow notes, Church History.
5. Frances Thompson Hill reminiscences, Church History.
6. *The Independent Democrat* (newspaper), July 3, 1862.
7. Quoted in *Christian Science History* by Septimus J. Hanna, first printing, p. 36.
8. *The Quimby Manuscripts,* ed. Horatio W. Dresser (New York: University Books, 1961), pp. 230–232.
9. Church History document A11043.
10. Church History document A10342.
11. Tomlinson notes, Church History.
12. *Ibid.*
13. *Science and Health,* pp. 184–185.
14. Tomlinson notes, Church History.
15. *Science and Health,* First edition (1875), p. 351.
16. *Science and Health,* p. 573.
17. Psalm 46:1.
18. *Science and Health,* Third edition (1881), p. 156.
19. *Miscellaneous Writings,* p. 24.
20. Tomlinson diary: September 9, 1907, Church History.
21. John 16:7–14.
22. *Science and Health,* p. 295; Church History document A11047.
23. *Science and Health,* p. 455.

CHAPTER 4

1. Tomlinson notes, Church History.

2. *Miscellaneous Writings,* p. ix.

3. Luke 9:58. In November 1868 Mary wrote to her friend Sarah Bagley, "if you . . . could understand the spiritual or rather scientific sense of the 9th Cha[pter] of Luke you would see my life in its truer meaning."—Church History document L08307.

4. Luke 9:62.

5. Wilbur, p. 134.

6. *Miscellaneous Writings,* p. 380.

7. "My first writings on Christian Science began with notes on the Scriptures. I consulted no other authors and read no other book but the Bible for about three years. What I wrote had a strange coincidence or relationship with the light of revelation and solar light. I could not write these notes after sunset. All thoughts in the line of Scriptural interpretation would leave me until the rising of the sun. Then the influx of divine interpretation would pour in upon my spiritual sense as gloriously as the sunlight on the material senses." *Miscellany,* p. 114.

8. *Miscellaneous Writings,* p. 380.

9. Wilbur, pp. 140–141.

10. Abigail Dyer Thompson reminiscences, Church History.

11. Margaret E. Harding reminiscences, Church History. At the time of this healing Mrs. Glover told Mrs. Norton of a store in Boston "where straps might be adjusted to brace the feet and legs of the boy until they were stronger. These were later secured and were afterwards found to be unnecessary, since strength came rapidly to the legs and feet of the boy, who afterwards became a mechanical engineer and lived a useful and happy life."

12. Church History document A11070.

13. Wilbur, pp. 142–143.

14. Church History document A10224.

15. Tomlinson notes, Church History.

16. Church History document A10062b.

17. Historical File: Hiram Crafts, February 23, 1902. Church History.

18. Wilbur, p.165; Tomlinson notes, Church History.

19. Church History document A09000.

20. Notation in Mrs. Eddy's handwriting in the margin next to Psalm 103: "My brother, Albert raised me up from a sick bed by reading to me this Psalm." The Book of Psalms (New York: American Bible Society, 1879), Mary Baker Eddy Bible collection, AA16, Church History. (See p. 53.)

CHAPTER 5

1. Very soon after the healing, one of the doctors told Mrs. Glover that Mrs. Gale was addicted to morphine, taken for relief from consumption, which had been healed at the same time as the pneumonia. Mrs. Glover then felt the need to pray day and night about the addiction. In three days it was cured. Historical File: Henry Robinson, Church History; see also *Miscellaneous Writings,* p. 242.

2. Clara Shannon reminiscences, Church History.

3. Mary Baker Eddy, *Pulpit and Press,* p. 54; Robert W. Peel, *Mary Baker Eddy: The Years of Discovery* (Boston: The Christian Science Publishing Society, originally published by Holt, Rinehart and Winston, 1966), pp. 223–224.

4. Church History document A11065.

5. *Boston Traveller* supplement, Communion season, 1900; Tomlinson, *Twelve Years,* p. 56.

6. Church History document A11351.

7. Church History document A10088.

8. Wilbur, pp. 186–187.

9. Church History document L03919.

10. Elizabeth Moulton statement in Historical File: Alfred Farlow, Church History.

11. Church History document L11061.

12. Tomlinson notes, Church History.

13. Church History document A11071.

14. Samuel P. Bancroft, *Mrs. Eddy As I Knew Her In 1870* (Press of Geo. H. Ellis Co., 1923), p. viii.

15. Church History document F00362.

16. Bancroft, p. 119.

17. Emma Shipman reminiscences, Church History.

18. Lida W. Fitzpatrick reminiscences, Church History.

19. *Science and Health,* p. 458.

CHAPTER 6

1. Church History document A10328.

2. Matthew 13:46.

3. Mary Baker Eddy, *Manual of The Mother Church,* Art. XXVI, Sect. 2.

4. Church History document L09662.

5. Fitzpatrick reminiscences, Church History.

6. *Ibid.* See also *The First Church of Christ, Scientist, and Miscellany* 105:7–10. At that time it was believed that spiritualists were able to heal others.

7. *Lynn Transcript,* February 3, 1872.

8. Mary Baker Eddy Bible collection, AA9, Church History.

9. Church History document L10106.

10. *Science and Health,* First edition (1875), p. 5.

11. *Ibid.*

12. *Lynn Transcript,* January 13, 1872.

13. John 17:11–21.

14. *Science and Health,* First edition, p. 352.

15. *Ibid.,* p. 353.

16. Helen A. Nixon reminiscences, Church History.

17. John Randall Dunn reminiscences, Church History.

CHAPTER 7

1. Twenty years after the fact Mrs. Eddy spoke of her experience of first writing *Science and Health* to a guest at her home: "I could not originate such a book. Why, I have to study it myself in order to understand it. When I came to the writing each day, I did not know what I should write until my pen was dipped in the ink and I was ready to begin." James Gilman reminiscences, Church History. She also wrote of this in an article for the *Boston Herald* (December 3, 1900), "It was not myself, but the divine power of Truth and Love, infinitely above me, which dictated "Science and Health with Key to the Scriptures." I have been learning the higher meaning of this book since writing it." *Journal,* January 1901; *Miscellany,* p. 114.

2. *Message to The Mother Church for 1902,* pp. 15–16.

3. Church History document A11060.

4. *Science and Health,* First edition (1875), p. 4.

5. *Ret.,* p. 38.

6. Church History document L02043.

7. *Miscellany,* p. 105.

8. Church History document A10328.

9. Calvin Frye diary: October 9, 1901.

10. Matthew 5:6.

11. Church History document L12666.

12. It's interesting to note that most of the early editions of *Science and Health* were bound in vibrantly colored covers of blue, green, red, and purple.

13. Church History document L07808.

14. Church History document L07816.

15. *Ret.,* p. 15.

16. Church History document L08737.

17. Annie M. Knott reminiscences, Church History.

18. Church History document L02051. Mrs. Eddy originally intended the Second edition of *Science and Health* to be "a book of over five hundred pages" that would give a "fuller synopsis of our metaphysical system." The printer's proofs were so filled with typographical errors that Mrs. Eddy could only salvage 167 pages and so had to publish a considerably smaller edition of her textbook. She labeled it "Vol. II" because she wanted the public to consider it in conjunction with the First edition/volume published three years earlier. [Quotes from Second edition, p. 5]

19. Minutes of the Church of Christ (Scientist), 1879–1889, Church History.

CHAPTER 8

1. Minutes of the Christian Scientist Association, Church History.

2. Church History document L02655.

3. Helen M. Grenier reminiscences, Church History.

4. Church History document L13362.

5. Mary B. G. Billings reminiscences, Church History.

6. Mary Baker Eddy, *Christian Healing,* p. 16.

7. Church History document L09676.

8. *Miscellaneous Writings,* p. 223.

9. *Ibid.*

10. *Science and Health,* p. 451.

11. *Science and Health,* Third edition (1881), p. 167.

12. *Science and Health,* p. 361.

13. *Ibid.,* p. 92.

14. Robert W. Peel, *Mary Baker Eddy: The Years of Trial* (Boston: The Christian Science Publishing Society, originally published by Holt, Rinehart and Winston, 1971), pp. 95–96.

15. Matthew 18:15.

16. Minutes of the Christian Scientist Association, Church History; Peel, *Years of Trial.,* p. 99.

17. Tomlinson notes, Church History.

18. "Christian Science," *Mind in Nature,* June 1885. (Mrs. Eddy was responding to two previous articles by Bishop Samuel Fallows, who labeled Christian Science as "telepathic power" and *"un*-Christian.") See also *The Christian Science Journal,* February 1885, p. 5.

CHAPTER 9

1. Letter to Clara Choate. Church History document L02496.

2. Letter to Julia Bartlett. Church History document L07689.

3. Church History document L10642.

4. Church History document L02499.

5. Tomlinson notes, Church History.

6. Church History document L12626.

7. Mrs. Eddy and some of her students had established the College at the end of 1880, receiving a charter from the state in January 1881.

8. Mary Baker Eddy Bible collection, AA2, Church History.

9. Church History document L04885.

10. Church History document L04093.

11. *Science and Health* 109:11–16.

12. Church History document A9000, 41:2–3. Compare with *Science and Health* 291:13–16 (to ,).

13. Church History document A9000, 593:9–14. Compare with *Science and Health* vii:13–15 *Truth,* and 224:22–27.

14. After much revision and expansion, "Historical Sketch of Metaphysical Healing" was published in 1891 as the book *Retrospection and Introspection.* The same treatment was given "Defense of Christian Science," which was later issued as *No and Yes.*

15. Church History document L02069. She lectured on the Bible text "Whom do men say that I am?"

16. *Miscellaneous Writings,* p. 54.

17. Delia S. Manley reminiscences, Church History.

18. *Ibid.*

19. Christian Scientist Association minutes, Church History.

20. Church History document V00915. "Softening of the brain" is a literal description of a degenerative disease sometimes connected to senile dementia or paralysis.

21. Church History document L02633.

22. Philippians 2:5.

CHAPTER 10

1. *Miscellaneous Writings,* p. 95.

2. *Ibid.,* pp. 95–98.

3. Christian Scientists Association minutes: May 6, 1885, Church History.

4. *Ibid.,* February 4, 1885.

5. William B. Turner reminiscences, Church History.

6. Christian Scientists Association minutes: January 7, 1885, Church History.

7. Revised and reprinted in *Miscellaneous Writings,* p. 242.

8. The Prospectus issued by the College stated that the Primary class was comprised of twelve lessons, spread over three weeks, the first six lessons taught on consecutive days. The Normal class, intended to train teachers, was open only to students who had taken the Primary class, and indicated that students needed "to practice [Christian healing] from one to two years before entering."

9. Peel, *Years of Trial,* p. 186.

10. Church History document L11013.

11. Church History document L14725.

12. Lewis Prescott reminiscences, Church History.

13. Church History document H00042. For more information about Gill's healing see Peel, *Years of Trial,* p. 194.

CHAPTER 11

1. Mrs. Eddy had renamed the *Journal of Christian Science* to this in 1885.

2. *Journal,* March 1888, p. 629. Mrs. Eddy's definition of "baptism" in the Glossary of *Science and Health* (p. 581) is "Purification by Spirit; submergence in Spirit."

3. *Journal,* May 1888, pp. 93–94. The questions the twelve girls answered are noted in the *Journal.* There is no record of the answers given.

4. Church History document L03470.

5. Abigail Dyer Thompson. See Biographical Glossary, pp. 381–382.

6. Abigail Dyer Thompson reminiscences, Church History department of The Mother Church. See also the *Christian Science Sentinel,* October 3, 1931, p. 94.

7. Harriet O'Brien reminiscences, Church History.

8. Bertha Reinke reminiscences, Church History.

9. The substance of this address can be found in *Miscellaneous Writings,* pp. 98–106. Susan B. Anthony, a leader in the women's suffrage movement, was in the audience.

10. *Boston Evening Traveller,* June 23, 1888.

11. Emilie B. Hulin reminiscences, Church History.

12. Church History document A10273.

13. Church History document L12804. Caroline Frame letter, *Journal,* July 1888, p. 201.

14. Church History document L13004. The parable Mrs. Eddy is referring to is in Luke 20.

15. Church History document V01069.

16. Mary Baker Eddy, *Poems,* pp. 6–7.

17. Clara Shannon reminiscences, Church History.

18. Church History document L04491.

19. *Science and Health,* p. 103.

20. Christian Scientist Association minutes, Church History.

21. Church History document L08683.

22. Church History document L12782. Peel, *Years of Trial,* p. 252.

23. Christian Scientist Association minutes, Church History.

24. Church History document L10677.

25. Church History document L11172.

26. Church History document L03502.

27. Church History document L13091.

28. Church History document L05956.

29. Mrs. Eddy made it clear that this applied only to the Boston Church: "Be it understood that I do not require Christian Scientists to stop teaching, to dissolve their organizations, or to desist from organizing churches and associations." (*Journal,* December 1889, p. 434)

30. *Journal,* June 1889, p. 156; July 1889, p. 204; January 1890, pp. 477–478: "The fact is, I withdraw from an overwhelming prosperity, and was never better satisfied with my own demonstration of *Christian Science.* My dear students never expressed such a grateful sense of my labors with them as now, and were never so capable of relieving my tasks as at present."

31. *Journal,* December 1889, p. 431. Also, *Miscellaneous Writings,* pp. 355–359.

CHAPTER 12

1. Church History document L08229.

2. *Science and Health,* Fiftieth edition (1891), pp. 55–56. See also current edition, p. 162.

3. *Journal,* December 1905, p. 572.

4. Church History document L04139.

5. Church History document L08931.

6. Peel, *Years of Trial,* pp. 267–268.

7. Ellen Brown Linscott, C.S.D.

8. Church History document L11026.

9. Church History document L12650.

10. Church History document L08565. See *We Knew Mary Baker Eddy* (Boston: The Christian Science Publishing Society, 1979), pp. 90–91.

11. Arthur A. Maxfield reminiscences, Church History. Captain Eastaman gave this testimony a few years later in the Original Edifice of The Mother Church: Eloise M. Knapp reminiscences, Church History.

12. David Easton letter, September 30, 1891, Church History.

13. Church History document L04680.

14. With the 1892 Deed of Trust, Mrs. Eddy began to drop the congregational model, moving toward the centralization of authority to run the affairs of the Church, under the *Church Manual,* by The Christian Science Board of Directors. Thereafter, she reduced and ultimately eliminated the congregation as a decision-making body.

15. *Journal,* March 1892, p. 488. See also *Miscellaneous Writings,* p. 91.

16. In 1895, these Rules and By-Laws were compiled and published as the *Manual of The Mother Church.*

17. To Alfred Farlow. Church History document L01584. There is very likely a connection between Mrs. Eddy's use of the word "storm" in this letter to describe church organization difficulties and an incident she noted on a flyleaf in one of her Bibles [AA 9]: "Opened to Jeremiah 29th—7 to 20th ver. In my sweet home when I calmed the terrible storm that was coming (Concord N.H. June 25 1892)."

CHAPTER 13

1. Adelaide Morrison Mooney reminiscences, Church History.

2. Anna White Baker reminiscences, Church History.

3. Ludie M. Waldron reminiscences, Church History.

4. Church History document L03485. See also Robert W. Peel, *Mary Baker Eddy: The Years of Authority* (Boston: The Christian Science Publishing Society, originally published by Holt, Rinehart and Winston, 1977), p. 41.

5. *Journal,* January 1894, p. 429. See also *Miscellaneous Writings,* p. 374.

6. To Edward Kimball. Church History document L07433. See also Peel, *Years of Authority,* p. 60.

7. Church History document L05974.

8. Church History document L05458.

9. Clara Shannon reminiscences, Church History.

10. Church History document L02748. See also Julia Michael Johnston, *Mary Baker Eddy: Her Mission and Triumph* (Boston: The Christian Science Publishing Society, 1974), pp. 134–135.

11. Emilie B. Hulin reminiscences, Church History.

12. Church History document L05082.

13. *Christian Science Sentinel,* September 12, 1903, p. 24. See also *Miscellany,* p. 230.

14. Evening meetings were changed from Friday to Wednesday in 1898.

15. Church History document L05043. See also *Journal,* April 1895, pp. 40–42, and December 1939, p. 469; and *Christian Science Weekly* [*Sentinel*], October 6, 1898, p. 4.

16. John 16:7–14.

17. Emma C. Shipman reminiscences, Church History.

CHAPTER 14

1. *Miscellaneous Writings,* pp. 120–125.

2. *Journal,* February 1897, p. 550.

3. Church History document L03453, Church History.

4. Charles Carroll Howe reminiscences, Church History.

5. Church History document L05911. *Christian Science Sentinel,* April 4, 1936, p. 610.

6. Church History document L05459. *Sentinel,* March 28, 1936, p. 590.

7. See also *Miscellaneous Writings,* p. 317.

8. Minnie Ford Mortlock reminiscences, Church History.

9. *Ibid.*

10. *Journal,* March 1897, p. 575.

11. Church History document L03524.

12. Church History document L03528.

13. See "Dedicatory message," *Miscellany,* p. 183.
14. The months in this paragraph coincide with the dates of Mrs. Eddy's correspondence when she instituted these changes. The notices of them in the Christian Science periodicals were published at later dates.
15. Church History document L02402.
16. See chapter 15, pp. 183–184.
17. Church History document A10125. See also *Journal,* April 1898, p. 3.
18. Church History document A10125.
19. Mary E. Dunbar reminiscences, Church History.
20. Revelation 22:2.

CHAPTER 15

1. Church History document: Walther 583CH007.
2. Church History document L07610.
3. Matthew 22:1–14.
4. *Message for 1900,* p. 15.
5. Christian Scientists Association, January 17, 1883, Church History. See also Clifford P. Smith, *Historical Sketches* (Boston: The Christian Science Publishing Society, 1992), p. 166.
6. Clara Shannon reminiscences, Church History.
7. Church History document L11198.
8. Church History document L09748.
9. Marie Chalmers Ford reminiscences, Church History.
10. *Miscellany,* pp. 131–133.
11. *Sentinel,* January 16, 1902, p. 321.
12. Church History document L04317.
13. *Journal,* February 1900, p. 735. See also *Poems,* p. 79.
14. Church History document L14525.

15. Church History document L00155.
16. Church History document L08043.
17. Church History document L03744.
18. Joseph I. C. Clarke, *My Life and Memories* (1915), p. 337.

CHAPTER 16

1. *Miscellany,* p. 111.
2. For the origin and further background of the marginal headings, see the editorial *"Science and Health:* textbook for self-improvement" in the September 1993 issue of *The Christian Science Journal.*
3. Whereas the 1902 reading was for the purpose of making corrections, *Science and Health* xii:20–22 refers to her reading the textbook in 1907 specifically for the purpose of "elucidat[ing] her idealism."
4. Church History document L08403.
5. Church History document L14299.
6. Church History document F00246.
7. Church History document V00274.
8. Church History document L03057.
9. Church History document L15516.
10. Church History document L08352.
11. Church History document H00071.
12. Clara Shannon reminiscences, Church History.
13. Lottie Clark reminiscences, Church History.
14. Church History document L04273.
15. *Sentinel,* September 12, 1903, p. 24. Reprinted in *Miscellany,* pp. 229–230.
16. Church History document L00383.
17. Church History document L01365.

CHAPTER 17

1. Church History document H00094.

2. George Kinter reminiscences, Church History.

3. Mary Crane Gray reminiscences, Church History.

4. *Boston Herald,* June 11, 1905.

5. Matthew 10:38.

6. *Miscellany,* p. 4.

7. Church History document L10930.

8. Church History document L08548.

9. Church History document L14627.

10. Church History document V00698. See also Lyman P. Powell, *Mary Baker Eddy: A Life Size Portrait* (Boston: The Christian Science Publishing Society, 1991), p. 234; Tomlinson, *Twelve Years,* p. 269.

11. Church History document L15400.

12. Church History document V03226.

13. *Science and Health,* p. xii. The dictionaries of Mrs. Eddy's day defined "idealism" as a term applied to metaphysical systems.

14. *Ibid.*

15. Church History document L13998. General Booth lived to be eighty-five, passing away in 1912.

16. *We Knew Mary Baker Eddy,* p. 182.

17. The "Masters" consisted of a judge, a psychiatrist (then known as an alienist), and an unbiased attorney. They were to determine Mrs. Eddy's competence to conduct her own financial affairs.

18. Tomlinson, *Twelve Years,* p. 71. See also Part Two, pp. 278–284.

19. Victoria Murray reminiscences, Church History.

CHAPTER 18

1. John Lathrop diary, Church History. Mr. Lathrop was one of

Mrs. Eddy's secretaries at the time. See pp. 338–339.

2. *Ibid.*

3. *Sentinel,* January 18, 1908, p. 391.

4. *Science and Health,* p. 107.

5. *Ibid,* p. 455.

6. Adam H. Dickey *Memoirs,* Church History.

7. This statement also appeared in *Journal,* May 1908, and was reprinted in *Miscellany,* p. 286.

8. Church History document L09772.

9. Church History document L08756. See also *Miscellany,* p. 275.

10. *Science and Health,* Second edition, 1878, p. 166.

11. *Miscellany,* p. 353.

12. Alexander Pope, "An Essay on Man," 1733, epistle I, line 274.

13. *Miscellaneous Writings,* p. 4.

14. Church History document L03466. Two weeks after this, Mrs. Eddy abolished the Communion service in The Mother Church to stop the annual pilgrimage of multitudes of Christian Scientists from outside the Boston area.

15. Church History document A11333.

16. *Manual of The Mother Church,* p. 49.

17. Church History document L13481.

18. Church History document 006CH729.

19. Church History document L01572.

20. *Science and Health,* p. 269.

21. William Rathvon reminiscences, Church History.

22. Church History document L01775.

23. Helena Hoftyzer reminiscences, Church History.

24. Church History document L01953.

25. Elsie Bergquist reminiscences, Church History.

26. Rathvon reminiscences, Church History.

27. Church History document L13841.

28. Church History document L04726.

APPENDIX

1. Clara Shannon and Janette Weller reminiscences; Historical File: Irving Tomlinson notes, Church History.

2. Milmine, *The Life of Mary Baker G. Eddy,* p. 108.

3. Historical File: Eddy—Family—Abigail Tilton, Church History.

4. Anna Baker reminiscences, Church History.

5. Church History document F00182. Mark 8:18.

6. Historical File: Eddy—Family—Elizabeth Baker, Church History.

7. Historical File: Tomlinson notes, Church History.

8. Church History document A11025. English philosophers John Locke and Francis Bacon, French philosopher and writer François de Voltaire, and Scottish philosopher David Hume.

9. Historical File: Tomlinson notes, Church History.

10. Samuel Bancroft, *Mrs. Eddy As I Knew Her in 1870,* p. 8.

11. Harriet Betts reminiscences, Church History. Irving Tomlinson also relates this healing in his book, *Twelve Years with Mary Baker Eddy,* pp. 54–55.

12. Clara Brady reminiscences, Church History.

13. James Brierly reminiscences, Church History.

14. Clara Choate reminiscences, Church History.

15. Mary Dunbar reminiscences, Church History.

16. Chestnut Hill: #202—Joseph Eastaman, Church History.

17. Ruth Ewing reminiscences, Church History.

18. Marie Chalmers Ford reminiscences, Church History.

19. Church History document L02011.

20. Alice French reminiscences, Church History.

21. Historical File: Alfred Farlow—January 1907 Lewis Strang letter, Church History.

22. Mary Crane Gray reminiscences, Church History.

23. Historical File: Alfred Farlow—C.E.L. Green statement, Church History.

24. Helen Grenier reminiscences, Church History.

25. Margaret E. Harding reminiscences, Church History.

26. Emilie B. Hulin reminiscences, Church History.

27. Arthur Maxfield reminiscences, Church History.

28. *Miscellaneous Writings,* pp. 98–106.

29. Historical File: Archibald McLellan, Church History.

30. *Ibid.*

31. Adelaide Mooney reminiscences, Church History.

32. *Ibid.*

33. *Miscellany,* 345.

34. Minnie Ford Mortlock reminiscences, Church History.

35. *Ibid.*

36. Victoria Murray reminiscences, Church History.

37. Church History document L02865.

38. *Journal,* December 1929, p. 506.

39. *Journal,* March 1902, p. 739.

40. Elizabeth Norton reminiscences, Church History.

41. Church History document L11127.

42. Harriet O'Brien reminiscences, Church History.

43. Mary Godfrey Parker reminiscences, Church History. See also *We Knew Mary Baker Eddy,* pp. 4–6 and 9–10.

44. Historical File: Mary Godrey Parker, Church History.

45. Church History document L14551.

46. This letter was sent to Mrs. Eddy by her cousin and legal counselor, Henry M. Baker, May 3, 1899, Church History.

47. Charles MacFarland, *Lyman Pierson Powell, Pathfinder in Education and Religion* (New York: Philosophical Library, 1947), p. 215.

48. Julia Prescott reminiscences, Church History.

49. *Ibid.*

50. *Ibid.*

51. Historical File: Lyman Powell—Correspondence—January 13, 1931.

52. The published *Manuscripts* were edited by Horatio Dresser, who had previously written of them: "One searches his manuscripts in vain for a clear explanation of his method of silent cure." *A Message to the Well* (New York: Putnam, 1910), p. 88.

53. *Miscellany,* pp. 306–307.

54. William Rathvon reminiscences, Church History.

55. *Ibid.*

56. *Ibid.*

57. *Ibid.*

58. Else Buchenberger account, Bertha Reinke reminiscences, Church History.

59. Samuel Bancroft, *Mrs. Eddy As I Knew Her in 1870,* p. 10.

60. Joseph Mann's healing is related in *We Knew Mary Baker Eddy,* pp. 167–170. John Salchow reminiscences, Church History.

61. *Ibid.*

62. Laura Sargent reminiscences, Church History.

63. Clara Shannon reminiscences: August 16, 1927, letter, Church History.

64. Emma Shipman reminiscences, Church History.

65. Historical File: Daniel Spofford, Church History.

66. Augusta Stetson, *Reminiscences, Sermons, and Correspondence,*

1884–1913 (New York: G. P. Putnam's Sons, 1926), pp. xi–xii.

67. Mary Baker Eddy Bible Collection: AA27; R. F. Weymouth, *The New Testament in Modern Speech* (London: James Clarke and Co., 1903), Church History.

68. Adelaide Still reminiscences, Church History.

69. *Ibid.*

70. Marguerite Sym reminiscences, Church History.

71. Abigail Dyer Thompson reminiscences, Church History.

72. *Ibid.*

73. *Ibid.*

74. Historical File: Alfred Farlow - Affidavits, Church History.

75. Tomlinson, *Twelve Years,* p. xvii.

76. Tomlinson reminiscences, Church History.

77. William B. Turner reminiscences, Church History.

78. *Ibid.*

79. Ludie Waldron reminiscences, Church History.

80. Annah E. Davis reminiscences, Church History.

81. *Ibid.*

82. Church History document L13426.

83. Historical File: Wentworth family, Church History

84. Peel, *Years of Discovery,* p. 95.

85. Church History document L13931.

86. Church History document A10994.

87. Robert W. Peel, *Christian Science: Its Encounter with American Culture,* p. 112.

88. *Miscellany,* pp. 317–319.

89. Church History document L02164.

90. Tomlinson reminiscences, Church History.

91. Woodbury, *War in heaven,* 1897, p. 5.

92. Church History document L02652. Mrs. Woodbury was admitted to The Mother Church on two years' probation in 1895, but expelled one year later for continuing misbehavior.

93. Alice Wool reminiscences, Church History.

94. Matthew 7:14.

95. Mary Baker Eddy Bible Collection, AA9, Church History.

INDEX